W9-CSI-079

COLS WRIGHT STATE UNIVERSITY
UNIVERSITY LIBRARY

0 00 13 0239412 5

NATURAL CLASSICISM

Essays on
Literature and Science

NATURAL CLASSICISM

Essays on Literature and Science

by Frederick Turner

Paragon House Publishers
New York

PN
55
,T87
1985

Printed in the United States by
PARAGON HOUSE PUBLISHERS
2 Hammarskjold Plaza
New York, New York 10017

Copyright 1985, by Paragon House Publishers

All rights reserved. No part of this book may be
reproduced, in any form, without permission unless
by a reviewer who wishes to quote brief passages.

Library of Congress Cataloging-in-Publication Data

Turner, Frederick, 1943—
  Natural Classicism.

  Bibliography:
  1. Literature and science—Addresses, essays,
lectures. I. Title.
PN55.T87 1985   801'.09   85–19195
ISBN 0-913729-13-2

Text and jacket designed by Paul Chevannes.

Contents

Acknowledgments

I have had the privilege of working closely with men and women whom I regard as among the creators of the future in the arts, the sciences, and the humanities. It seems to me significant and encouraging that the times have produced so many extraordinary, vigorous, undamaged, and utterly original human beings: I see them as constituting a cultural movement of great scope and importance, though I suspect that in the fierce honesty of their independence every one of them might at points decline to be counted as a part of it. This book is an attempt to gather together and synthesize their insights into the most economical and elegant whole I could make of them, and thus to speak for the incipient movement at its birth.

There are too many of these contributors to be able to name them all, but I would like to take this opportunity to thank the following: First, my father, Victor W. Turner, and the group of brilliant anthropologists and performance experts who gathered about him, especially Richard Schechner, Roy Wagner, Barbara Myerhoff, and John MacAloon. Next, J. T. Fraser, whose new theory of time has provided much of the intellectual skeleton of this book; and many other members of the International Society for the Study of Time, especially the physicist David Finkelstein and the evolutionist Harry Jerison. Next, a remarkable group of poets: Dick Allen, Lois Bassen, James Bertolino, Julia Budenz, Amy Clampitt, Frederick Feirstein, Dana Gioia, Emily Grosholz (whose profoundly original work on the philosophy of mathematics has also influenced me deeply), Brooks Haxton, Jascha Kessler, Nicholas Kilmer, James Merrill, Judith Moffett, Michael Newman, Wade Newman, John Frederick Nims, Edwin Watkins, and Theodore Weiss. Perhaps the most immediate source of ideas and information was the Werner Reimers Stiftung study group on the biological foundations of aesthetics: all the members of this group should be thanked, but I shall single out the psychophysicists Ernst Pöppel and Ingo Rentschler, the anthropologist Wulf Schiefenhovel, the human ethologist Irenaeus Eibl-Eibesfeldt, the neurologist Gunther Baumgartner, the musicologist David Epstein, and the chemist Heinrich Zollinger. I also wish to thank Carl Djerassi for his friendship, patronage, and intellectual influence; Ihab Hassan and many of his fellow workers at the Center for Twentieth-Century Studies; Bernard Beckerman, Bernice Kliman, and many of my other colleagues in the 1982 Folger Institute on Shakespeare in Performance, who provided me with a crucial link in my argument from ritual to literature; Robert Kellogg, John Miles Foley, and other members of the MLA Anthropological Approaches to Literature Section; Michael Wood, who pointed out the relationship of my notion of the performed reader to "reader response" theory; Lynda Sexson, who showed me the sacred in the ordinary; and Peter Jennings, the software magician who confirmed my sense of the computer as a divine toy.

Many of my colleagues at Kenyon College have contributed ideas, encouragement, criticism, and inspiration. Among them are Clifford Weber, William McCulloh, James Hans, Robert Cantwell, Jerry Irish, Kirk Emmert, Frederick Bauman, Pamela Jensen, Richard Hoppe, John Coats, and Jay Tashiro. The composer George Crumb and the folklorist Lewis Hyde contributed vital insights, as did Guy Davenport, George Steiner, Martin Esslin, Howard Eiland, Harvey Wheeler, Christopher Crocker, Edward Holt, Emily Lyle, Andrew Lyons, Harriet Lyons, and Nathan Sivin. My gratitude is due also to Patricia Bosch, who transformed my illegible handwriting into clear type.

"Performed Being: Word Art as a Human Inheritance" was commissioned for the new periodical *Oral Tradition*. "The Neural Lyre: Poetic Meter, the Brain, and Time" first appeared in *Poetry*, August 1983, where it won the Levinson Prize. "The School of Night" was published in *Corona*, 1985. "Reading as Performance" was commissioned for a volume to be published by Methuen entitled *Shakespeare in Performance*. "Reflexivity as Evolution in Thoreau's Walden" was commissioned for a volume of essays entitled *The Anthropology of Experience*, edited by Edward Bonner, University of Illinois Press, 1985. "Technology and the Future of the Imagination" was originally a paper delivered to the LOGON conference in Bozeman, Montana, July 1983; it was published in an abridged form in *Harper's Magazine*, November 1984, under the title "Escape from Modernism." "Kalogenetics: Bibliographical Notes on Recent Developments in the Scientific Study of Aesthetics" was originally commissioned for the *Journal of Social and Biological Structures*.

Introduction

The title of this book, *Natural Classicism*, may be a sort of litmus test for the philosophical assumptions of the reader. For some it may even be a paradox: the diehard lover of classical high culture may value precisely that about the classic which defies and transcends nature. The romantic lover of nature, on the other hand, might well boggle at the implication that nature, innocent, free, and spontaneous as it is, could ever produce or endorse so sophisticated, restrictive, and artificial a notion as classicism. This book offers an invitation to both such readers to change their conceptions radically.

Another reader, educated in the Aristotelian, the Renaissance, or the Thomist tradition, might interpret "natural" as pertaining to natural law and might find nothing remarkable in the title: the classical, in the sense of the excellent, ought to follow nature. Such a reader may find much to agree with in this book; but in some ways there may be just as deep, if more subtle, a difference in world view. The "nature" to which I am referring is not the nature of Aristotle, Aquinas, or even the Florentine neoplatonists. Rather, it is nature as we have come to know it through late twentieth-century science: a nature which may indeed possess and exhibit all those values which were once attributed to it, but which must do so within the constraints of mechanisms and processes that can be strictly described in empirical language and reproduced in the laboratory. Nevertheless, the new nature seems to allow more room for those values than has seemed possible for the past two hundred years. In fact there is another kind of reader, one educated in the nineteenth-century scientific doctrines of strict determinism and reductionism, who might object to my title for the reason that classicism is a human fantasy that can have nothing to do with the iron laws of natural necessity, except as a psychological symptom designed to disguise the unpleasant truths of our condition. This reader, too, is invited to consider a different perspective: one which will not, I believe, threaten the gloomy honor of his position.

Another reader, of a European phenomenological persuasion, may question my title on the ground that Being, the proper subject of the arts and literature, lies only in experience, and not in some technical or scientific naturalism; the latter is, they might argue, the imposition of a false cultural consciousness upon the purity of the *Dasein*. This reader, too (though there is something impenetrable indeed about this position, like solipsism) will be asked to consider an alternative view, if only for the reason that the inspired amateurishness of the universe, as the new science shows it to us, is so much more interesting and lovely than Being is. But this reader may be consoled by the very high—indeed the constitutive—

position which experience is accorded in the ontological criticism presented in this book.

When John Crowe Ransom called for an ontological criticism he meant something very different from what will be developed here. Indeed, his position would have fallen somewhere among those of the classicist, the romantic, and the phenomenological objectors to my title. But an ontological criticism, nevertheless, is what is being attempted in this book: that is, a view of literature which sees it as continuous with all other kinds of reality, without reduction or inflation, while preserving intact many of the hard-won insights on every side of the barriers that have separated the humanistic, the scientific, the religious, the philosophic, and the artistic disciplines. Indeed, this book strives to demonstrate that those barriers themselves are illusions. It is an ontological criticism in another sense: a criticism of the various truncated, and thus deformed, ontologies which those barriers protect and preserve, and an attempt to make them whole by grafting together the most healthy and vital parts from them all.

That whole of which I speak is, like a solid as opposed to a plane or a curve, not easily scanned, expounded, or even described by a single line of argument. Each of the essays in this book is a kind of cross-section of a volume; from the shape of each cross-section, together with the points where each cross-section intersects the others, the reader may build up a sense of that rather unusual and comprehensive literary world view which is the book's subject. A topologist, given a circle, an ellipse, a parabola and a hyperbola, intersecting with each other, can infer the exact specifications of the cone of which they are sections. Just as an ellipse and a parabola have their own mathematical integrity, each essay can be taken as a statement in itself. But that integrity is the integrity only of a curve or a plane; when they are put together, the higher integrity of the solid may appear.

The points of intersection, to change the metaphor, are the recurring themes of this volume. I shall list a few of them, so that they will the more readily spring to the mind when they appear. First, and most general, is the assertion that a non-reductive reconciliation of natural, psychological, aesthetic, pragmatic, and ontological descriptions is always available for any subject: there is no need for that despair that leads to specialization.

The second, closely related to the first, is the extended use of the evolutionary model of the universe as a reliable ordering device for connecting the most diverse subject matters in a meaningful way: through evolution every part of the world bears on every other part.

The third is that that order is both hierarchical and dynamic: it is rule-governed, rule-creating (nomogenetic), and generative.

The fourth is the contemporary collapse of ontology into epistemology: the universe *is* the mutual affecting, registering, sensitivity, and measurement of its parts; and as it is made only of arrangements, new arrangements with new sensitivities really alter the universe.

From this there follows another theme: the recent death of materialism, that system of belief which has been dominant since shortly after the Renaissance. Matter and mind are different arrangements, the latter much more complex than, and subsuming, the former.

The sixth theme is in turn related to the fifth: the death of modernism as an aesthetic, moral, and philosophical movement, and its imminent replacement by an even more coherent, if much more comprehensive, set of cultural paradigms.

We may in some senses—our seventh theme—be about to pass once more through a "renaissance" phase of history, but in the opposite direction, so to speak—on the way to, rather than out of, a conception of a great chain of being. But the new chain of being will be evolutionary, dynamic, and both proved and empowered by the achievements of the great detour the West took through materialistic empiricism.

The eighth theme is the overlap between the last phases of human biological evolution and the early phases of human cultural evolution, an overlap that printed both predispositions and procedures of cultural behavior into our genes. Humankind has a nature; that nature is cultural; that culture is classical.

The ninth theme is the ramifying set of implications that follow from the recent discovery of endorphins, those potent brain-rewards by which certain mental behaviors are motivated. Explanations of human motivation which reduce it to sublimations of economic or sexual drives are no longer necessary: the long celebrated joys associated with moral virtue and philosophical insight have their own independent physiological basis.

The aesthetic pleasure of beauty itself—the tenth theme—is similarly mediated by brain chemistry, and evolved as a reward for that astonishing human behavior of internal world construction: a behavior which we share with some species of higher animals, but which was enormously reinforced and developed under the selective pressure of early human ritualization. The arts, sciences, and religious practices of civilized humankind are rooted in the rituals of our *Homo erectus* and *Homo sapiens* ancestors, and there are pan-human neurophysiological aptitudes for their performance.

The eleventh theme is that since literature, like all the other arts, originated in performance—and we can trace this development by studying traditional oral literature—the neurophysiology of literature itself is the neurophysiology of a performing art, and if we ignore this fact it is at our peril. Performance studies remind us of the determi-

nateness, willed transience, and active nature of performance, and may serve as a vital corrective to the excesses
of hermeneutic ambiguity. Performance is also *personal*,
and the self is itself perhaps the product of a performance:
all the world's a stage.

Related to this point is the twelfth theme—that literature shares with legislation, game-rule stipulations, religious invocations, and certain other types of utterance
the characteristics of "performative" statements: that is,
those statements which legitimately create a new reality
by verbal fiat. The Renaissance, with its special interest
in the relationship between nature and art, in political
foundings, bonds, rhetoric, magic, the creation of currency, and religious legitimacy, investigated what we call
"performatives" much more thoroughly than the mod-
erns have done, but the tradition of American pragmatism may have found a scientifically acceptable way back
to their insights.

The thirteenth theme is that the reflexiveness that
postmodern critics have admired in literary art is not rare
at all, but constitutes the normal process of growth in
nature. Self-referentiality can be said to be one way of
describing the intensity of being in a given organism; it is
a standard survival strategy in the physical universe. The
observer problem is the substance of time.

The fourteenth and last theme is that of the process of
creation, which constitutes an expansion of the universe
and a continuation of the work of evolution.

The six essays that follow explore and connect these
themes in a variety of modes and ways. The first, "Performed Being: Word Art as a Human Inheritance," uses
the tradition of oral literature as a starting point for the
development of an evolutionary theory of literary art.
The second, "The Neural Lyre: Poetic Meter, the Brain,
and Time" is a close investigation of the neurophysiology
of poetic meter. It leans heavily on important experimen-

tal data collected by the psychophysicist Ernst Pöppel, of the Institute for Medical Psychology in Munich, and also on some of his ideas about those results. The third essay, "The School of Night," is in a very different mode, being an historical essay on the opinions and communications of a brilliant circle of poets, magicians, philosophers, humanists, scientists, statesmen, and explorers in the English Renaissance. Its central focus is on the idea of creation out of nothing, on the essentially interdisciplinary character of the creative process, on the Renaissance idea of art as a continuation of nature's own innovative tradition, and on the question, what kind of universe *can* be created by fiat? The fourth essay, "Reading as Performance," is a brief illustration of how literature might be taught to students, given the conception of it that this book develops. In the fifth essay, "The Anthropology of Experience: Reflexivity as Evolution in Thoreau's *Walden*," a single literary work provides the material for a discussion of the relationship between transcendentalism, American pragmatism, and the birth of American anthropology. But Thoreau is more than a subject. He is a guide on the path from natural to human creation, an adept of the reflexive process common to both, and a living example of that mysterious identity which can exist between scientific experiment and the experience of Being. The sixth essay, "Technology and the Future of the Imagination" attempts to prophesy the major patterns of the new cultural movement which, given the revolution in contemporary understanding celebrated in this book, will succeed modernism. The last essay is an annotated bibliography of the scientific study of aesthetics, which discursively outlines some of the reading and research which led me and others to the natural classical viewpoint.

In view of the interdisciplinary nature of this book, a few words of warning seem appropriate. The first concerns my use of the word "performance." In the field of experimental psychology, the term is sometimes used in a positivist sense, as opposed to "competence," or even as strategically delineating the legitimate and measurable material of scientific study from the merely subjective or experiential. I use the word in a different sense, closer to "enactment" (though "enactment" lacks some of the fertile ambiguities of "performance"), a sense by no means exclusive of the intentional and the experiential.

My use of an externally similar word, "performative," also needs some explanation. Although I originally borrowed this term and its very powerful philosophical meaning from J. L. Austin, I have greatly extended the range of its application, even allowing an intentional contamination from the dramatistic, anthropological, and liturgical senses of "performance." Whether this debauching of the strict philosophical meaning of "performative" is justified, I leave it to the reader to judge, only urging the maxim "by their fruits ye shall know them."

Thirdly, and with more gravity, I must warn the reader that some of the research cited in this book, especially on the human brain, is speculative and controversial; and that some of my interpretations of contemporary experimental evidence might not be endorsed by the experimenters without professional reservations. However, I have taken care to stay within the spirit, if not always the letter, of the work of the best theoreticians and experimentalists, and I believe that everything I have said in this book on specialized scientific subjects would find defenders among their ranks.

In two specific areas, lateral brain function and brain rewards, further defense is necessary. I am aware that I have placed greater emphasis on the left-right axis of differentiation in the brain than on the fore-hind and upper-lower axes. Some of the distinctions of brain function I have analyzed, and the cooperation they imply, may apply better, for instance, to the fronto-limbic/posterior cortical convexity axis than to the left-right one.[1] For me the interesting issue is the existence of the differentiations, and especially the cooperations, themselves: the nature of the language that brain research finds most useful and powerful, rather than the particular things that are said in that language—which may be subject to the vicissitudes of further empirical confirmation. I do not believe that the main arguments of this book stand or fall by the exact results of future research into the brain; rather, they are based on what I take to be the fundamental paradigms by which that research is generated and informed. The same applies to the use of endorphin and brain reward research. Whatever the exact neurochemistry of aesthetic delight turns out to be, the significant implication of current research in this area is that it makes sense to ask the question, that the question is not reductive, and that indeed if the question is inadmissible, then so too is the claim of psychology to be a science. Likewise, the adaptive function of the capacity for aesthetic experience is not a mere finding of evolutionary biology, but a logical implication of its fundamental principles. That is, if there is no adaptive function in the aesthetic capacity, then either the theory of evolution is weakened or there is no such thing as an aesthetic capacity.

Contemporary brain research is engaged in one of the grandest, most demanding, and most promising intellectual enterprises of the human mind. Neither the humanist nor the artist can afford to be left out.

1. See, e.g., K. H. Pribram, "A Review of Theory in Physiological Psychology," in Penguin, (New York: 1969.) K. H. Pribram, ed. *Brain and Behaviour*, vol. 1, *Mood, States and Mind*

INTERCHAPTER I

The project that this first essay sets for itself is to show how a connection might be made between the study of the arts, in this case the literary arts, and the main body of science. This connection follows three main logical pathways: The first runs from literature to the performing arts; from the performing arts to human ritual performance; and from human ritual to animal ritual, with its sexual, social, psychological, and evolutionary implications. The second runs from literature to the oral tradition; from the oral tradition to its culturally universal mnemonic, rhythmic, and narrative devices; from these devices to the neurophysiological aptitudes and structures that underlie them; and from human neurophysiology to human physical and cultural evolution. The third runs from literature to the arts in general; from the arts to aesthetics; from aesthetics to the evolutionary development and function of the sense of beauty; and from the adaptive value of beauty to the general evolution of brain functions. The strength of the whole approach is best demonstrated by weaving these three logical threads together, as I do in this essay. The resulting fabric of hypothesis and research will be elaborated and tested in the subsequent essays.

Performed Being: Word Art as a Human Inheritance

The study of the oral tradition presently lies at the crossroads of several new lines of research that promise to transform the shape of literary criticism and critical theory forever. The nature of this change is best indicated by an analogy with the revolution in the study of biology which was brought about by the theory of evolution. Before Darwin and Wallace proposed the mechanism of natural selection, biology was essentially disconnected from the other sciences of the physical world. Various strategies or approaches existed for the pursuit of biological studies: the descriptive (corresponding to the routine descriptive criticism one finds in the standard surveys of literature), the taxonomic (corresponding to classical genre study), the functional (corresponding to the study of rhetoric and reader response), the developmental (corresponding to biographical and historical criticism), the anatomical (corresponding to the New Criticism and Structuralism), the mystical/vitalist (corresponding to

Deconstructionism), and the ecological (corresponding to "influence" criticism). But no single principle unified these strategies; no way of relating living matter to other forms of organization existed; no concrete connection appeared between higher and lower forms of life; and no opportunity was offered for the use of mathematical models on one hand and experimental analysis on the other, though these tools had proved extremely powerful in understanding less complex physical entities such as planetary motions and chemical compounds.

The evolutionary perspective, however, provided a single underlying principle uniting all branches of biological science. It opened the way for the development of biochemistry, which links nonliving with living matter and derives the latter from the former. It showed how the higher forms of life derived from the lower. It spawned population genetics and the elegant statistical mathematics of gene pool models. It not only provided a starting point for biological experimentation, but it also demonstrated that many "experiments" already existed in the form of isolated evolving ecosystems like the Galapagos Islands, or in the selective breeding of domesticated species. Above all, evolutionary theory provided the biological phenomena of the present moment with a deep history, so that their significance sprang suddenly into three-dimensional clarity. The result of these changes was to transform biology—as a discipline—from a hobby of gentleman scholars to a central and vital element of public life and cultural development.

Would it not be a worthy goal for the literary scholar to seek an equivalent unifying idea? The various schools of critical theory and practice all have their successes, but taken together their differences cloud rather than sharpen the student's vision. We have no theory of the relation between literature and the other arts, and those human activities such as religion and politics; we have little coherent idea of the connections between high-brow literature and folk and popular literature; we have not seriously studied how literature might be understood in terms of the organs which produce and appreciate it—the linguistic and auditory systems of the brain; and we have no way of constructing genuine literary experiments because we have no basic language for asking the questions experiments are designed to answer. (A merely random reshuffling of linguistic elements, which characterizes much modern "experimental" literature, is not, for this reason, truly experimental at all.) We do not know what existed before literature that made literature come to be possible, and thus cannot recognize the relationship between its archaic "grammar" and its expressive novelty. Literary study remains the intellectual pursuit of a leisured minority, despite the pervasive importance of the arts of words in the lives of all human beings.

Even the analogy of a unifying paradigm in a natural science is productive in that it suggests requirements for a working body of knowledge that have neither been exacted nor met in literary criticism. Perhaps, indeed, the analogy should not be taken too far. Literary criticism is a field of humane studies, not a science. But to the extent that the achievements of evolutionary theory in biology provided that discipline with the humblest common-sense rational virtues—consistency, unity of language, fertility of hypothesis, clear criteria of significance—the criticisms implicit in the analogy should not be rejected. Surely literary criticism should never be an exact quantified science. But then by the same token neither should biology: life, after all, is itself a survival strategy of finesse against the cold numbers of entropy, complexifying the molecular game, raising the stakes, delaying the payment of physical debt, changing the rules so as to keep ahead of the literalistic determinism of thermodynamics. Evolutionary theory did not falsify by reduc-

tion the complex and qualitative richness of the bio-
sphere: rather, it helped us to reveal it.

Several characteristics qualify the oral tradition to be
the Galapagos Islands,[1] so to speak, where a unifying
literary theory may begin to take shape. First, its antiquity, for the roots of oral tradition reach back as far as our
scholarship can trace. Second, its origins in ritual, a kind
of behavior which we share in part with other animals
and which appears to be fundamental to human nature.
Third, its association, in practice, with pleasure, on
which there is now an increasing body of neurophysiological research. Fourth, its use of psychic technologies such
as rhythmic driving and mnemonics. Fifth, its cultural
universality, which points to a shared human inheritance. Sixth, its nature as a tradition of *performance*—an
activity now increasingly recognized as having its own
rules and structures, which may in turn cast light on the
literary arts in general. Seventh, its complex and profound involvement with speech acts and "performative"
utterances, forms of language which linguistic philosophy has recently begun to explore and which are in turn
connected to the most fundamental questions of truth,
reality, and being.

The oral tradition is the one branch of literary studies
which reaches back far enough in time to invite a
consideration of that crucial period in human prehistory
when biological evolution overlapped cultural evolution.
During this epoch the physiological adaptations which
produced modern *Homo sapiens* were not complete, but
according to paleoanthropology, there is unmistakable
evidence that quite complex cultural behaviors, including speech, were already in place and in process of further
development. The length of this period is a matter of
vigorous controversy among anthropologists, archaeolo-
gists, and human ethologists. The shortest estimates,
however, are in at least hundreds of thousands of years—

many authorities would say millions.[2] A large proportion of those physical characteristics which are uniquely human and which mark us off from the other primates evolved during that period of overlap; and—most significantly of all, though the natural divisions between subdisciplines have obscured it until recently—those human characteristics of body and brain must have evolved under the strong influence and selective pressure of the earliest forms of culture. In other words, the human brain and body is at least as much the product of human culture as human culture is the product of the human body and brain! *We* are a domesticated species—self-domesticated, or, better still, domesticated by culture even before we had what we might truly call a human self. There was ample time for *cultural* requirements to become genetically embodied in human tissue, and thus we are hairless, oversexed, brainy, long-lived, infantile, and artistic. Thus also, perhaps, we like stories and poetic rhythm. Of this more later.

The point is that we can no longer look at human cultural activity—especially the very ancient kind, like oral performance—as simply arbitrary in form and structure. There are real artistic rules, just as the classical critics maintained (though for different reasons). Our brains and bodies will be happy, facile, vigorous, and inventive—radiant and porous, as Virginia Woolf puts it[3]—when they use one kind of artistic structure, and not when they use another kind. We are better at telling stories than at throwing together utterances that don't make some kind of story. Babies prefer nursery rhymes to other kinds of sounds. We are better at reciting three-second chunks of language than eight-second chunks. Perhaps the "rules" of human art are quite exact and complex, and are discoverable, and may form the basis of a coherent literary criticism.

The oral tradition is linked to one of the most funda-

mental of human activities: ritual. Indeed, it would be
hard to think of an occasion in which a traditional oral
performance would not itself be part of a ritual occasion,
and nearly as difficult to imagine a ritual without some
kind of traditional oral performance. However, the significance of this relationship has not been entirely clear,
largely because the oral tradition has been the province of
folklorists and literary scholars, while ritual has belonged
to anthropology, religious studies, and ethology. Furthermore, it is only fairly recently that certain aspects of
ritual have come to light, which have very exciting
implications for the oral tradition as well.

Ritual, until the last few years, was often regarded as
little more than superstitious, repetitive, neurotic, backward, and conservative behavior, beneath the notice of
humane scholars, and discussed by social scientists as
part of the flummery by which the harsh economic
realities of society were disguised. Now, however, ritual
is increasingly considered as one of our most vital,
creative, and healthy activities. Three new discoveries
have helped bring about this change. First, in anthropology and religious studies, it became clear that ritual, far
from being a mindless activity, is often (indeed in many
societies, exclusively) the place where society stands
back from itself, considers its own value system, criti-
cizes it, and engages in its profoundest philosophical and
religious commerce with what lies outside it, whether
divine, natural, or subconscious. In ritual human beings
decide what they are and stipulate that identity for
themselves, thereby asserting the most fundamental freedom of all, the freedom to be what they choose. The great
life-crisis, calendrical, sacrificial, celebratory, and mystical rituals propose counter-structures to the normal
structures of society, as Victor Turner has argued, and
thereby constitute a large part of a society's evolutionary
and adaptative potential.[4] Like the recombinations of

genes which take place in sexual reproduction, they introduce variability and hybrid vigor into their society. What Turner calls *"communitas"*—the recognition of human siblinghood—comes to the fore in rituals and is reinvigorated for the sake of social cohesion. Rituals, moreover, are by no means static and unchanging, but are continually reinvented at that fertile interface between the individual and the collectivity. Students of the oral epic and the ballad will be quite familiar with this process.

Second, it is becoming obvious that human ritual is not entirely unique but belongs to a set of ritualized behaviors to be found among many species of higher animals. The great ethologists, Huxley, Lorenz, and others, have shown how pervasive is that marvelous counterfactual activity we call ritual among our fellow inhabitants of the planet.[5] One of the chief priorities of contemporary ethology is to *avoid* drawing the obvious analogies between human and other animal rituals. Mating, aggression, territory, home-building, bonding, ranking, sexual maturity, birth all have their ritual behaviors, human and animal. In fact the only major aspects of the life of an animal which are ritualized by human beings but not by other animals seem to be time and death.

But there is another, much greater difference between human and animal ritual. Animal rituals are passed down from one generation to another by essentially genetic means. The specific "fixed action patterns" that act as mutual triggers in ritual interaction are either expressed automatically in a healthy animal or lie ready to be released by some stimulus (such as hearing the species-specific birdsong of a conspecific). The inborn ritual instincts of animals can be distorted by natural or artificial interference, but such distortions can only lead to permanent changes in a species' ritual if the new behavior has a genetic basis and that genetic alteration confers a selective advantage upon the breeding individuals that possess it.

Human ritual, on the other hand, is passed down, in its particular details and even in many of its large structures, by means of tradition: a process of teaching and learning which need not wait for genetic changes to produce real novelty from one generation to the next. It may seem strange to describe tradition as a means of rapid change, but compared to genetic evolution, tradition is a veritable hotbed of newfangledness. Some animals—the classical example is the Japanese macaques[6] which invented the art of potato-washing and spread it through the whole population—can pass down simple technological innovations from one generation to another by means of tradition. But only humankind does so with ritual.

This does not mean that humankind does not inherit a genetic predisposition to ritual behavior in general; its universality and its evident psycho-physiological basis attests to an important genetic element. Further, there are many particular behaviors and forms which seem to be common to much human ritual and which are no doubt related to inherited anatomical, neural, and behavioral features of our species: rhythmic chanting, body decoration, *communitas*, tripartite structure, storytelling, and so on. But the crucial point is that we do not genetically inherit particular rituals, as other animals do, but rather a disposition to ritual in general and a fundamental grammar and lexicon of ritual elements with which we can generate an infinite variety of rituals. Moreover, we can very rapidly change the rituals we already possess, through that reflexivity that the anthropologists have observed in ritual practice.

All the foregoing of course applies to the oral tradition. Beneath the oral tradition we can dimly make out its roots in more general primate and mammal ritualization; and if we look carefully we may begin to discern the inherited grammar and lexicon that we unconsciously use to make oral performances, and perhaps to make literary art.

Thus at the heart of human artistic performance we find an archaic genetic armature of mammalian/primate ritual. Surrounding this core we find a layer composed of the new, genetically-transmitted, grammar and lexicon of human ritual performance, created by the interplay of biological and cultural evolution. Next, we find the oral tradition itself, culturally evolved but directly reliant on the genetic structures which it itself imposed by selective pressure upon the species. Next above that is the recorded tradition, in which the limits of human memory are transcended by the technology of writing and print. Finally we encounter the realm of exegesis, criticism, and metacriticism, activities themselves conducted within the subtle ritual space of literature. This concentric structure is also the record of a historical development of increasing reflexivity, and at each point the leap from a more archaic system to a more sophisticated and reflexive one takes place through the needs and pressures of performance. The performance of the ancient genetic rituals led to their imitation, with variation, by the young, and the birth of the ritual tradition. The performance of the traditional rituals exerted selective pressure on the nervous systems of our ancestors—those who could not perform the rituals would not get a mate or even survive—which ingrained the performance "grammar" into the genes. In turn the demand of the priest-actors for external memory storage of complex ritual dramas led to the development of literary recording; and the performance of literary productions led to the need for exegesis and criticism, as recorded directorial notes to the actors, so to speak.

From this perspective it becomes clear that the arts should properly be regarded as the most fluid, sophisti-

8

cated, and reflexive subset of the broad general category
of ritual performance, and the oral tradition as one of the
crucial areas connecting the arts with the rest of the
ritual continuum. As we shall see, the implications of
this way of looking at the arts are especially striking for
literary criticism.

The third exciting development in the study of ritual
has been the recognition that ritual activity is tuned to
observable mechanisms in the human brain and nervous
system. The groundbreaking book *The Spectrum of Ritual: A Biogenetic Structuralist Perspective* has explored
ritual trance and the massive cognitive, emotional, perceptual, somatic, and social changes it involves; and has
shown that it performs indispensable functions for the
human individual as well as the group. Further, the book
describes specific ritual techniques by which the trance
state—whether light and barely noticeable or heavy and
obvious—is brought about; the varieties of types of trance
ranging from meditation to frenzy; and their characteristics in terms of brain chemistry, brain rhythms and the
functions of the ergotrophic, trophotropic, sympathetic
and parasympathetic systems, and the left and right
hemispheres of the brain. Most interesting of all for our
purposes are two points: the close resemblance between
the subjective effects of ritual trance and aesthetic pleasure; and the observation that the rhythmic driving of an
endogenous brain rhythm by a synchronized external
beat is one of the chief means by which those changes in
brain state are produced. Ernst Pöppel, the German psychophysicist, and I have investigated the curious fact that
all human poetry possesses regular lines that take roughly three seconds to recite. (Our findings are reported in
chapter three.[8]) We concluded that poetic meter is a way
of inducing much larger regions of the brain than the
left-brain linguistic centers to cooperate in the poetic
process of world construction, and that one of the chief

techniques of that world construction is the creation and maintenance of a hierarchy of temporal periodicities which makes sense of past events and is powerfully predictive of future ones. Recent work on the preferences of babies for nursery rhymes has confirmed our findings.[9]

One of the most interesting questions in the contemporary study of the biology of aesthetics concerns the biological basis and evolutionary necessity of pleasure in general and aesthetic pleasure in particular. We participate in oral performances, just as we look at sculpture or listen to music, not primarily to be informed or edified, but to be delighted. To an evolutionary biologist, pleasure, like any other activity of an organism, serves an adaptive function, in this case, reward. The neuropsychologist James Olds and others[10] have begun a close study of the reward systems of the brains of higher animals, with special attention to human beings. Theorists in the same field, such as Lionel Tiger, have postulated an extensive group of very large peptide molecules which the brain can produce and in turn take up, and which are associated with the various subjective sensations of pleasure, ranging from high arousal to deep relaxation. Henry N. Wagner and his collaborators have obtained images of opiate receptors in the living human brain.[11] The peptide molecules are large enough—only one step removed from the proteins—to carry information on their own account. Like most great scientific discoveries, this one was in a sense obvious, but only once it was pointed out. All it took was the question, "Why do opiates and cocaine produce such great pleasure?" Obviously our species could derive no adaptive advantage from consuming the resins of certain Oriental poppies or South American shrubs, nor were they available to most members of the species. Thus the presence of the specific receptors in the brain which respond so sensitively to these chemicals cannot have anything to

do with poppies or coca as such. They must then be
designed to respond to internally generated chemicals
which are crudely mimicked in structure by those herbal
resins.

It soon became obvious that the internally-generated
brain rewards were more powerful, by many orders of
magnitude, than the conventional motivators proposed
by crude materialists and behaviorists. Rats will ignore
the pangs of extreme hunger and thirst, and the presence
of strong sexual stimuli, in order to press a bar which will
either deliver the chemicals of delight or electrically
stimulate their own brains to do so. If even rats do not
live by bread alone, *a fortiori* neither do humans.

It is becoming clear that the "higher pleasures" of
creative mental effort, of beauty, of goodness, of truth are
indeed independent pleasures of their own and not merely perverted or sublimated versions of sexual or nourishment drives. The endorphins, as the endogenous brain
chemicals are called, are clearly involved in aesthetic
pleasure. Let us now return to our earlier questions: What
is the adaptive significance of aesthetic pleasure? Why
should we be designed to appreciate beauty and to enjoy
it with an intensity which is potentially much greater
than that of hunger or lust?

One clue is afforded us by the fact that the "pleasure-
chemicals" are by no means automatic in their effect.
Indeed they can even apparently be painful if adminis-
tered without warning and without the control of the
subject.[12] Thus these pleasures must be associated with
the autonomy, the power over the future, and the predictive capacities of the organism. Yet the sense of beauty is
not the same as the exultation of power, though it can
resemble it. We associate beauty with a certain set of
perceived objects, and with a certain manner of perception, cognition, and emotional comprehension, but not
necessarily with action as such; some of the strongest

experiences of beauty take place in response to our own endogenous imagery of dream, fantasy, or memory. The feeling of beauty, then, is a reward for a certain autonomous activity of the brain, one which gives the brain a grip on the future, which is, however, not necessarily involved with immediate external actions to change the environment. We are rewarded powerfully by the pleasures of taste and sex, for the metabolically expensive activities of foraging and reproducing ourselves. Otherwise we might not bother. But the creation and appreciation of beauty is much more metabolically expensive, and is rewarded by a pleasure for which humans will happily neglect the delights of sex and eating. What activity can be so much more important than nourishment and reproduction?

The answer to this question necessitates an understanding of the ethological term *Umwelt* in the special sense that Von Uexkull used it when describing the behavior and perception of animals.[13] Every animal has a species-specific world, a set of relevant factors in its environment which its receptors—its senses—are designed to detect and its effectors—its limbs and other active organs—to act upon. Outside that world, that umwelt, nothing exists as far as that animal is concerned. For instance, visual phenomena have no existence for an eyeless species, nor subterranean ones for an animal not equipped for digging. For those animals with simpler nervous systems the umwelt is a crude one containing only a few unrelated elements: there is a fairly direct link between stimulus and action, without much intermediate interpretation of the various sensory inputs. For advanced species, on the other hand, with a much higher ratio of nervous tissue to body weight and complex cortical development, the evidence from many receptors is continuously integrated into a coherent universe of enduring objects in motion relative to each other and to the organism, with their own smell, sound, taste, touch, and their own sensitivity to each other and to the organism that perceives them. Nowhere in physics is it asserted that such entities as enduring objects exist. They come into existence, as far as we know, as the highly elegant constructs of the brains of higher animals. Physics knows only a complex interplay of the four fundamental forces at various intensities, wavelengths, and vectors. The concrete universe of objects as we, the higher animals, know it, is just the most parsimonious, ordered, powerful, coherent, and comprehensive hypothesis that will reconcile our inherited expectations with our experience.

When we encounter words like "elegant," "parsimonious," "ordered," "powerful," "coherent," and "comprehensive," we are already in aesthetic territory. There is no prior reason, logical or empirical, why the world should be elegantly and economically organized, nor is it necessarily better, in a moral sense, that it should be. It is simply more beautiful that way, and can therefore be dealt with more efficiently. Before a species can reproduce itself or even eat, it must enter a consistent working relationship with its world, its umwelt, which will generate predictions to be confirmed or deconfirmed by experience. Such a relationship is harder to maintain the more information an organism is capable of absorbing and the more it is capable of doing; and this is why the human brain uses about one-third of the body's oxygen and nutrients. So the world constructing, cosmogenetic activity is provided with a very powerful inducement and motivation. World creation is hard work, and must be richly rewarded.

What distinguishes artistic performance from ritual in general is that the sense of beauty, the aesthetic, is more directly and specifically involved in the former. Thus we may say of oral performance, which lies toward the

artistic end of the ritual spectrum, that it is a cosmogenetic activity, perhaps vital to the maintenance of
the human umwelt. Further, we might speculate that
because the human umwelt is itself much more learned
than inherited—though we inherit a predisposition to
learn a complex umwelt—the activity of world construction is for humans much more vital, much more difficult,
and much more highly rewarded than it is among the
other animals, whose umwelt is relatively more inherent
in their genes. Thus the tradition of oral performance
may be much more closely tied to our survival as a
species than we think, since it is our specialization to
create worlds to be tested against sensory experience, as
it is the mole's to dig and the bird's to fly.

It should, moreover, be stressed that world creation is
not a metaphor, or rather not a metaphor *only*. As we
know from quantum physics, the precise characteristics
of the fundamental constituents of the physical universe
are not decided until they are registered or measured by
some other system that is selectively sensitive to those
characteristics themselves.[14] This in fact follows, as does
relativity theory, from the basic scientific principle that
the only things that can be said to exist are those things
which are measurable. All entities selectively measure
each other, and thus we can say that the universe is
exactly and only what its constituents appear to each
other to be. Thus human world construction is a perfectly genuine activity, with as much ontological legitimacy
as the reaction of any particle to any other particle,
indeed, more, because human perception and cognition
sifts out much more severely than does an elementary
particle any phenomena that are not highly probable and
mutually confirming. Of course human world construction is more effective if it has already, by scientific
observation and experiment, canvassed the reactions of a
good sample of non-human entities and placed itself in a

position which can be construed as being in agreement
with them, or at least not in contradiction. But anything
about which the universe is not already in agreement
with itself is not yet decided, and there remains an
infinite number of topics which have not yet come up for
consideration. Human ritual, performance, and art are
ways of setting the stage, creating the frame, arranging
the agenda, and picking the topic in such a way as to give
human beings a home court advantage in making the
ontological contract. Much human art and ritual does not
even need, and would be embarrassed by, confirmation by
non-human participants. Fiction is explicitly counterfactual, as are the phantom antagonists in the triumph-
ceremony of the geese; and a congregation would be
rightly horrified to find the contents of the chalice to be
arterial red, sticky, and prone to swift clotting.

But how exactly are the brains of individuals prepared
and synchronized with each other to work the marvelous
transubstantiation of artistic and ritual performance?
Here the study of oral tradition is especially valuable.

We have already touched on the power of rhythmic
repetition as a psychic technology. Perhaps the fundamental characteristic of the oral tradition is its use of
rhythmic language. By extending the region of the brain
that is at work on its integrative, cosmogenetic functions, rhythmic language prepares us for that active
inventive imposition on the world of our own cultural
umwelt, our own construction of it.

There is increasing evidence[15] that it is the exchange of
information between right-brain and left-brain modes
which constitutes the human capacity to make sense of
the world. At present fascinating research is being done
by Colwyn Trevarthen, Robert Turner, and others, using
new Nuclear Magnetic Resonance Scanning techniques
to examine the myelinization (that is, the activation of
neural fibers by acquisition of a coating of myelin) of the

corpus callosum, the body that connects the left with the right side of the brain. This research may show how acculturation actually changes the active structure of the brain, wiring together various brain elements across the commissure.

But the cooperation of left and right brain which is sponsored by rhythmic language does not only make us more intelligent and creative, but also increases the power of our memory enormously. Here we may note a remarkable convergence between the work of the psycho-physiologists on the bilateral asymmetry of brain func-tion, the brilliant investigations of traditional mnemonic systems by Frances Yates and others, and the ground-breaking work of Parry, Lord, and their modern followers on methods by which illiterate epic poets are able to perform thousands of lines of poetry.

Yates[16] describes the Renaissance memory system as essentially a mapping of the discourse to be remembered onto the interior of a large house with many rooms. On each of their imagined walls there are niches containing objects associated with the topics of the discourse. The niches were also called "places" or "commonplaces"; a common-place book was a notebook of memorable obser-vations. By imaginatively walking around the "memory theater" in a particular order of rooms, an orator can recall a highly complex series of points with great exact-ness, and even be able to retrace his steps or take a different route.

A brain scientist would instantly recognize this proce-dure as a way of translating left-brain temporal sequence, for which we have a very poor memory—telephone numbers are only seven digits long because any more would overload our short term memory buffer—into the right-brain spatial gestalt mode. We can remember very complex locations and images, and with some subjects, for instance dwelling-places, our powers of recall and recognition of spatial patterns are astonishing. Thus mnemonic systems remedy the deficiency of left-brain memory by means of the pattern-recognition talents of the right brain. (Essay three describes a remarkable group of Renaissance artists and scientists who put this integrative psychic technology to work.)

Oddly enough, the procedure of memorizing a sequence by mapping it onto a series of rooms in a house has also been described to me independently by a flamenco guitarist and a jazz musician, when asked how they remember musical compositions. But sometimes the connection is reversed. A composer informs me that he sometimes records a musical phrase in his memory by associating it with the rhythm of a quotation from the Bible that he knows by heart. Here a right-brain pattern is remembered by its connection with a left-brain sequence. Perhaps the fundamental point is that any memory is safer if kept in both modes, left and right. We might go so far as to say we only *know* something truly when we have translated it back and forth between the two sides of the brain a few times. The great authority on lateral brain function, Jerre Levy, has indeed said just this.[17]

Do we not find a similar basic strategy in the techniques of the oral epic?[18] Homer and the Yugoslav epic poets evidently strung formulaic half-lines upon the melodic gestalt geography of a plotline, reinforcing the mnemonic properties of their words by poetic rhythm, calling into play by the "driving" mechanism the affective capacities of the midbrain, and activating the right brain by means of significant metrical variation. The muses may indeed be daughters of memory, in this sense.

In such a perspective plot or story becomes crucially important. The "unity of action" Aristotle talks about— the homecoming of Odysseus, the wrath of Achilles, the avenging of Agamemnon—functions as a sort of connected series of rooms, containing places for memory storage. Plot, moreover, with its capacity to organize large units of time, extends the harmonious patterning of temporal periodicities that we find in poetic meter to larger and larger scales, organizing a voluminous body of material and broadening the temporal horizon of memory and expectation. The "now" or present moment of a story (if "now" is, say, Odysseus's journey home) can cover a length of many years. Once the "now" of a story reaches out to include even the death of the hero or heroine, tragedy and the highest forms of literary art become possible. What makes us human, what enables us to transcend the world views of other animals, is our greater capacity to organize and comprehend time.[19] Perhaps this is the reason why rituals of temporality and funeral are unique to human beings.

Plot not only unites right-brain pattern recognition with the left-brain capacity to deal with large units of time, it also connects these cortical functions in turn with the limbic system and its powerful rewards. It does this by the process of identification. If the self is the governing subset of mental relations, including a set of symbols reflexively representative of that subset, then other persons that I know, including characters in a story or drama, are smaller subsets with their own symbol clusters. The integrative activity of relating those subsets with each other and especially with one's self-subset is rewarded neurochemically by the subjective feelings of love, sympathy, insight, pity, or satiric triumph. Further, the self is the focus of those sensations of fear, desire, anger, and so on with which the organism responds to its environment, sensations under the control of the limbic system. Identification makes us feel the character's emotions as if they were our own. Thus plot promotes and exercises the relations between cortical world construction and limbic reward. We shall return to the issue of plot later on, in a literary critical context. Suffice it to say here that the modernist tendency to dispense with or demote plot may have been a grave mistake.

The fact that comprehension and memory demand the literal cooperation of both sides of the brain, and that the cortex as a whole is motivated and rewarded by the limbic system, may afford us fascinating insights into the nature of symbolism. The arts inherited the technique of symbolism from earlier forms of ritual, where it served a purpose not unlike that of rhythmic meter. On the cortical level a symbol evidently acts as a connective between a left-brain linguistic proposition, or network of propositions, and a right-brain image or image cluster. This may explain why the more obvious forms of allegory and emblem are sometimes tiresome, unmemorable and insipid, for they connect only linguistic with linguistic, left-brain with left-brain information, and do not possess the fertile suggestive tension and memorability which comes about when the corpus callosum must translate, with only partial success, from one mode to the other.

As Victor Turner has pointed out,[20] symbols also connect the higher brain with the lower. Symbols possess two poles: ideological (cortical) and orectic (limbic). The great ritual and artistic symbols are reward systems of their own, relating pleasurable emotion or sensation with the higher values, and priming the pump of self-reward.

In a memory system symbols correspond to the suggestive objects, which are to be found in the niches or places of the memory theater. From the analysis it follows that mere images in themselves, without a left-brain discursive component, will be insignificant and insipid and that symbolism only makes sense when it is set in the context of a comprehensible and reproducible sequence of places, rather than jumbled up together as in much modernist literature. To the extent that symbolists and imagists abandoned argument, plot, and discursive reason, they broke the mysterious and fertile connection between left

cortex, right cortex, and limbic system. Eliot's phrase in
The Wasteland, "a heap of broken images," is very apt;
and we may now see this poem, despite the disorganizing
interference of Ezra Pound, as an attempt to restring
those images together upon the primeval sequences of
ancient myth. And to turn from heroic pathology to
heroic health, consider the Shield of Achilles passage in
the *Iliad*, or even the whole of the *Divine Comedy*, as a
memory theater within which symbols, themselves
memorably uniting left with right and higher with lower,
are in turn memorably and significantly positioned in a
varied metrical medium along a temporal plotline and
within a spatial, gestalt geography. These passages are
summative statements of the healthy and productive
human psyche, and also of the cosmos that is generated
by the performative fiat of such a psyche; and appropri-
ately they have delivered to generations of reader/
performers the sweet shock of endorphin reward.

It may be that modern literary criticism, by treating
literature as if it were merely a linguistic left-brain
art—with the authority, one might speculate, of Lessing's
Laocoön, which insisted on purity of medium in the
arts—was doing literature a grave disservice. Once literature becomes only a pattern of "differences," of words
translating other words, and the left brain is cut off
from the right and from the limbic system, then the
way is open to the vacuity and anti-cosmos that the
deconstructionists perceive at the heart of all literary art.
It is interesting that the modernist period was also the
period in which the poetic narrative was replaced by
more exclusively left-brain prose genres, the plotless
"new novel" replaced the traditional "page-turner" of
Austen and Tolstoy, and free verse replaced metered
poetry. Story and rhythm, plot and image, image and
rhythm, were increasingly separated. Meanwhile in the
visual arts the Renaissance dictum *ut pictura poesis*—a

bilateral epigram—was set aside, as, in modernist music, tonality, melody, recognizable rhythm, and articulated temporal structures were often abandoned. Even in modern architecture there has been what almost seems to be a conspiracy to detach the left brain from the right, by creating spatial structures which are so uniform and repetitious that pattern-recognition becomes impossible and we are reduced to counting to find our way through them. And "functionalism" sometimes appears to be a way of denying the viewer the comfortable and organic rewards that are provided to the limbic system. In the sixth essay this critique of modernism will be developed further, with alternatives suggested.

The neurological perspective also offers insights into the matter of discursive argument and logical persuasion in literature. In Plato's *Dialogues*, which at points are little removed from the philosophical exchanges in Sophocles and Euripides, we can clearly see that the origins of argument and discourse can be found in plot and story. Argument is basically a kind of story, the story of a war of words between heroic verbal antagonists. As such it possesses the integrating properties, in neural terms, that I have already described. Like a story, a good argument is memorable and transcends, because of its hierarchical organization of larger and larger temporal units, the left-brain weakness in recalling mere lists (the limitation that the spatial mapping of the memory system is designed to overcome). What follows from this analysis is that when the treatise succeeds the dialogue we have stepped away from the integrative properties of a plotline. We only hear one side of the story, so to speak; and unlike Plato, Aristotle must replace the gestalt structuring of plot with a sort of geometrical structure of logical dependence. Aristotle, without the continuing story of the actors in the dialogue, cannot afford those delightful wayward changes of subject which we find in Plato, unless he has already prepared a logical place for the new block of discursive masonry. Yet even the stonemason Socrates, the oral philosopher, is one step away from the agonistic story of the Atreides.

The lesson to be learned for literature, if we are to preserve its ancient ritual powers of psychic and cosmic integration, is that discursive argument has a vital place in literature, as long as it preserves its primal ties with story, or else replaces those ties with powerful integrative symbolism.

It might be argued that despite evolution, ethology, and brain chemistry, the study and practice of oral performance does not necessarily require a "deep grammar," a set of natural classical rules, an explanatory evolutionary paradigm, such as I am postulating here. However, a serious consideration of the matter from a cross-cultural perspective reveals, across a wide range of human activities and types of culture and social organization, an extraordinary unanimity of cultural forms that points to a powerful and significant common inheritance. I quote a remarkable list, compiled by the anthropologist George Peter Murdock, "of items . . . which occur, so far as the author's knowledge goes, in every culture known to history or ethnography . . . age-grading, athletic sports, bodily adornment, calendar, cleanliness training, community organization, cooking, cooperative labor, cosmology, courtship, dancing, decorative art, divination, division of labor, dream interpretation, education, eschatology, ethics, ethnobotany, etiquette, faith healing, family, feasting, firemaking, folklore, food taboos, funeral rites, housing, hygiene, incest taboos, inheritance rules, joking, kin-groups, kinship nomenclature, language, law, luck superstitions, magic, marriage, mealtimes, medicine, modesty concerning natural functions, mourning, music, mythology, natal care, pregnancy usages, property rights, propitiation of supernatural beings, puberty cus-

toms, religious ritual, residence rules, sexual restrictions,
soul concepts, status differentiation, surgery, tool making,
trade, visiting, weaning, and weather control."[21]

Murdock would probably not object if we added to this
list combat, gifts, mime, friendship, lying, love, storytelling, murder taboos, and poetic meter; and it would be
tempting to propose that a work of literary art can be
fairly accurately gauged for greatness of quality by the
number of these items it contains, embodies, and
thematizes. They are all in the *Iliad*, *The Divine Comedy*, *King Lear*, and *War and Peace*; and most of them can
be found in relatively short works of major literature,
such as Wordsworth's *Intimations* ode, or Milton's *Na-
tivity* ode, or even—very compressed—in Yeats' *Among
School Children*. These topics virtually exhaust the content of the oral tradition; taken together they constitute a
sort of deep syntax and deep lexicon of human culture. In
the essay that follows a similar universality is demonstrated for poetic meter, which may constitute part of a
corresponding "deep syntax." It is the function of the oral
tradition to preserve, integrate, and continually renew
this deep syntax and lexicon, while using it to construct
coherent world-hypotheses. Literature, which is to the
oral tradition as the oral tradition is to ritual, extends
these functions by means of that greater reflexiveness
and sophistication obtained by the technological prosthesis of script and books, so that those world-hypotheses
gain in power, predictiveness, and beauty.

The relative universality of a given theme or form in
human linguistic art can serve to test its legitimacy as a
correct usage of the genetically inherited cultural grammar and lexicon. If we find a story (the descent into the
underworld, for example) or a technique (poetic meter,
for example) which is repeated in hunter-gatherer, peas-
ant, city-state, and technopolitan cultures, then we know

that we have encountered a paradigm declension or definition of a pan-human verbal artistic element. Further, as artists, and even as critics searching for a way to describe an unusual literary work, we can use the rich variations on those themes and forms in human verbal art as a storehouse of sound, handy, and vital ideas. Cultural universals are to our new ontological criticism what Darwin's voluminous collection of examples of adaptation in nature were to his theory of natural selection.

Perhaps we can see the same phenomenon at work in the remarkable similarity of mythic story elements from all over the world. Joseph Campbell's magisterial new atlas of human mythology extends his earlier important work on "the hero with a thousand faces" to many other mythic ingredients than the hero.[22] James Frazer, Claude Lévi-Strauss, and David Bynum have explored in depth yet other themes.[23] Perhaps the instinct of some of the greater modernists—Yeats, Joyce, Eliot, Lawrence, Mann —to seek in ancient myth the coherence that the modern world did not seem to offer, was a wise one. However, it seems to me that the kind of grasping for a mythic lifebelt that we find in "Sweeney Among the Nightingales," for example, is not entirely healthy. The ebullient and cavalier luxuriance of mythic invention that is characteristic of the better works of contemporary science fiction such as Lindsay's *Voyage to Arcturus*, Herbert's *Dune*, Wolfe's *New Sun* tetralogy, and Le Guin's *Left Hand of Darkness* is to my mind the sign of a much healed culture.[24] Like the classical Greeks, late medieval Florentines, and Renaissance Elizabethans, such writers naturally and confidently adapt the old mythic grammar and lexicon to new uses. Science fiction has its own vocabulary of critical terms, one of which is "time-binding." The phrase is almost untranslatable into ordinary critical language but it is unmistakably referring to the mapping of left-brain temporal modes of understanding onto right-brain spatial gestalt modes, and vice versa.

We need not even go out into ancient or foreign cultures to find rich sources of insight into the "deep language" of human word art. The oral tradition continues in our own culture in at least two realms: liturgy and theater. Liturgy and theater can serve the same function for our new theory of criticism that the practices of domestication and selective breeding served for Darwin's theory of evolution. They are, as it were, a vast experiment lying close at hand, familiar to all, and even a warrant in advance of the practical applications of the theory. And when we consider in these contexts the practice of rehearsal, the relationship between script (whether a text or a verbal tradition) and performance, the structure and articulation of a performance, the relationship between actor and audience, priest and congregation, the special uses of dramatic and liturgical language, the nature of dramatic and liturgical suspense, the relationship between actor and role, the changes in mental state during performance, the relationship between actuality and possibility in church or theater, and between theme and variation, we may see many elements which have remained unchanged since prehistoric times and which can serve as a framework and animating principle for a truly ontological criticism.

The crucial idea here is *performance*. It was pointed out earlier that it is performance that drives the reflexive, innovative and evolutionary tendency of human ritual and art. And now that we are privileged to have had a half-century of subtle research into the nature of performance by such figures as Stanislavsky, Jerzy Grotowski, Richard Schechner, and Victor Turner,[25] we possess the materials for a new integration of literary criticism based on the very definite structures, effects, and requirements of successful performance.

Perhaps the most prosaic requirement for effective performance is the fundamental triadic structure, described by Aristotle as beginning, middle, and end, and by Victor Turner as the ritual sequence of separation—liminal period—re-aggregation. Simple as this structure seems, it has profound implications. One is that if an audience—or even a single reader—is not introduced into a work by a proper beginning, conducted out of it by a satisfactory ending, or given a space in between and matter to play with in that space, the grammar of human art is being violated, the carrier-wave of significant communication is swamped with noise, and the endorphin reward is aborted.

More interesting still, the sequence implies motion into, through, and out of a concentric entity, a passing through, a trial, a risk, an experiment, an experience. The Latin *periculum*, from which we get "peril," is related to "experience," and "experiment;" the word is cognate with the Germanic "fear." The beginning and the end are the gates into and out of a realm which, by definition, cannot be of this world, and may be dangerous, but which is essential to our sentient life. We find the threefold structure elaborated in the five acts of a Shakespearean play, and in the sevenfold divisions of Greek tragedy; and the concentric pattern is repeated in the architecture of the arenas, stupas, temple-plots, shrines, and theaters where the performance event takes place. The Globe Theater is paradigmatic. We find it also in the mandala, a visual instrument of meditation analogous to chanting, which is the corresponding acoustic instrument. Walt Disney's Magic Kingdoms in California, Florida, and Tokyo have the same concentric labyrinthine shape. The deep meaning of this shape is, I believe, reflexivity: the beginning and the end are like mathematical parentheses, or better, quotation marks, that distinguish the unreflexive "use" of a word from the reflective "mention" of it, as the philosophers would say. One of the earliest strategies of living matter was to envelop itself with a membrane of lipids which were hydrophobic at one end and hydrophilic at the other, and which attracted each other at the sides, thus constituting a cell. The cell is a sort of parenthetical comment on the rest of physical reality, containing a controlled environment isolated from the world by a semipermeable skin. The "three-act" structure is a full *experience* of what life is, a passing through from the outside to an inside and thence back to the outside. Or it might even be more accurate to say that the beginning and the end of an imaginative performance are where we pass out of the common world and return into it. To the extent that we are not our environment, each person is a little piece of not-world, of counterfactuality guarded by a membrane, a seven-gated city with armed warriors—teeth or antibodies or critical reason—on guard at the gates. Art can be a passport—or the branch of golden leaves—that allows us to enter and to leave.

But to stand outside the wall and consider it as we are doing now is to constitute ourselves as another outer wall, surrounding the inner wall. What does this new outer wall look like from outside? If we back up to see, we make yet another wall beyond; the "I" that contemplates the "myself" is in turn reduced to a "myself" that is contemplated by a new "I." Thus concentric structures tend to multiply themselves, as two mirrors will when confronted with each other. If one mirror is square and one is round, the shape one sees when one is in between is the shape of the mandala, which possesses hypnotic qualities: the city is surrounded by many walls, the living organism by a richer and richer integument of membranes, which include senses, limbs, and nervous system. Or perhaps the elaboration of skins takes place in an inward direction, and the neocortex is the innermost skin of all. So thought Henry David Thoreau, whose anthropology of experience is described in essay five. Consciousness is the moment-by-moment accumulation of memory of one's previous self, a continuous growing of new rings; subjective time is simply the experience of that growth. From the point of view of the hearing system, each "ring" is three seconds thick, the length of a moment, of an iambic pentameter.

These last two paragraphs might be taken as a kind of gloss on the statement "all the world's a stage." There is a deep paradox in this statement which points us to another universal element of performance, another rule of human artistic language. Simply put, we cannot detach the sense of "act" as "pretend, counterfeit" from the sense of "act" as "do." Really to do something is by definition not to merely counterfeit something; and yet there is a terrifying wisdom in the stubborn resistance of the word "act" to being claimed, as it were, by either of its two senses and thus losing its strange logical tension. To do, says the word "act," always involves a pretence, just as to win a kingdom is first to be a pretender to the throne. Any true act we do is a pushing out into the realm of the unaccustomed (otherwise it would not be an act but merely part of our regular being); it is to step out of our previous identity and into another. The same ambiguity is found in the word "perform:" "I pay you for performance, not to put on a performance." So also a plot, a story, is also always a deceptive conspiracy. The free play of a system, when it is doing what naturally is proper to it, is after all only "play." Every real stage we go through is only a stage. The person is a mask; the character is only what is scratched or engraved onto a surface to make it mean something it did not mean

before. The agon is an agony; "agere" means both to drive
and to do; an agent is not necessarily the real doer of a
legal deed. To make something is to make it up; its
makeup or constitution is perhaps only makeup or cos-
metics. "Art" itself implies artifice, even wiles and
charms.

What we learn from this relentless pattern of lexical
paradoxes is that to pretend to be something is to go a
long way to becoming it. St. Paul uses the normal word
for dressing-up when he says "Put ye on Christ." By
putting Him on, the Christian becomes his Christ—a
becoming garment indeed. And all action involves a risk
of deception, or even a perilous loss of self. The "passing
through" of experience is perhaps a proper cause for fear.
For the literary artist or critic one consequence is plain: a
completely honest literary art cannot exist, if honesty
implies no fiction, no "making up," no departure from
the self as it is up to now. Literature is not a record of
experience, but an experience, if literature is true to its
roots in performance. To take us in to it, a literary work
must deceive us, indeed, take us in. The lyric poem
which honestly and accurately sets down the poet's
sensations or feelings without artifice is not in this sense
art, or poetry (which means, literally, "making up") at all.
And "real life" is the same: the only way one attains a
real autonomous self, if these linguistic paradoxes are
accurate, is to assume one, to play or act or playact
oneself so convincingly that like the First Player in
Hamlet one forces one's soul to one's own conceit.[26]

In this way the old Romantic problem, of the conflict
between spontaneity and self-consciousness, is exploded.
Consciousness, or reflexivity, if it is actively affecting the
very person that is generating it, always immediately
loses itself and becomes spontaneous in the amplifying
reverberations of its own feedback system. It is the
attempt to cling to an unreflective "natural" self that is

paralyzing: and this, not excessive consciousness, is the real source of the malaise that Wordsworth, Coleridge, and Keats complain of. The highest kind of "flow," to adopt the language of Mihaly Csikszentmihalyi,[27] who contrasts the spontaneity of "flow" with the reflexiveness of "frame," occurs when reflexiveness itself has reached its specific "speed of light" and is so total that it has lost the awkwardness of ordinary self-consciousness. Stage actors describe this experience as being like flying, and insist that it occurs only and essentially in performance.[28] Yet readers, too, report the same near-breathlessness, the slight rising of the hair and gooseflesh, the pricking of incipient tears, the mixture of total control with total freedom as the limits of one's consciousness-system are reached, transcended, and recreated. Is reading, at its best, a kind of performance, then? If so, our critical theory must be largely overhauled.

Literature is not usually referred to as a "performing" or "lively" art at all. But the perspective we have developed here would deny that distinction. If literary art is truly descended from the oral tradition, then indeed it is performed. In a later chapter, "Reading as Performance," some of the implications of this suggestion will be explored.

Given the conception of reader as performer, another central element of performance becomes crucially important. What Stanislavsky showed was that an actor must have a clear, single objective (even if it is a very profound one) in order to perform convincingly. Modern literary criticism, with its love of ambiguity, multiple meanings, dialectical hermeneutics, and deconstructive unraveling of contradictory significations, has provided every work of literature, *as a text*, with a divine plenum of viable interpretations. The text is an infinite and eternal set of possibilities. Like an electron before it is detected, which can only be described as a finite (if usually infinitesimal)

likelihood of an electron-type event spread throughout
the entire universe from its beginning to its end, with a
strong peak of probability in a particular region, the text
for a modern critic is essentially indeterminate, unactual-
ized, and perhaps unactualizable.

But a reading—like a reading on an instrument designed to make an electron declare itself—if it is a true
performance, must choose an objective and must sacrifice the divine indeterminacy and infinitude of possibility for the tragic and concrete finitude of actuality. It is
simply impossible to perform a reading and keep the text
of the modern critic. The text dies into its reading as the
divine incarnate victim dies into the eucharistic sacrament. The honor, the sadness, and the glory of true
theatrical performance lies partly in the consciousness of
all the participants that the work of art is dying with each
reverberation into the air at the very moment that it is
actualized.

What are the implications for the critic? Perhaps if she
or he is a virtuoso performer, it is to give so lucid, so
definite a reading that the work is actualized and made
concrete before us, and reincarnated into the deepest
idiom and costume and dialect of our own time. The
implications of this approach for the teacher of literature
are explored in essay four.

Perhaps ambiguity is less of a virtue than we have
come to think. The universe began as a soup of chance,
and its evolution into the exquisite forms of life and
intelligence was a cumulative process of greater and
greater lawfulness, definiteness, and certainty, carrying
with it, of course, greater and greater gradients of possible
fall back into the ambiguous chaos of its origins.[29] Anything ordered, beautiful, actual, and concrete, stands
tragically high above the precipice of undifferentiated
"hermeneutic richness." Great literature is the achievement of an unmistakable clarity and intelligibility in the

teeth of the proclivity of every word, every sentence, to collapse entropically into divine indeterminacy. The only legitimate use of ambiguity in literature is perhaps as part of a finesse toward greater actuality of coherent meaning —as builders of sandcastles may, to achieve greater compactness, wet the sand they use with the very element that will destroy their creation when the tide comes in. In a performance multiple meanings only work if they redundantly resonate the carrier-wave of its lawfulness; the proper contradictions of literary language, like the ones implicit in Shakespeare's use of the word "act," are like the facing mirrors in a laser that organize the plenum of wavelengths and phases in a light beam into a coherent pulse of energy. Only with such an instrument can truly three-dimensional images be wrung like ghosts from the plot, rhythm, symbolism, and argument of a literary work, as a split laser beam can actualize the image implicit in the grooves of a hologram.

Recent developments in the philosophy of language lend unexpected confirmation to the theory of criticism that is implied here. Modernist philosophy was based on the brilliant skepticism of the seventeenth century: Bacon's, which resulted in empiricism, and Descartes', which resulted in rationalism. It is beginning to look now as if even that skepticism itself was a presumptuous and implicitly metaphysical act of faith. (The history of the resulting religion of materialism is sketched in essay six.) That kind of certainty which modern skepticism found so disappointingly absent in the traditional view of reality now appears meaningless and nonsensical, for instead of a world of objects and a world of knowledge about them (which should correspond) we now confront a world in which knowledge is another kind of object, and objects are made up of the knowledge other objects have of them.[30] Descartes' and Hume's powerful critiques of empirical knowledge have been seconded by Popper, who defines empirical knowledge, as such, as knowledge which is falsifiable.[31] We deal regularly in physics with events which would have been quite different had we come to know them in a different way.[32] The neurological description of the brain as a damped, driven feedback system whose capacity for enormous variation resulting from miniscule differences in initial conditions, and whose active role in the construction of reality makes impartial objective observation impossible, is profoundly subversive to the requirements of empirical knowledge. The very complexity of the brain, with its 10^{10^9} possible brain states,[33] exceeds the theoretical computing capacity of the rest of the physical universe; thus no objective check on the legitimacy of its activities could be carried out.

This is not to say that empirical knowledge, knowledge by experience and the evidence of the senses, is invalid. But its validity cannot be sought within itself. If we know something empirically, we cannot empirically know that we know it. Strangely enough, the same kind of problem arises even for rational knowledge, that inner sanctum of certainty to which Descartes retreated. I oversimplify, but I shall here take rational knowledge to be the same thing as logical truth, truth by definition, or analytic truth. An example is that a plane triangle contains one hundred eighty degrees in its interior angles. Another is that bachelors are unmarried. But the problem with rational knowledge is, as Gödel showed, that there is no system of axioms which is capable of proving the truth of its own axioms.[34] Every system of logic rich enough to make meaningful propositions will contain a proposition of this form: "This statement is not provable," a statement which is true but not provable, and which therefore distinguishes truth from provability within the system. One must leave the system in order to be able to assert the proposition's truth. In doing philosophy in language, for instance, where do we stand when asked to give a definition of the word "definition" or of the word "refer?"

Thus the twin foundations of modern knowledge seem to be no longer foundations at all, but perhaps, like the seeming-solid planet Earth itself, in free fall. What kind of knowledge *can* we believe in for sure? Is the "knowledge" model of language-use the most accurate one anyway? Suppose language-use were conceived less as a collection of cognitive propositions, and more as a set of actions?

The philosopher J. L. Austin identified an interesting group of utterances, called which he characterized as "performative" statements, closely related to speech acts, in which the speaker performs an action by what he or she says, rather than states a belief or a piece of knowledge.[35] Performative utterances rely neither on an unreliable correspondence with empirical fact, nor on the unreliable truth of a set of unprovable axioms. My own favorite example is the dealer in a poker game who stipulates that in the game she is dealing, red threes will be wild. Once she makes this statement, red threes are indeed wild; yet they are in no sense wild by definition (another dealer could choose one-eyed Jacks instead), nor would her statement yield to empirical falsification. No player could check his hand and complain that he had a red three that happened not to be wild. A poker chip could conceivably fall upward, as a result of some extraordinary cosmological freak of gravity or quantum-statistical freak of probability; or a whole group of poker players might hallucinate it falling upwards. But the red three is wild.

In other words, performative truth can be more reliable than empirical or logical truth in certain situations. Those situations are often very important: though the stipulation of game-rules may be the purest example,

promising and contract-making are also performative, as
are marrying, legislating, religious invocations and sacraments, and perhaps even the scientific decision to base a
system of measurement upon a particular type of question asked of the physical universe. An instance here is
the stipulation of radioactive cesium decay as the basis of
time measurement, replacing astronomical measures.

In what circumstances can a performative statement
legitimately be made? First of all, there must be what I
shall call a "performative community:" a universe of
beings *for* whom a performative utterance shall be true.
Performative truth pays for its certainty by giving up its
claim to apply to entities outside its community. Secondly, the utterer must be empowered by that community to
make the performative stipulation. Third, the performative utterance can stipulate reality only where previous
legislation within the performative community and still
in force is not declared to be in contradiction with it.
These limitations introduce an intriguing feature of performative truths: they are always certain, but they can
vary in strength and effectiveness, depending on the size
of their performative community. To win and keep a
large community, a performative must be in a relation
with the past constitution of its universe that is parsimonious, consistent, coherent, powerful, predictive, and
elegant—in a word, beautiful. Beauty is the fourth requirement of performative truth.

At this point we may see how empirical truth and
logical truth find a place within the broader framework of
the performative which restores to them much of the
legitimacy they have lost to rigorous twentieth-century
analysis. (Ironic that Reason, inductive and deductive,
must be rescued by an appeal to the fundamental principle underlying the medieval ideas of faith, authority, and
revelation!) Empirical observation and experiment can
now be seen not as an independent source of truth value,

but as a way of enlarging the performative community so as to include not only persons but also non-personal and non-living organisms; and of establishing what kind of utterance can be true for them. Newton's inverse square law of gravitation relied on the establishment of a performative community including the moon, the planets, apples, and dropping cannonballs, which had a language in common. In a sense it did not matter how the law itself was proposed: in any case it would have constituted a definition of space. Newton wished to keep space flat and Euclidean, so he made the gravitational attraction proportional to the inverse square of the distance. Einstein, on the other hand, preferred to make the gravitational attraction constant and vary the curvature of space. Which we choose depends finally on how beautiful—as already defined—the resulting universe game is.

Rational or logical truth also finds a place within the performative universe. When we state an axiom we are in fact making a performative utterance. "A straight line is the shortest distance between two points" cannot be tested for logical consistency with its axioms: it *is* an axiom. If we are in the performative community of the geometer, we accept his dictum here; and what persuades us to join and remain in that community is partly the beauty of the universe generated by that axiom. By their fruits, not their grounds, we shall judge them: for there are no grounds. The universe, our cosmologists tell us, began in chaos and nonexistence, so the final ground of any appeal is utterly unreliable;[36] and the world won its way to such consistency as it has through a long and bitter process of selection by consequences. In this light the American pragmatist tradition of philosophy is quite consistent with the performative view of truth: we make, or even make up the truth, and keep it if it works. William James's conception of the "will to believe"[37] —in which he defends ungrounded faith by arguing that it can bring about the reality it stipulates—is essentially a performative one.

Perhaps those quantum measurements of electrons, which force them to declare their position or energy, and the use of polarizing filters to make photons "make up their mind" which orientation they are vibrating in, are performative communications with nature. Indeed, there is an element in any coherent scientific experiment which consists of a declaration of groundrules, a delimitation of the region of significant events. Though science is a process of questioning, it is scientists who decide what questions to ask.[38]

It should already be clear that there is a close relationship between performative utterance and performance in literature, in the oral tradition, and in ritual, human and even animal. Mating rituals among animals stipulate not previously existent beings (the "enemy" in the triumph ceremony) and bring into being a real entity, the pair bond, as well as a new individual of the species. At a Catholic mass, the bread and wine performatively *are* the body and blood of Christ (for the faithful, that is one of the things that the word "Christ" means, and they after all have a right to decide what a word means for them). When a storyteller says, "Once upon a time," or "I sing of that man skilled in all ways of contending" the subjunctive world is welded to this one and becomes part of it, yielding up its divine infantile indeterminacy as an electron does when it is measured. When a poet writes and an actor speaks the line, he "gives to airy nothing A local habitation and a name;" performs new being into existence.[39]

Toward the end of *The Origin of Species* Darwin permitted himself a metaphor—that of the branching tree of life, whose every twig was a species and whose branches represented ancient genera, families, classes, and kingdoms.[40] Freud, too, illustrated his theory of the psyche in society with a myth—that of the primal horde.[41] Socrates began the practice, perhaps, and it is originally on his authority that a sort of *Gedanken-experiment* or myth is offered here.

The function of the myth is to bring together the various perspectives explored in this essay: human evolution's role in the development of the linguistic arts; ritual as the root of the oral tradition and ultimately of literature; the adaptation of brain chemistry, structure and function to the forms and substance of those arts; their cultural universality; their essential nature as types of performance; and their philosophically performative validity. The myth is also intended to dispel any suspicion that the theory proposed here is a reductionist one—that is, behaviorally or biologically determinist. At the same time the myth rejects the opposite view, which has in fact cooperated with the reductionist view in preserving a sterile dualism: that is, the conception of literary art as *sui generis*, without connection with the vital history of our species. The myth also takes up anew the fertile Renaissance debate about the relationship between nature and art which was aborted in the seventeenth century by the rise of Reason, rational and empirical, and in the nineteenth century by the romantic idea of Nature as innocent and unreflexive; but the debate is now enriched by the greater effectiveness of our technology, by the collapse of epistemology and ontology in quantum theory, and by the full elaboration of the theory of evolution.

Once upon a time, then, there was a clever race of apes. Like many other species of higher animals, they possessed a sophisticated though instinctual system of vocal communication; they engaged in play activity when unoccupied; they possessed elaborate instinctual rituals, especially surrounding the functions of reproduction; their ranking system promoted wide variations in reproductive success; and like other higher primates they used rudimentary tools and passed their use down to the next generation by instruction as well as by genetic inheritance.

It took only one individual to combine these capacities in such a way that the Word became incarnate as a seed of culture and began to mold its host species into a suitable soil for it to flourish in. The competition for mates was intense; a competition which in other species had evolved structures as impractical as the antlers of the giant elk and the feathers of the peacock, and behaviors as contrary to survival as the mating dance of March hares or the courtship of the blue satin bowerbird. At the same time the border between play behavior and mating behavior was paper-thin. One individual, then, discovered that the desired mate responded favorably to playlike variation in the instinctual mating ritual: it was an improved lovesong that began the human race, for their mating ritual already involved a prominent vocal element.

This first pair was imitated by others, and those which did so achieved greater reproductive success. They were in turn imitated by their young, who had inherited a slightly improved capacity to override the genetic hardwiring of their ritual inheritance by playlike variation on it. (This contrast, between inherited norm and playlike variation, will be preserved later in the general information processing system of human beings, where a regular carrier wave is systematically distorted to carry meaning; and specifically where a regular poetic meter is tensed against the rhythm of the spoken sentence, or musical meter is stretched or compacted by rubato, or even where visual symmetry is partly broken by the pleasing proportions of the golden section.)

Thus was born what we might call the Freedom and Dignity Game: for as it became elaborated, it developed vocal forms which, like the phantom opponent of the triumphal geese, had at the time no referents—honor, soul, purpose, good, love, the future, freedom, dignity, the gods, and so on. But those vocal forms were performative utterances, and so for the performative community of the tribe those mysterious entities actually came into existence. As if they were real all along, those abstract entities became independent sources of active determination, even though the medium of their being and of their continuity was no more than a communal convention. But after all, our bodily structures are maintained as realities not by themselves but by a mere arrangement of genes.

The ritual game indeed rapidly evolved. It developed cells of active reflexivity and self-criticism. Each generation altered it competitively, introducing new complexities: kinship classification, decorative art, food taboos, hygiene, household conventions, law, storytelling, and all the rest. And in turn these complexities exerted irresistible selective pressure upon those wise apes. They developed an adolescence, with special hormones to promote rebellion against the traditional ritual. Infancy was protracted, to help develop and program the huge brain that was required to handle the complexities of the ritual, and lifespan was prolonged to accommodate the extra programming-time. A massive sexualization took place in the species, so that male and female were continuously in heat, females experienced orgasm like males, and they copulated face-to-face, thus transforming sex into a form of communication. The reward system of the brain was recalibrated to respond most powerfully to beauty, which is the quality which characterizes the ritual's dynamic relationship of stability and increasing coherent complexity. Body decoration and clothing banished body hair. The hands turned into expressive instruments. The otolaryngeal system was elaborated into an exquisitely sensitive medium of communication and expression. The two sides of the brain became specialized, one for recognizing and holding an existing context in place, the other for acting upon it and transforming it in time. The indeterminacy of the world was lumped together into a new concept, the future, which was carried by the dissonance between right brain pattern and left brain sequence. The present was born as the realm of the act.

At a certain point in the Neolithic Age the performative community began to expand beyond the limits of the genus—which we may already recognize as *Homo*. Certain plants and animals—wheat, dogs—had joined the performative community in subordinate roles, their gene structures changing in response to the human ritual game. It was, in comparison with the five million years the ritual had existed, but a moment before large regions of physics, chemistry, and biology had joined the human game and had been taught by scientific experimentation and instrumentation to speak the same language as we. Contemporary technology is the concrete continuation of the performative fiat with which we began.

But the moment that other, non-human entities began to join the game, the selective pressure it had exerted upon its performative community ceased, for the bookkeeping functions which the game had relegated to the genes could now be taken up by our servants the plants, the animals, and the minerals. Reproductive success no longer depended on proficiency in the game, and eventually there arose a celibate priesthood which entrusted its entire informational inheritance not to its genes but to the prosthetic seeds—semen, semantics—of music, writing, and the visual arts.

Our genetic inheritance, then, was frozen at the point it had reached in the Neolithic Age, and thus its fundamental grammar must be ours. For us to use the marvelous instrument of our brains properly we must figure out that grammar. And when we have done so we may be able to reinvigorate that pallid, decadent and degenerate descendant of the great ritual, literature, with an infusion of the wild stock. We may do so partly by the mediation of the oral tradition, a healthy strain even in advanced technological culture, partly by breeding from our own performance and performative genres, and partly by hybridization with the ritual play of other cultures all over the world.

Nor will this work of revitalization be only a recuperation, an attempt to recover in part what has been lost. Rather, it will represent a new phase of evolution in the great game, the phase in which the game contemplates itself as a whole with the most meticulous scholarship, and directly guides its own development using what it has learned. In so doing it will have taken to itself the powers once allocated in hope and terror to uncontrolled deities which were neither kind nor humane, and will have begun to fulfill the promise of many religions, of the incarnation of the Word as reality rather than just as a seed. Nor need we fear that the process of the spirit will become tame and commonplace, for the more we know ourselves, the more radically the "knower" is thrust into the unfathomable mystery surrounding the cosmos, in the attempt to step back to get a better view. There is no conflict between consciousness and spontaneity: It is only the consciousness which holds back from full commitment that is impotent.

What are the immediate consequences for literary criticism of the new theory of the word arts as it emerges?

First, perhaps, a dethroning of the text as the central locus of the act of literary art. Thus hermeneutics loses its specific relationship to literary studies and becomes a branch of the general process of analysis as it is used in the sciences, the social sciences, engineering, linguis-

tics, and so on. Hermeneutics remains a useful but
unprivileged technique among others in the study and
appreciation of literature. But the emphasis will shift to
literary performance; in non-oral literature, that performance is curiously divided between the writer and the
reader, and the text that connects them floats in a limbo
of potentiality. The interest that the text may possess as a
complex structure in itself may be great, but it is no
different from the interest that a living cell, a complex
polymer, or an atomic nucleus possess. The interesting
involution of structure may in fact have little to do with
its actual value as a work of literary art: *Finnegan's Wake*
is surely more complicated, and a lesser work of art, than
the *Iliad; The Faerie Queene* than *King Lear.* Instead
of the text we shall be most interested, as literary folk, in
the instantiation—the incarnation in concrete action at a
particular time—of the work in performance. One good
sign that a person truly possesses a work of literature is
that one can remember, without having consciously
memorized them, large passages of the work, and that
those passages are recalled at those moments when they
can make life more lucid and meaningful. The capacity to
go through the work and do a hermeneutic or structural
analysis of it may have nothing to do with this real
possession of it.

An aspect of literary study which has been largely
ignored by the theorists becomes important here: oral
performance. One activity which really fastens a work of
literature to a human life is reading it aloud; and learning
to do that well may be more important than the technique of critical analysis (though good recitation will
surely involve, as a subordinate activity, some analysis).
Literary activity takes place largely in the classroom:
there is no harm in this, but given our altered view of
literature the classroom situation appears in a new light.
The classroom is to the literary ritual as the temple or

shrine is to religious ritual, as the theater is to drama or as the *dojo* or practice-ground is to the martial arts school. The teacher should recognize that the role of teacher requires something of the probity of a priest and the charisma of the actor. The class should enter into the spirit of comedy when a comedy is the subject; and there should be in the classroom that slight touch of danger, of the possibility of personal transformation that one finds in real performances and ritual action. (In the fourth essay such a classroom experience is described.) When Paulina in Shakespeare's *The Winter's Tale*, about to bring the statue to life, says, "Those that think it is unlawful business I am about, let them depart," the full force of that statement should be felt in the classroom as it should be in the theater. It ought to be dangerous to bring the dead to life, and real drama is doing precisely that, by performative fiat, just as in the eucharist the bread performatively becomes the body of Christ.

The reading of literature in the classroom ought to be explicitly related to the life values of the individuals present and of the community as a whole. The performances of Aristophanes and Sophocles at the feast of Dionysus in Athens, which implicitly joined the debate about the Peloponnesian War, are models in this sense.

This is not to say that the other half of the performance —the writer's own strange quiet frenzy over the page— should be ignored. A large part of literary study should be reconstructive, that is, it should most carefully enter the imaginative world of the author and reconstruct, with the author, the work of literature as it is being created; just as a priest at a Mass will reenact the movements and words of Jesus as he broke the bread; as the priest/actor in an Indonesian ritual drama will take on the role and actions of Hanuman the Monkey-God; or even as the Dalai Lama is all previous Dalai Lamas reincarnated. Standing where Shakespeare stands in the original com-

posing and performing of *The Tempest* or where Woolf
stands delivering *A Room of One's Own* will do more
to help us possess those works of art than any amount
of hermeneutics, though hermeneutics may be one way of
helping us get to that place. To possess a work of
literature is the purpose of trying to comprehend it. One
does not necessarily "comprehend" one's own eye or
one's own hand; and a great work of art can be as
valuable, as intimate, an organ.

Another consequence of the new view of literature
applies especially to us who are the heirs of modernism.
Great literary art calls us back to the work of making
ourselves human and remaking the world so that it more
richly expresses itself. Religion, literature, legislation,
science, and technological choice are all parts of the same
world constructing activity. We modernists, like angry,
indolent, rebellious adolescents, have neglected that
work for many decades, and have gone after anything
which did not seem as if it might be of enduring human
value. The result has been a systematic deprivation of the
inner pleasures, those brain rewards that are associated
with cosmogenesis. Perhaps, as will be argued in essay
six, we have turned to narcotics and to nuclear weapons
for exactly the same reason: to provide by artificial means
the sense of crucial value, value worth sacrificing for, that
we gave up when we rejected the human ritual and the
oral tradition. It is indeed part of our heritage that we
should rebel, that we should alter the ritual, generation
by generation. But the illumination occurs when both
sides of the mind—the innovative and the pattern-
holding—are mutually translated, when the new material
of the world is grafted so cunningly with the old than the
seam cannot be detected.[42]

We are on the verge of a new classicism, which I call
"natural classicism," based upon the deep lexicon and

syntax of human artistic nature as we are now coming to understand it. That new classicism, unlike the old, will not conceive of standards as an eternal and ideal perfection which can only asymptotically be approached, but rather as an aura, a mysterious and ghostly scaffold that precedes the growing edge, the concrescence of the world as it is performed into actual being. But there will be standards, and they will be neither relative nor pluralist in their fundamental character, though they will be so richly generative that they will perhaps appear to exemplify pluralism and relativism. Consider the myriad musics, poetries, and paintings of the world's culture's: How wholesome they are in the main; how recognizable they are, as human, to an anthropologist; how they obey the deep laws of proportion, color, meter and tone; and how they embody those essential human interests in kinship, cookery, and the soul; yet how diverse they are. The new classicism will be a single house, but like the Kingdom of Heaven a house of many mansions. And it will be also a house which is growing, to which wings are continually being added; it will be hierarchical, but the hierarchy of its values and genres will not signify a static Chain of Being but a dynamic evolutionary tree of life.

One of the unifying principles in natural classicism will be the use of poetic meter as a way of breaking the monopoly of the left temporal lobe in literature. The new investigation and use of the integrative relationship between biological and mental life will involve a re-innervation of the limbic system, and even of the body as a whole, by the conscious cortex, and a reinnervation of the left with the right sides of the brain. We shall reach back to ancient technologies such as meter, as well as forward to the science of neurology and the technology of prosthesis, to accomplish this act of enlightenment. But we must recognize that like an athlete or an adept at

meditation, a skilled reader of verse requires training and
discipline—training and discipline of which our children
have been increasingly deprived.

We shall, perhaps, reconcile ourselves to the fact that
there is no substitute for plot and story in literary art. If
our valuation of character, symbolism, imagery, theme,
and imitative form replaces our concern for the fundamental value of plot—if we dismiss story as having been
exhausted—then we have taken a step toward relinquish-
ing that mastery over time which makes us peculiarly
human. We each know how to go on being a conscious
person, how to construct a moral existence, how to win
meaning from the fact of change, because we have stories
that we can use as control-tests to sift out significant
variation in experience, and, even more important, to
resonate with significant constancies. Some writers, notably Deleuze and Guattari,[43] suggest that freedom consists in abandoning the coherence of self and of cosmos
and destroying the future as a significant conception.
Perhaps when we are no longer in danger of destroying
the entire species by such attitudes, we can try them out.
Voluntary prefrontal lobotomy would be a good start, for
it would abort our natural tendency to make sense of the
world. Meanwhile, we need stories to keep us alive; as
David Bynum puts it: "I know the chief use or function of
fabulous narrative traditions everywhere is to *make men
adaptable in their minds,* to enlarge the scope of their
mental lives beyond the confines of their actual experience socially, psychically, and in every other way. I am so
far persuaded of this that I have come to think of fabulous
story-telling, and even of the stories so told in tradition,
as proper aspects of human biology . . ."[44]

We shall rediscover the value of the genres as embodying anciently-tested constellations of rules, whole syn-
taxes in themselves, tuned to the human nervous system.
We will no longer dismiss as technological coincidence

the independent rediscovery of epic, for instance, by the authors of *Gilgamesh*, the *Iliad*, the *Mahabharata*, the *Heike*; or of tragic drama by the Japanese, the Chinese, the Indonesians, the Greeks, and the Aztecs.

We shall perhaps, as literary folk, take up once again the responsibility for singing the world into being; and now our capacity to do this has been immensely strengthened by the scientific and technological enlargement of our performative community to include large areas of nature. An ontological criticism implies an ontological literary art: our stories will be histories, our metaphors will be concrete realities, our acting will be action.

Notes

1. I refer, of course, to Darwin's study of the flora and fauna of the Galapagos Islands, especially the finches, which he undertook during the voyage of the *Beagle* and which demonstrated to him the effects of adaptation within a closed system.
2. For instance, depending on whether we confine the term "human culture" to *Homo erectus* and beyond, or include the pithecines, Jane B. Lancaster in *Primate Behavior and the Emergence of Human Culture* (Holt, Rinehart, 1975) would date the "overlap" from either one or five million years ago to about twelve thousand years ago when the agricultural revolution began (p.35). John C. Eccles, in *The Human Mystery* (Springer, 1979), estimates that the period extended from one million to one hundred thousand years ago (p.94). A. Irving Hallowell proposes, in "The Protocultural Foundations of Human Evolution" in *The Social Life of Early Man*, Sherwood L. Washburn, ed. (Aldine, 1961), a protocultural stage of human evolution, in which some but not all of the cultural features of modern humanity were in place, well before the major expansion of the brain, among the early hominids. This could, according to some estimates, be as much as twenty-five to fifty million years ago. Edward Sapir, in *Language: An Introduction to the Study of Speech* (Harcourt Brace, 1921), and Grace

Andrus De Laguna, in *Speech: Its Function and Development* (Indiana University Press, 1963) believe that language, and thus *a fortiori*, culture, were co-original with tool use, which would give us a period of up to fifteen million years. But Mary LeCron Foster, in "The Symbolic Structure of Primordial Language" in *Human Evolution: Biosocial Perspectives*, disagrees, placing the origin of language only fifty thousand years ago. However, she does not rule out the possibility of prelinguistic culture. G.F. Debetz, the Soviet anthropologist, dates the origin of human culture to the origin of tool-*making*, rather than tool use, which might give us three million years. (See "The Social Life of Early Man as Seen through the Work of the Soviet Anthropologists" in *The Social Life of Early Man*, S.L. Washburn, ed. Peter J. Wilson, in his excellent book, *Man the Promising Primate* (Yale University Press, 1980), also argues that tool-making implies genuine human culture, and regards *Homo habilis* (1.9-3 million years ago) as fully human in this sense. Perhaps the clearest and most unambiguous description of the origin of distinctively human culture is in F. Clark Howell's "Recent Advances in Human Evolutionary Studies," *Perspectives on Human Evolution*, S.L. Washburn and Phyllis Dolhinow, eds. (Holt, Rinehart, 1972). He asserts that the genus *Homo* is coterminous with human culture, which would give about three to five million years of overlap between the final phases of human biological evolution and the early ages of cultural evolution.
3. Virginia Woolf, *A Room of One's Own* (Harcourt Brace, 1957).
4. See, especially, V.W. Turner, *The Ritual Process* (Aldine, 1969), and *The Drums of Affliction* (Oxford University Press, 1968).
5. I. Eibl-Eibesfeldt, *Ethology: The Biology of Behavior* (Holt, Rinehart, 1975); K. Lorenz, *King Solomon's Ring* (Signet, 1952); J.S. Huxley, "The Courtship Habits of the Great Crested Grebe (Podiceps cristatus); with an "Addition of the Theory of Sexual Selection," *Proceedings of the Zoological Society of London*, 35, 1914.
6. Kinji Imarishi, "Social Behavior in Japanese Monkeys," *Macaca fuscata*, *Psychologia*, Vol. 1, 1957.
John E. Frisch, "Research on Primate Behavior in Japan," *American Anthropology*, Vol. 61.
M. Kawai, "Newly Acquired Pre-Cultural Behavior of the

Natural Troop of Japanese Monkeys on Koshima Islet," *Primates*, 6, 1965.

J. Itani, "On the Acquisition and Propagation of a New Food Habit in the Troop of Japanese Monkeys at Takasakiyama," *Primates*, 1, 1958.

7. E.G. d'Aquili, C.D. Laughlin, Jr., and J. McManus, eds., *The Spectrum of Ritual: A Biogenetic Structural Analysis*, Columbia University Press, 1979.

8. In *Poetry*, Aug. 1983.

9. S.M. Glenn and C.C. Cunningham, "What Do Babies Listen to Most?", *Developmental Psychology*, 19, 1983.

10. James Olds, "Behavioral Studies of Hypothalmic Functions: Drives and Reinforcements," *Biological Foundations of Psychiatry*, Vol. 1, R.G. Grenell and S. Babay, eds. (Raven, 1976); A. Routtenberg, *Biology of Reinforcement: Facets of Brain Stimulation Reward* (Academic Press, 1980); Solomon H. Snyder, "Opiate Receptors and Internal Opiates," *Scientific American*, March, 1977; Roger Guillemin, "Peptides in the Brain: The New Endocrinology of the Neuron," *Science*, 202, 1978. See also the chapter on "Joy" in Melvin Konner's *The Tangled Wing: Biological Constraints on the Human Spirit* (Holt, Rinehart, 1982). Neuroreceptors in the living human brain were first imaged by Henry N. Wagner and his collaborators, as reported in *Science*, September, 1983: "Imaging Dopamine Receptors in the Human Brain by Positrin Tomography." The first imaging of an actual opiate receptor is reported by this group in *The Journal of Computed Tomagraphy*, February, 1985.

11. Lionel Tiger, *Optimism: The Biology of Hope* (Simon and Schuster, 1979). See also J.C. Willer, H. Dehen, and J. Cambier, "Stress-Induced Analgesia in Humans: Endogenous Opioids and Naxolone Reversible Depression of Pain Reflexes," *Science* 212, 1981.

12. E.S. Valenstein, *Brain Control* (Wiley, 1973).

13. Jacob von Uexkull, *Umwelt and Innenwelt der Tiere* (Springer, 1921).

14. J.A. Wheeler, "Genesis and Observership," in *University of Western Ontario Series in the Philosophy of Science*, R. Butts and J. Hintikka, eds. (Reidel, 1977). David Finkelstein, "Coherence and Possibility: The Logic of the Innermost Universe," *Kenyon Review*, New Series, Spring 1982.

15. Jerre Levy, "Psychobiological Implications of Bilateral Asymmetry," *Hemisphere Function in the Human Brain*, Stuart J. Diamond and J. Graham Beaumont, eds. (Wiley, 1974, pp. 166-167); see also Jerre Levy, "Interhemispheric Collaboration: Single-Mindedness in the Asymmetric Brain," *Developmental Neuropsychology and Education: Hemispheric Specialization and Integration*, C.T. Best, ed. (Academic Press, 1984); and Jerre Levy, "Cerebral Asymmetry and Aesthetic Experience," to be published in *Biological Aspects of Aesthetics*, D. Epstein, I. Eibl-Eibesfeldt, I. Rentschler, F. Turner, eds. (Not yet published.) This latter paper was first given at the Biology and Aesthetics Research Group meeting in January 1983 at the Werner Reimers Stiftung, Bad Hamburg, W. Germany.
16. Frances Yates, *The Theatre of the World* (University of Chicago, 1969).
17. Jerre Levy, "Interhemispheric Collaboration," op. cit., pp. 31-33.
18. Milman Parry, *The Making of Homeric Verse*, Adam Parry, ed. (Oxford University Press, 1971).
   Albert B, Lord, *The Singer of Tales* (Harvard University Press, 1960).
19. See J.T. Fraser, *Of Time, Passion and Knowledge* (Brasiller, 1975, part III.
20. V.W. Turner, *The Forest of Symbols* (Cornell University Press, 1967).
21. George Peter Murdock, "The Common Denominator of Cultures," *Perspectives on Human Evolution*, Vol. 1, S.L. Washburn and Phyllis C. Joy, eds. (Holt, Rinehart, 1968, p. 231).
22. Joseph Campbell, *The Historical Atlas of World Mythology*, (Times Books, 1984).
23. James G. Fraser, *The Magic Art and the Evolution of Kings* (Macmillan, 1911). Claude Lévi-Strauss, *The Raw and the Cooked* (Harper, 1984). David Bynum, *The Daemon in the Wood* (Harvard University Press, 1973).
24. David Lindsay, *A Voyage to Arcturus* (Ballantine, 1963); Frank Herbert, *Dune* (Berkely, 1965); Gene Wolfe, *The Book of the New Sun* (Pocket Books, 1980, 1981); Ursula K. Le Guin, *The Left Hand of Darkness* (Harper and Row, 1969).
25. Konstantin Stanislavski, *An Actor Prepares*, Elizabeth Reynolds, tr. (Hapgood, Theatre Arts Books, 1946).

Jerzy Grotowski, *Towards a Poor Theatre* (Odin Teatrets Forlag, Holstebro, 1968).

Richard Schechner, *Essays on Performance Theory, 1970-1976* (Drama Book Specialists, 1977).

——, "Performers and Spectators Transported and Transformed," *Kenyon Review*, New Series, Fall, 1981.

Victor W. Turner, From Ritual to Theatre (Performing Arts Journal Publications, 1962).

——, Dramas, Fields and Metaphors (Cornell University Press, 1974).

26. Stephen Greenblatt, *Renaissance Self-Fashioning: From More to Shakespeare* (Chicago University Press, 1980).

27. Mihaly Csikszentmihalyi, *The Experience of Play in Work and Games* (Jossey-Bass, 1975).

28. Ellen O'Brien, "Actors' Perspectives on Tragedy," to appear in *Shakespeare in Performance*, B. Beckerman, C.J. Gianakaris, C. Mazer, and F. Turner, eds. (Methuen, 1986).

29. Manfred Eigen and Ruthild Winkler, *Laws of the Game: How the Principles of Nature Govern Chance* (Knopf, 1981).

30. The history of this change is nicely charted in the evolution of Wittgenstein from the *Tractatus Logico-Philosophicus*, C.K. Ogden, trans. (Kegan Paul, 1933) to the *Philosophical Investigations*, G.E.M. Anscombe, trans. (Macmillan, 1955).

31. Karl Popper, *The Logic of Scientific Discovery* (Basic Books, 1959).

32. Werner Heisenberg, *Physics and Philosophy* (Harper, 1966).

33. J.T. Fraser, "Out of Plato's Cave: The Natural History of Time," *Kenyon Review*, Winter, 1980, p. 153.

34. Kurt Gödel, *On Formally Undecidable Propositions* (Basic Books, 1962).

35. J.L. Austin, *How to Do Things with Words* (Oxford University Press, 1976).

36. Alan H. Guth and Paul J. Steinhardt, "The Inflationary Universe," *Scientific American*, May, 1984, p. 123.

37. William James, *The Will to Believe and Other Essays in Popular Philosophy* in *The Works of William James* (Harvard University Press, 1979). See also H.S. Thayer, "The Right to Believe: William James' Reinterpretation of the Function of Religious Belief," *Kenyon Review*, Winter, 1983.

38. Thomas Kuhn, *The Structure of Scientific Revolutions* (University of Chicago Press, 1962).
39. William Shakespeare, *A Midsummer Night's Dream*, V. i. 16-17.
40. Charles Darwin, *The Origin of Species by Means of Natural Selection* (Collier Books, 1982, p. 121).
41. Sigmund Freud, *Civilization and Its Discontents* (Norton, 1981, pp. 46-48).
42. See William Shakespeare, *The Winter's Tale*, IV. iv. 72-103.
43. Gilles Deleuze and Felix Guattari, *L'Anti-Oedipe* (Editions de Minuit, Paris, 1972).
44. Op. cit., p. 27.

INTERCHAPTER II

The perspective offered in the previous essay can only prove its value by the fertility of the research it makes possible. The following essay takes up one element of literary art, poetic meter, and treats it as a specific neurophysiological aptitude with identifiable adaptive functions, a demonstrable basis in psychophysics, and a plausible mechanism in terms of known brain structures.

The general hypothesis of the first essay implies certain predictions about poetic meter: it should, even in the precise details of its operation, be culturally universal; its temporal periodicities should match observable cyclicities in the auditory cortex; it should be associated with changes in brain chemistry; and it should enable the brain to do things beyond the capacity of ordinary linguistic activity. In the following pages these predictions are tested against new and existing research.

More crucial to the humanist is whether the picture of meter that emerges from such scientific studies of it matches the actual aesthetic experience of it. I believe that far from diminishing meter to some kind of brutish automatism this approach actually enhances its dignity and importance as a truly human activity. Indeed, the place it gives meter is a much higher one than the official guardians of the arts, particularly modernist literary theorists, have allowed it. Ironically, the scientific investigation of meter may rescue it from artistic obscurity and lead to renewed vitality in an ancient and potent artistic practice.

The Neural Lyre:
Poetic Meter, The Brain,
and Time

This essay brings together an old subject, a new body of
knowledge, and a new scientific paradigm, which have
not previously been associated with one another. The
subject is poetic meter, a universal human activity,
which despite its universality and obvious importance in
most human cultures, has received very little attention
from humanists, except for the studies of a few literary
prosodists, and virtually none at all from science. The
new body of knowledge consists in the findings of that
intense study of the human brain which has taken place
in the last few decades. The new scientific paradigm has
been developed by the International Society for the Study
of Time. Its major postulates are that an understanding of
time is fundamental to an understanding of the real
world; that time is not simple, but composite; that time
is a hierarchy of more and more complex temporalities;
that the more complex temporalities evolved as part of
the general evolution of the universe, and in a sense the

evolution of time *constitutes* the evolution of the universe; and that the hierarchical character of time as we know it reflects and embodies the various stages of its evolution.[1]

The radically interdisciplinary nature of this essay is not simply a consequence of the need to seek explanations across the boundaries of different fields. It represents also a commitment and a belief not only that this type of study will cast light on its specific subject (poetic meter), but also that the scientific material will be reciprocally enhanced in value, taking its place within a framework which gives it greater predictive power; "understanding" itself consists in just such a union of detailed knowledge with global significance.

At this point it might be helpful to review the major characteristics of human cortical information-processing, as it has been provisionally determined by studies in perceptual psychology, brain-chemistry, psychology, brain evolution, brain development, ethology, and cultural anthropology.[2] Individually the characteristics of human brain-activity which are listed below are commonplace and uncontroversial for the most part; collectively they constitute a new picture of the human mind. This new picture replaces older, simple models of it, such as the unextended rational substance of Descartes, the association-matrix of Locke, the *tabula rasa* of Hume, the passive, reinforcement-driven animal of Skinner, and the genetically hard-wired robot of the sociobiologists, though it does include the elements which led those writers to construct their models.

Human information-processing is, on the crude level of individual neurons, *procrustean*. That is, it reduces the information it gets from the outside world to its own categories, and accepts reality's answers only if they directly address its own set of questions. In the macrocosm our perception of electromagnetic radiation cuts out all but heat and the visible spectrum; in the microcosm, a given neuron in the visual cortex will fire only if certain characteristics—say, a moving vertical light contrast—are met by the retinal image, and will ignore all others. We possess, as it were, a certain domineering and arrogant quality in our dealings with sensory information, and our brain will 'listen' only to replies to its own inquiries. In quantum physics the familiar procrustean questions (Waves or particles? Which slit did the photon pass through? Is this ray of light polarized north-south or east-west?) force reality into a certainty and definiteness which it did not naturally possess. This insistence on unambiguity is rooted in our neurons themselves.

Thus we may say that human information processing is, secondly, *determinative.* That is, it insists on certainty and unambiguity, and so is at war with the probabilistic and indeterminate nature of the most primitive and archaic components of the universe. This insistence on definiteness, however, is in a grand tradition: matter itself is a condition of energy which severely limits the probabilistic waywardness of its elementary particles; large clumps of organized matter, like crystals, have overcome much of the vagueness and unpredictability of their primary constituents (though they pay for their certainty by becoming liable to entropic decay). Indeed, the replication of living matter could be said to be another stage in the suppression of physical ambiguity, for it implies an exact continuity and stability of structure which survives even the matter of which it is composed. Thus the human neural insistence on determinateness is in line with a general tendency of nature, and is related to the syllogistic proposition that homeostatic systems tend to endure and survive.

Third, and in contrast to the "conservative" tendency just described, the human nervous system seems designed to register differences. It is *habituative*. That is, it tends to ignore repeated and expected stimuli, and to respond only to the new and unexpected. Though it asks the questions, it is more interested in odd answers than ordinary ones. Temporally it hears changes and sees movements; spatially it sees contrasts and borderlines. Deprived of its sacchades, the eye sees nothing, for it sees no differences.

Fourth, human nervous activity is fundamentally *synthetic* in its aim. It seeks gestalts even when they are not there, and there is a serious ontological question as to whether they do in fact come to exist when we find them there.

Fifth it is *active* rather than passive, it constructs scenarios to be tested by reality, vigorously seeks confirmation of them, and painfully reconstructs them if they are deconfirmed. The brain is at least as much an organ of action as it is an organ of knowledge. [David Marr's *Vision* (New York: W.H. Freeman, 1982) came to my hand as this was going to press. It contains a brilliant account of visual perception which confirms the hypothesis I have presented here.]

Thus, sixth, it is *predictive*. The patterns it extrapolates or invents are patterns which involve specific expectations of what will happen next, and in the more distant future—expectations which await satisfaction and are tested by the senses. Dreaming, it would seem from the testimony of Shakespeare, Descartes, Kékulé, and Freud, is the formative stage of pattern-creation. Out of dreams come *A Midsummer Night's Dream*, skeptical philosophy, the benzene ring, and a viable ego. So dominant is the human adaptation for predictive calculation, that it might be said that the human senses exist as a check on our predictions rather than, as in most other animals, triggers for appropriate behavior. Memory itself might be said to be an instrument of prediction. It is hard to imagine what other adaptive function it serves.[3] If this is the case, it carries an interesting implication. Memory would be useless in an entirely random and indeterminate universe; therefore the very fact that the metabolically expensive neural machinery of memory evolved and proved adaptive is a kind of odd proof that the universe is at least locally predictable, to justify such an investment.

But on the other hand an entirely deterministic and predictable universe would have no use for memory either. The umwelt of the lower animals, as determined by their affectors and receptors, is so limited that, to the extent that organisms survive, such an umwelt constitutes a predictable universe; therefore they possess no memories but only fixed action patterns triggered by appropriate stimuli. Memory only makes sense in a world of many possible futures, a world not fully determined. Otherwise we could be programmed to perform an automatic and invariable set of behaviors, which would exactly fit our adaptive needs. All futures share a common past, and thus memory gives us a handle on any possible future.

It could be objected, however, that the universe is indeed deterministic and predictable, but so complex that no animal can exactly predict its behavior, and that the very complex nervous systems of the higher animals developed precisely in order to improve their predictive powers. Such an argument produces an interesting dialectic, which might be worth following. It could be replied to this objection that a the nervous systems of human beings are many orders of magnitude more complex than the physical universe they are, it is claimed, designed to predict. There are billions of times more possible brain-states in a single human brain than there are particles in the physical cosmos. The relations of the brain's parts carry usable information, whereas the relations between particles in the physical universe do not.

There might, however, be a rejoinder to *this* argument, in turn. Human brains are part of the universe, and they merely make the job of predicting it more difficult without altering, by their presence, its actual determinateness. The fact that a major predictive function of human brains is to predict the complex behaviors of each other, in no way weakens the proposition that the world is predictable.

But even this argument can be countered. For it implicitly yields the point that the world is *in practice* unpredictable, because any mechanism complex enough to predict events outside itself would also be so complex as to pose an insuperable problem to another predicting-mechanism, unless that other mechanism were in turn more complex still. It would not, moreover, be able to predict its own behavior. If Apollo gives prophesies, we should perhaps believe him, because he knows the mysteries of things and all human thoughts. But if Zeus, who also knows what Apollo is thinking, and who thus knows what Apollo will do, makes a contrary prophesy, we should believe Zeus instead. But Zeus does not know what Zeus will do, so perhaps we should not even believe Zeus at all.

Our original objector might still be able to argue that the predictability of events is only theoretical, not practical. But this argument must fail too, for when we are dealing with the whole universe, the practical *is* the theoretical. If something is practically impossible for the whole universe, that is a way of saying it is theoretically impossible.

Finally, our antagonist might fall back to the position that future events are *determined* but not *predictable*. But since predictability would be the only conceivable scientific *test* of determinateness, such a statement would be semantically empty. A system whose complexity is increasing faster than any theoretical prediction-system could operate would therefore not be fully determined. In such a universe free choice based on memory would be a powerful survival strategy.

The peculiar logical form of this digression—which uses the infinite regress as a way of proving a negative proposition by means of a *reductio ad absurdum*— illustrates the peculiar predicament that the human brain at once evolved to handle and at the same time helped to create for itself. The very structure of the thinking process itself reflects the increasing levels of complexity the brain was called upon to deal with.

Human information processing is therefore, seventh, *hierarchical* in its organization. In the columns of neurons in the sensory cortex a plausible reconstruction of the world is created by a hierarchy of cells, the ones at the base responding to very simple stimuli and passing on their findings to cells programmed to respond to successively more complex stimuli. Likewise, motor decisions are passed down a long command-chain of simpler and simpler neural servomechanisms.

The coordination of these hierarchial systems, in which many kinds of disparate information must be integrated, some requiring more processing-time and some requiring less, requires a neural pulse within which all relevant information is brought together as a whole. For instance, in the visual system many levels of detail-frequency, color, and depth must all be synchronized, or we would not be able to associate the various features of a visual scene.[4] Thus brain processing is, eighth, essentially *rhythmic*. That these rhythms can be "driven" or reinforced by repeated photic or auditory stimuli, to produce peculiar subjective states, is already well known.

More controversial in detail, but in general widely accepted, is the proposition that the brain's activities are, ninth, *self-rewarding*. The brain possesses built-in sites for the reception of opioid peptides such as enkephalin—the endorphins—and also other pleasure-associated neurohumors such as the catecholamines. It also controls the manufacture and release of these chemicals, and it has been shown that behavior can be reinforced by their use as a reward. The brain, therefore, is able to *reward itself* for certain activities which are, presumably, preferred for their adaptive utility. Clearly if this system of self-reward is the major motivating agent of the brain, any external technique for calibrating and controlling it would result in an enormously enhanced mental efficiency. We would be able to harness all our intellectual and emotional resources to a given task. (Indeed, I will argue later that this is exactly what an aesthetic education, including an early introduction to metered verse in the form of nursery rhymes, can do.) It is, I believe, precisely this autonomous and reflexive reward system which underlies the whole realm of human values, ultimate purposes, and ideals such as truth, beauty, and goodness.

Associated with the brain's capacity for self-reward is, tenth, that it is characteristically *reflexive*. It is within broad limits self-calibrating (partly because of the habituation response). And it seems, unlike a computer, to have a more or less general capacity to convert software into hardware—short-term memory into long-term memory, for example—and vice versa, to examine by introspection its own operations, so that its hardware can become its input or even its program. In the brain the observer problem becomes most acute. In fact we might define consciousness itself as the continuous irresolvable disparity between the brain as observer of itself and the

brain as the object of observation. The coincidence between the words for consciousness and conscience in
many languages points, incidentally, to the relationship
between self-awareness and self-reward.

The human nervous system, we know now, cannot be
separated from the human cultural system it was designed to serve. Its operations are, eleventh, essentially
social. It is not only specific skills and communicative
competences that are learned in a social context, but also
the fundamental capacities of arousal, orientation, attention, and motivation. Clearly we possess genetic proclivities to learn speech, elementary mathematical
calculation, and so on; but equally clearly we require a
socio-cultural context in which to release that potential.
On the other hand, human society itself can be profoundly changed by the development of new ways of using the
brain; take, for instance, the enormous socio-cultural
effects of the invention of the written word. In a sense
reading is a new synthetic instinct, input which becomes
a program and which in turn crystallizes into neural
hardware, and which incorporates a cultural loop into the
human nervous circuit. This "new instinct" in turn
profoundly changes the environment within which
young human brains are programmed. In the early stages
of human evolution such new instincts (speech must
have been one) had to wait for their full development
while sexual selection established the necessary elaborate vocal circuitry in the cortex. Later on we were able to
use our technology, which required much less time to
develop, as a sort of supplementary external nervous
system. A book is like an R.O.M. chip we can plug in to
our heads.

One of the most exciting propositions of the new brain
science is that human information processing is, twelfth,
hemispherically specialized. Here some important distinctions must be made. There are strong logical objec-

tions to the popular and prevailing view that the right brain is emotional while the left brain is rational, and that artistic capacities, being emotional, are located in the right brain. Both sides of the brain are capable of rational calculation; it is surely just as rational to "see" a geometric proof—which is the function of the right brain—as to analyze a logical proposition—which would be done on the left. And both sides of the brain respond to the presence of brain chemicals, and thus both must be said to be "emotional" in this crude sense. The right brain may be better able to recognize and report emotions, but this capacity is surely a cognitive one in itself, and does not necessarily imply a judgment about whether it *feels* emotions more or less than the left. Above all, art is as much a rational activity as it is an emotional one, so the location of art on the "emotional" right is surely the result of a misunderstanding of the nature of art. More plausible is the position of Jerre Levy, who characterizes the relationship between right and left as a complementarily of cognitive capacities.[5] She has stated in a brilliant aphorism that the left brain maps spatial information onto a temporal order, while the right brain maps temporal information onto a spatial order. In a sense understanding largely consists in the translation of information to and fro between a temporal ordering and a spatial one—resulting in a sort of stereoscopic depth-cognition. In Levy's view the two "brains" alternate in the treatment of information, according to a rhythm determined by the general brain state, and pass, each time, their accumulated findings on to each other. The fact that experienced musicians use their left brain just as much as their right in listening to music shows that their higher understanding of music is the result of the collaboration of both "brains," the music having been translated first from temporal sequence to spatial pattern, and then "read," as it were, back into a temporal movement. The

neurologist Gunther Baumgartner suggests that the forebrain acts as the integrating agent between specialized
left and right functions, and it is in this integrative
process that I would locate the essentially creative capacities of the brain, whether artistic or scientific. The
apparent superiority of the isolated right brain in emotional matters may well reflect simply the fact that
emotions, like music, are temporal in nature and their
articulation requires the sort of temporal-on-spatial mapping that is the specialty of the right.

Finally, thirteenth, human information-processing can
be described as *kalogenetic*, a word coined from the
Greek καλος, "kalos," for beauty, goodness, rightness;
and γενεσις, "genesis," begetting, productive cause, origin, source.[6] Another word for this characteristic, coined
in jest by Ernst Pöppel, is *monocausotaxophilia*, the love
of single causes that explain everything. William James
called it "the will to believe." Laughlin and d'Aquili use
the term "the cognitive imperative," or the "what is it?"
syndrome, while Zollinger has identified it in the scientific urge to confirm and affirm a given hypothesis, rather
than to deconfirm it (as Karl Popper would have us do).
Baumgartner's notion of the integrative function of the
forebrain also partakes of the same idea. The human
nervous system has a strong drive to construct affirma-
tive, plausible, coherent, consistent, parsimonious, and
predictively powerful models of the world, in which all
events are explained by and take their place in a system
which is at once rich in implications beyond its existing
data and at the same time governed by as few principles
or axioms as possible. The words that scientists use for
such a system are "elegant," "powerful," and "beautiful;" artists and philosophers use the same terms and also
"appropriate," "fitting," "correct," "right," all of which
can translate to the Greek καλος.

If this tendency *is* a true drive, then according to the

theory of reinforcement, it is an activity for which the
brain rewards itself; and if there were techniques by
which the endogenous reward system could be stimulated and sensitized, then those techniques would enable
us to greatly enhance the integrative powers of our
minds.

Any such technique would have to meet certain quali-
fications. First, it would probably be culturally universal,
since it would be based on neural and biochemical
features common to all human beings.[7] Secondly, it
would be very archaic, identifiable as an element of the
most ancient and the most primitive cultures. Third, it
would be likely to be regarded by its indigenous
practioners as the locus of an almost magical inspiration
and as a source of wisdom; it would have the reputation
of having significantly contributed to the efficiency and
adaptiveness of the societies in which it is practiced.
Fourth, it would be associated with those social and
cultural activities which demand the highest powers of
original thought and complex calculation, such as education, the organization of large-scale projects like war and
co-operative agriculture, and the rituals which digest for
social uses the dangerous and valuable energies implicit
in sexuality, birth, death, sickness, and the like.

Metered poetry, the use of rule-governed rhythmic
measures in the production of a heightened and intensi-
fied form of linguistic expression, nicely fulfills these
requirements. Jerome Rothenberg's collection of ancient
and "primitive" poetry, *Technicians of the Sacred*,[8] contains poems or excerpts from poems from about eighty
different cultures, past and present, in Africa, North
America, South America, Asia, and Oceania; W.K.
Wimsatt's excellent collection of essays, *Versification:
Major Language Types*, describes the metrical features of
Chinese, Japanese, Hebrew, Greek, Latin, Slavic, Uralic,
Germanic, Celtic, Italian, Spanish, French, Old English,

and Modern English, and apologises (p.17) for omitting
the Vedic-Indic verse system, the Arabic, including Swa-
hili, and the Persian.[9] Metered poetry is a highly complex
activity which is culturally universal. I have heard poetry
recited by Ndembu spirit-doctors in Zambia and have,
with the anthropologist Wulf Schiefenhövel, translated
Eipo poetry from Central New Guinea.[10] I can report, as a
poet, that the rhythm of Eipo poetry, when reproduced in
English, has much the same emotional effect as it does in
the original. Such a minute correspondence between
poetic techniques in such widely different cultures surely
points to an identical neurophysiological mechanism.

In nearly all cultures, metered poetry is used in the
crucial religious and social (and often economic) rituals,
and has the reputation of containing mysterious wisdom;
the learning of major poetic texts is central to the process
of education in most literate traditions. Many forms of
work—farming, herding, hunting, war, ship-handling,
mining—have their own body of poetry and song.

It may be objected, however, that we have simply
lumped together many different uses of language under
an artificial category of poetry. This objection is strongly
negated by the fact that poets themselves, who ought to
know, can recognize the work of their alien colleagues as
poetry despite cultural differences. But we do not have to
rely only on the reports of qualified native informants.
Objective, universal and specific traits can be identified
across the whole range of poetic practice throughout the
world and as far back into the past as we have records.
From these universal characteristics we can construct a
general definition of metered poetry which will hold up
from the ancient Greeks to the Kwakiutl, and from
Racine's France to Polynesia.

The fundamental unit of metered poetry is what we
shall call the LINE. We distinguish it by capitalization from
the normal use of the word, because some orthographic

traditions do not conventionally write or print the LINE
in a separate space as we do; and in other traditions there
are examples of a long line divided into two sections
by a caesura, which would, in terms of our classification, actually constitute a couplet of LINES. Sometimes,
on the other hand, what we would call a single LINE is divided in half on the page. The LINE is preceded and followed by a distinct pause (not necessarily a pause for
breath), which despite the presence of other pauses
within the line, divides the verse into clearly identifiable pieces. Metrically experienced poets can readily
recognize the LINE divisions of poetry in languages they do
not know, when it is read aloud. The LINE unit can contain
from four to twenty syllables; but it usually contains
between seven and seventeen in languages which do not
use fixed lexical tones, or between four and eight syllables in tonal languages like Chinese, in whose tradition
of recitation the metrical syllable takes about twice as
long to articulate. Most remarkable of all, this fundamental unit nearly always takes from two to four seconds to
recite, with a strong peak in distribution between two-
and-a-half and three-and-a-half seconds. A caesura will
usually divide the LINES in the longer part of the range;
sometimes (as with Greek and Latin epic dactylic hexam-
eters), the unit will be four to six seconds long, but clearly
divided by a caesura and constituting for our purpose two
LINES.

I have recorded and measured Latin, Greek, English,
Chinese, Japanese, and French poetry, and Pöppel has
done the same for German. Less systematic measurements, by syllable count, have revealed fully consistent
results for Ndembu (Zambia), Eipo (New Guinea), Spanish, Italian, Hungarian, Uralic, Slavic, Amharic, Finnish,
Russian, and Celtic. An average syllable in a non-tonal
language takes about one-quarter of a second to articulate, and in a tonal language about one-half of a second,

though recitation traditions vary in this respect. The Ndembu LINE averages ten syllables; Eipo poetry favors an eight- or twelve-syllable line; in Spanish the epic line of the *Poema de mio Cid* is about fourteen syllables, but most other poetry is octosyllabic or hendecasyllabic (eight or eleven). The classic Italian line is the eleven-syllable *endecasillabo;* Hungarian uses lines between six and twelve syllables long, with a preference for eights and twelves; Slavic has octosyllabics and decasyllabics, with an epic long line of fifteen to sixteen syllables; Celtic has sevens, eights, nines, and some longer-lined meters.[12]

Rather remarkably, I am informed by Deborah Was-serman, the authority on mime, that a phrase or beat in mime is usually about three seconds long—which sug-gests either that the three-second period is not only the "specious present" of the auditory information process-ing system, but also of human information processing in general; or that mime is, paradoxically, a linguistic art in some sense. An interesting test would be to time the intervals between pauses in congenitally deaf users of Standard American Sign Language, using as controls signers who were once able to hear, and signers with perfect hearing.

Among the poetic traditions that Poppel and I have investigated most closely, the results for LINE-length are as follows, giving a range of different meters:

JAPANESE

Epic meter (a seven-syllable LINE followed by a five-syllable one) (average)	3.25 secs.
Waka (average)	2.75 secs.
Tanka (recited much faster than the epic, as three LINES of five, twelve, and fourteen syllables) (average)	2.70 secs.

CHINESE

Four-syllable line	2.20 secs.
Five-syllable line	3.00 secs.
Seven-syllable line	3.80 secs.

ENGLISH

Pentameter	3.30 secs.
Seven-syllable trochaic line	2.50 secs.
Stanzas using different line lengths	3.00 secs., 3.10 secs.
Ballad meter (octosyllabic)	2.40 secs.

ANCIENT GREEK

Dactyllic hexameter (half-line)	2.80 secs.
Trochaic tetrameter (half-line)	2.90 secs.
Iambic trimeter[13]	4.40 secs.
Marching anapests	3.50 secs.
Anapestic tetrameter (half-line)	2.50 secs.

LATIN

Alcaic strophe	3.90 secs.
Elegiac couplet	3.50 secs.
Dactyllic hexameter (half-line)	2.80 secs.
Hendecasyllabic	3.80 secs.

FRENCH

Alexandrine (twelve-syllable)	3.80 secs.
Decasyllable with octosyllable (La Fontaine)	3.00 secs.

GERMAN

(sample of two hundred poems, collected by Pöppel)

LINE - length of under two seconds	3%
LINE - length of two to three seconds	73%
LINE - length of three to four seconds	7%
LINE - length between four and five seconds[14]	17%

This fundamental unit is nearly always a rhythmic, semantic, and syntactical unit as well: a sentence, a colon, a clause, a phrase, or a completed group of them. Thus other linguistic rhythms are entrained to—that is, brought into synchrony with—the basic acoustic rhythm, producing that pleasing sensation of "fit" and inevitability which is part of the delight of verse, and is so helpful to the memory. Generally a short line is used to deal with line subjects, while the long line is reserved for epic or tragic matters.

It is, we believe, highly significant that this analysis of the fundamental LINE in human verse gives little or no significance to breath, or "breath-units," as a determinant of the divisions of human meter. Thus our common-sense observation that breath in speech is largely under voluntary control, and that one could speak anything from one syllable to about forty in one breath, is vindicated. Systems of verse based on breath-units, such as "projective verse" and many other free verse systems, therefore have no objective validity or physiological foundation.

The second universal characteristic of human verse meter is that certain marked elements of the LINE or of groups of LINES remain constant throughout the poem, and thus serve as indicators of the repetition of a pattern. The three-second cycle is not merely marked by a pause, but by distinct resemblances between the material in each cycle. Repetition is added to frequency to emphasize the rhythm.

These constant elements can take many forms. Simplest of all is a constant number of syllables per line, as in Hungarian folk poetry; but here the strict grammatical integrity of each line is insisted upon, as if to compensate for the absence of other markers. Some verse forms (for instance, that of the *Poema de Mio Cid*) have a fixed number of stressed syllables per line, with an unfixed

number of unstressed syllables. Other meters (most European ones, for example) use small patterns of syllables,
distinguished by stress or length, to make feet, creating a
line out of a fixed number of feet. Tonal languages, like
Chinese, distinguish between syllables of an unchanging
tone and syllables which change tone, and construct
meters out of repeated patterns of changing and unchanging syllables. Celtic poetry uses prescribed cadences; Old
English uses systematic alliteration. Many languages use
some system of assonance, especially rhyme, which usually marks very strongly the ending of a line, and thus
forms a strong contrast-spike to divide off one line from
the next. Hebrew poetry uses semantic and syntactical
parallels between its pairs of half-lines. Often many of
these devices will be used at once, some prescribed by the
conventions of the poetic form, others left to the discre-
tion and inspiration of the poet. No verse-convention
prescribes all the characteristics of a line, so every poem
contains an interplay between prescribed elements and
free variation.[16]

Sometimes, as in the Spenserian stanza, or in the
Greek or English ode, or in the invented stanzas of Donne
or Yeats, a whole group of lines of different lengths will
itself constitute a repeated element. When lines of different lengths are used together, as in Milton's *Lycidas*, the
rhyme (which stresses the integrity of the line) and
the foot are given special emphasis to compensate for the
variation in the fundamental pulse—as if to insist on the
threshold dividing the carrier-wave from mere "noise."
And in variable-lined verses there is usually a normal-
length line which acts as an unconscious constant
against which the exceptions are measured as such.

At this point it should be pointed out that some of the
characteristics of metered poetry do not apply to songs
and lyrics derived from a song tradition. Music has its
own form of organization, which diminishes the impor-

tance of the line at the expense of the musical phrase. But in those traditions where we can see poetry emerging from song, such as the Latin lyric, there is an interesting tendency, as the musical order is forgotten, toward the establishment of the characteristically poetic forms of organization: the regular line, with variations, the distinction between different types of syllable (long and short, stressed and unstressed, tonally changing or unchanging), and the rest. Thus the fact that songs do not conform to the limits of poetic meter is negative proof of the relation of language and meter.

The third universal characteristic of human metrical verse is variation, or, more precisely, a pseudolinguistic generativeness created by the imposition of rules, which makes possible significant perturbations of an expressive medium. Robert Frost put it very well, in a negative way, when he described poetry without meter as being like tennis without a net. The net introduces a restriction which is paradoxically fertile in the elaboration of groundstrokes which it demands, and significant in that it distinguishes legal from illegal shots.

Variation does not necessarily mean departure from the rules (Romantic and Modernist theories of art sometimes make this mistake). Variation does not occur *despite* the rules but *because* of them. Freedom never means a freedom *from* rules, but the freedom *of* rules. It is important here for us to distinguish our general position from that of socio-biological and other purists of the genetic-deterministic persuasion on one hand, and from the pure cultural relativists, behaviorists or otherwise, on the other. Genetic determinists would be likely to assume, once a human universal such as metrical verse is pointed out to them, that this behavior indicates the presence of a set of biological constraints which act as an outer envelope, restricting possible human behaviors within a given repertoire, large or small. Cultural relativists would tend to deny the existence of such a human universal, or would be inclined to dismiss it as an analogous response to similar problems or stimuli, or as an artificial product of the investigator's definitional vocabulary and research method.

I will adopt a third position, which is already hinted by my use of the word "pseudolinguistic." As I see it, the similarities between metered verse in different cultures are real and do indeed indicate a shared biological under-pinning; but unlike the genetic determinists I do not regard this shared inheritance as a constraint, nor as an outer envelope restricting human behavior to a certain range. Rather, I would regard it as a set of rules which, though derived from the structure of the human auditory cortex and the brain in general, does not restrict, but enormously increase, the range of possible human behavior.

At first glance this position might appear paradoxical. How can the range of possibilities be increased by the imposition of rules governing their use? If rules are rules, then they must surely deny certain previously possible behaviors, and therefore decrease the total number of them.

The paradox is easily resolved. A mathematical analogy will help. Given four possible behaviors, A, B, C, and D, only four alternatives exist. If we now impose a rule, which is that these behaviors can only be performed two at a time, suddenly and strangely there are now not four but six alternatives: AB, BC, CD, AC, BD, AD. Of course, this is cheating, in a sense, because before the rule was mentioned, there was no hint that behaviors might come in groups. It could be pointed out that in terms of sets of behaviors, in fact sixteen possibilities exist: the ten already mentioned, the four groups of three, the whole group together, and the null set. But this is precisely what the rule has done: it has created the group of behaviors as a significant entity, as a behavior in itself, and therefore expanded the repertoire from four to six. Furthermore, those six permitted combinations now stand in relation to ten non-permitted ones, and their correctness marks them out as valuable and special, as opposed to the "incorrect" permutations. Thus the rule has introduced a) a greater repertoire of behaviors than was previously possible and b) a marker of significance and value. All game-rules work in this way, creating possible scenarios and desired goals out of thin air.

The linguistic rules of phonology, grammar, and the lexicon work in a generally similar way. Linguistic rules are, to an extent, arbitrary and culture-bound, but Chomsky has shown certain invariant characteristics in the way in which human languages use syntactical subordination, which are no doubt biological in origin (and probably related to the hierarchical nature of human brain processes). Meter, with its cultural variations in the syllabic markers but its invariance in LINE-length, shows a similar interplay of cultural and genetic forces, and, more important, it produces a similar increase in the repertoire of behavior and a similar capacity to create significance.

In fact it is this general strategy by which the DNA molecule of life and the nervous systems of the higher animals attained greater complexities than the physical universe out of which they evolved: by making permutations of elements significant through highly restrictive "rules," and therefore increasing, as it were, the "cardinality" of the number of bits of information that the organism could hold. We find, for example, a similar interplay between genetic and cultural factors in the human recognition of colors. A rather restricted set of anatomically-determined color sensitivities is combined by culture into a large, and often idiosyncratic, repertoire of tints and shades, many of them with strong ideological significance. The range, variety, and combinations of colored pigmentation used in animal ritual behavior attest to a corresponding extension and valorization of color distinctions among the higher animals.

Thus metrical variation can be seen as a code, or communicative device, and the various elements of meter can be neatly described in terms of information theory. The three-second LINE is the communicative medium or "carrier-wave," which must be distinguishable from mere "noise" or the random transmissions around it, by the recurrence of a pause at the LINE-ending, by the many regular metrical features—syllable-count, stress, quantity, tone, systematic assonance, etc.—that we have described, and by the coincidence of semantic, syntactic, and rhythmic units with the LINE unit. Metrical variation is the "message" which is transmitted upon the communicative medium—like a radio-transmission. It consists of a systematic distortion of a regular medium or wave, which nevertheless remains within the regular parameters of the medium so that at all times the transmission is distinguishable from random noise.

The "message" that metrical variation conveys, however, is rather mysterious. If it is a code, what kind of code is it? Metrical scholars have attempted to discover exact relationships between individual metrical variations and the semantic content of poetry.[17] But their conclusions have been disappointingly vague or arbitrary, reminiscent, in fact, of musicological attempts to assign fixed meanings to different musical keys, signatures, and variations, so as to make a symphony describe a scene or conduct an argument. Here the analogy between metrical and linguistic significance breaks down. Certainly a connection between metrical (or musical) and linguistic meaning exists, and in some cultural traditions (English Augustan poetry and European Romantic music, for instance), artists have developed a self-conscious repertoire of metrical or musical codes to convey specific meanings. But other traditions do not possess such codifications, or else use the same specific devices to convey entirely different ideas.

The predicament of the critic, in fact, can be likened to that of a viewer of a visual artifact who is so convinced that what he is looking at is a page of writing, that he does not realize that the artifact is actually a picture. Perhaps it is a picture of something he has never seen (or has never noticed), and thus his mistake is a natural one. But the attempt to extract a sort of linguistic meaning out of the planes, lines, corners, masses, and angles of a picture would be frustratingly arbitrary—especially if he had a whole series of paintings of different subjects, in which the same visual elements were used for entirely different purposes—the same curve for a face, a hillside, and the sail of a ship. Linguistic meaning and pictorial meaning are based on codes so fundamentally different that no code-cracking algorithm that would work on one could possibly work on the other. Their mutual intelligibility cannot be sought in the direction of analysis, but only within the context of a synthetic whole which contains both of them.

What we are suggesting is that a linguistic type of analysis of meter, as of music (or painting, e.g. Chinese landscape painting), is likely to be fruitful *only* when the composer has arbitrarily imposed linguistic meaning on the elements of the composition; and that the meaning of metrical variation must be sought in a fashion much more like that of the recognition of a tune or the subject of a picture. That is, metrical variations are not significant in themselves, like sememes: but rather they form, together, a picture-like Gestalt which is a distinct representation of something that we can recognize; and thus, like pictorial representations, or music, they are much less culture-bound than linguistic codes. But here, excitingly, we encounter a paradox stemming from the gross

structure of the human brain. Poetry, being an art of
language, is presumably processed by the left temporal
lobe of the brain. But meter, we are suggesting, carries
meaning in a fashion much more like that of a picture or
a melody, in which the meaning inheres more in the
whole than in the parts. There is no "lexicon" of metrical
forms. They are not signs but elements of an analogical
structure. And this kind of understanding is known to
take place on the right side of the brain. If this hypothesis
is accurate, meter is, in part, a way of introducing
right-brain processes into the left-brain activity of understanding language; and in another sense, it is a way of
connecting our much more culture-bound (and perhaps
evolutionarily later) linguistic capacities with the relatively more "hard-wired" spatial pattern-recognition faculties we share with the higher mammals.

If one asks the question "what does the ear hear?" the
obvious answer is "sound." What is sound? Mechanical
waves in the air or other medium. But this answer is not
very illuminating. One can, for instance, perceive mechanical waves by the sense of touch, yet it would be
inaccurate to say that a deaf man "heard" a vibrating
handrail with his fingers. What characterizes hearing as
such is not that it senses mechanical waves but that it
senses the distinctions between mechanical waves; just
as what characterizes sight is not the perception of
electromagnetic waves but the perception of distinctions
between electromagnetic waves.

For the sense of sight those distinctions (except for
color) are spatial ones; but for the sense of hearing they
are mainly temporal. To put it directly, what the sense of
hearing hears is essentially *time*. The recognition of
differences of pitch involves a very pure (and highly
accurate) comparative measurement of different frequencies into which time is divided. The perception of timbre,
tone, sound texture, and so on consists in the recognition

of combinations of frequencies; and the sense of rhythm and tempo carries the recognition of frequency into the realm of longer periods of time.

The sense of hearing is not only a marvelously accurate instrument for detecting differences between temporal periods, it is also an active organizer, arranging those different periods within a hierarchy as definite as that of the seconds, minutes, and hours of a clock, but one in which the different periodicities are also uniquely valorized. In the realm of pitch the structure of that hierarchy is embodied in the laws of harmony, and is well known (though it has not often been recognized that "sound" and "time" are virtually the same thing). New discoveries by Ernst Pöppel's group in Munich have begun to open up the role of the auditory time-- hierarchy in the structure and function of the brain. Out of this investigation is coming a comprehensive understanding of the general scheduling-organization of the human sensory-motor system, and a fresh approach to the production and understanding of language. We shall first briefly outline the auditory hierarchy.

Events separated by periods of time shorter than about three-thousandths of a second are classified by the hearing system as simultaneous. If a brief sound of one pitch is played to one ear, and another of a different pitch is played to the other less than three-thousandths of a second later, the subject will experience only one sound. If the sounds are a little more than three-thousandths of a second apart, the subject will experience two sounds. However, he will not be able to tell which of the two sounds came first, nor will he until the gap between them is increased ten times. Thus the lowest category in the hierarchy of auditory time is *simultaneity*, and the second lowest is mere temporal *separation*, without a preferred order of time. The most primary temporal experience is timeless unity; next comes a spacelike recognition of difference—spacelike because, unlike temporal positions, spatial positions can be exchanged. One can go from New York to Berlin or from Berlin to New York; but one can only go from 1980 to 1983, not from 1983 to 1980. Likewise, the realm of "separation" is a non-deterministic, acausal one. Events happen in it, perhaps in patterns or perhaps not, but they cannot be said to cause one another, because we cannot say which came first.

When two sounds are about three-hundredths of a second apart, a subject can experience their *sequence*, accurately reporting which came first. This is the third category in the hierarchy of auditory time, subsuming separations and simultaneities and organizing them rationally with respect to each other. But at this stage the organism is still a passive recipient of stimuli; one can hear a sequence of two sounds one-tenth of a second apart, but there is nothing one can do in response to the first sound before the second sound comes along: one is helpless to alter what will befall one, if the interval between the alert and its sequel falls within this range. Unlike the world of temporal separation, which is in a sense a realm of chance and pattern, the world of sequence is a realm of fate and cause. Events follow each other, and their temporal connections can be recognized as necessary, if indeed they are; but there is nothing one can do about it.

Once the temporal interval is above about three-tenths of a second, however, one enters a new temporal category, which I call *response*. Three-tenths of a second is enough time for a human subject to react to an acoustic stimulus. If two sounds are played to a subject a second apart, the subject could in theory prepare to deal with the second sound in the time given him after hearing the first. The perceiver is no longer passive, and events can be treated as actions in *response* to which the subject can perform actions and which can be modified before they happen if their cause is understood. For response to exist there must be simultaneities, a separation between them, a distinguishable sequence in the separation, and a further element which might be characterized as function or, in a primitive sense, purpose. The response to a given stimulus will differ according to the function of the responding organ and the purpose of the organism as a whole.

At several places in this analysis it has been pointed out that a given familiar temporal relation—chance, pattern, fate, cause, action, function, purpose—only becomes possible when there is enough time for it to exist in. The idea that an entity needs time in which to exist has become commonplace recently. An electron, for instance, requires at least 10^{-20} seconds of time (its spin period) in which to exist, just as surely as it requires 10^{-10} centimeters of space (its Compton wavelength). The corollary to this observation is that entities which consist only in spatio-temporal relations are not necessarily less real for that than material objects, for spatio-temporal relations are exactly what material objects consist of, too. But though a given period of time may be sufficient for an example of a given relation—chance, cause, function—to be recognized, it is not enough time for the concept of the relation to be formulated. It takes much less time to recognize or speak a word once learned than it takes to learn the word in the first place. Many examples of the sequence or response relation between events must be compared before a causal or purposive order can be formulated and thus recognized in individual cases. But comparison requires discrete parcels of experience between which the comparison may be made, and since the entities being compared are themselves temporal in nature, these parcels of experience must consist in equal periods of time. In like fashion the analysis of a picture (for transmission, reproduction, or identification of its details) might begin by dividing the picture up into "pixels" by means of a series of grids of various frequency; the highest-frequency grid representing the limit of the eye's acuity, the lower ones increasingly concerned with complex relations between details. The next lowest time-division beyond the three-tenths of a second response-frequency must be sufficiently long to avoid falling into the range of the characteristic time-quanta required for the completion and recognition of the temporal relations to be compared. The comparison of experience takes more time than experience itself; the recognition of a melody takes more time than the hearing of the single notes.

This fundamental "parcel of experience" turns out to be about three seconds. The three-second period, roughly speaking, is the length of the human present moment. (At least it is for the auditory system, which possesses the sharpest temporal acuity of all the senses. The eye, for instance, is twice as slow as the ear in distinguishing temporal separation from simultaneity.) The philosophical notion of the "specious present" finds here its experimental embodiment.

A human speaker will pause for a few milliseconds every three seconds or so, and in that period will decide on the precise syntax and lexicon of the next three seconds. A listener will absorb about three seconds of heard speech without pause or reflection, then stop listening briefly in order to integrate and make sense of what he has heard. (Speaker and hearer, however, are not necessarily "in phase" for this activity; this observation will be seen to be of importance later.)

To use a cybernetic metaphor, we possess an auditory information "buffer" whose capacity is three seconds' worth of information; at the end of three seconds the "buffer" is full, and it passes on its entire accumulated stock of information to the higher processing centers. In theory this stock could consist of about one thousand simultaneities, one hundred discrete temporal separations, and ten consecutive responses to stimuli. In practice the "buffer" has rather smaller capacity than this (about sixty separations); it seems to need a certain amount of "down-time."

It appears likely that another mechanism is involved here, too. Different types of information take different amounts of time to be processed by the cortex. For instance, fine detail in the visual field takes more time to be identified by the cortex than coarse detail. (Indeed, the time taken to process detail seems to be used by the brain as a tag to label its visual frequency.[17]) Some sort of pulse is necessary so that all the information of different kinds will arrive at the higher processing centers as a bundle, correctly labelled as belonging together, and at the same time; the sensory cortex "waits" for the "slowest" information to catch up with the "fastest" so that it can all be sent off at once. And this three-second period constitutes a "pulse."

Beyond the two horizons of this present moment exist the two periods which together constitute duration, which is the highest or "longest-frequency" integrative level of the human perception of time. Those two periods, the past and the future, memory and planning, are the widest arena of human thought (unless the religious or metaphysical category of "eternity" constitutes an even wider one). It is within the realm of duration that what we call freedom can exist, for it is within that realm that purposes and functions, the governors of response, can themselves be compared and selected. The differences between past and future, and the differences between possible futures, constitute the field of value, and the relations between low frequency objects and the more primitive high frequency objects of which they are composed constitute the field of quality.

It is tempting to relate this foregoing hierarchical taxonomy of temporal periodicities to the structure and evolution of the physical universe itself. The temporal category of simultaneity nicely corresponds to the atemporal umwelt of the photon, which reigned supreme in the first microsecond of the Big Bang. The category of separation resembles the weak, acausal, stochastic, spacelike temporality of quantum physics, within which there is no preferred direction of time: a condition which must have prevailed shortly after the origin of the universe, and of which the quantum-mechanical organization of subatomic particles is a "living fossil." The category of sequence matches the causal, deterministic and entropic realm of classical hard science, whose subject came into being some time after the origin of the universe, once the primal explosion had cooled sufficiently to permit the existence of organized, discrete, and enduring matter. With the category of response we are clearly within the umwelt of living matter, with its functions, purposes, and even its primitive and temporary teleology, which began about ten billion years after the Big Bang. Once we cross the horizon of the present we enter the realm of duration, which first came into being perhaps a million years ago (if it was roughly coeval with speech and with that development of the left brain which gave us the tenses of language). The evolution and hierarchical structure of the human hearing mechanism thus could be said to recapitulate the history and organization of the cosmos. The history of science has been the retracing of that path backwards by means of clocks of greater and greater acuity.

Cosmological speculation aside, it should already be obvious that a remarkable and suggestive correlation exists between the temporal organization of poetic meter

and the temporal function of the human hearing mechanism. Of general linguistic significance is the fact that
the length of a syllable—about one-third of a second—
corresponds to the minimum period within which a
response to an auditory stimulus can take place. This is
commonsense, really, as speech must, to be efficient, be
as fast as it can be, while, to be controllable, it must be
slow enough for a speaker or hearer to react to a syllable
before the next one comes along.

Of more specific significance for our subject is the very
exact correlation between the three-second LINE and the
three-second "auditory present." This extraordinary correlation is the major finding of this essay: it points to an
explanation of the prevalence of the three-second LINE.
The average number of syllables per LINE in human poetry
seems to be about ten; so human poetic meter embodies
the two lowest-frequency rhythms in the human auditory system.

The independence of poetic meter from the mechanism of breathing, which we have already noted, is thus
explained by the fact that the master-rhythm of human
meter is not pulmonary but neural. We must seek the
origins of poetry not among the lower regions of the
human organism, but among the higher. The frequent
practice when reading free verse aloud, of breathing at the
end of the line—even when the line is highly variable in
length and often broken quite without regard to syntax—
is therefore not only grammatically confusing but deeply
unnatural, for it forces a pause where neural processing
would not normally put it.

But at least there was a clear, if erroneous, rationale for
the doctrine of meter as made up of "breath-units."
Without this rationale, how do we explain the cultural
universality of meter? Why does verse embody the three-
second neural "present?" What functions could be served
by this artificial and external mimicry of an endogenous

brain rhythm? Given the fact, already stated, that poetry
fulfills many of the superficial conditions demanded of a
brain-efficiency reward control system, how might the
three-second rhythm serve that function? And what is
the role of the other components of meter—the rhythmic
parallelism between the LINES, and the information-
bearing variations upon that parallelism?

One further batch of data will help guide this line of
hypothesizing: the subjective reports of poets and readers
of poetry about the effects and powers of poetic meter.
Although these reports would be inadequate and ambiguous as the sole support of an argument, they may point us
in the right direction and confirm conclusions arrived at
by other means.

A brief and incomplete summary of these reports, with
a few citations, should suggest to a reader educated in
literature the scope of their general agreement. Robert
Graves speaks of the shiver and the coldness in the spine,
the hair rising on the head and body, as does Emily
Dickinson. A profound muscular relaxation yet an intense alertness and concentration is also recorded. The
heart feels squeezed and the stomach cramped. There is a
tendency toward laughter or tears, or both; the taking of
deep breaths; and a slightly intoxicated feeling (Samuel
Taylor Coleridge compared it to the effects of a moderate
amount of strong spirits upon a conversation). At the
same time there is an avalanche of vigorous thought, in
which new connections are made; Shakespeare's Prospero describes the sensation as a "beating mind" (and
repeats the phrase three times in different places in the
play). There is a sense of being on the edge of a precipice
of insight—almost a vertigo—and the awareness of entirely new combinations of ideas taking concrete shape,
together with feelings of strangeness and even terror.
Some writers (Arnold, for instance) speak of an inner light
or flame. Outside stimuli are often blanked out, so strong

is the concentration. The imagery of the poem becomes so intense that it is almost like real sensory experience. Personal memories pleasant and unpleasant (and sometimes previously inaccessible) are strongly evoked; there is often an emotional reexperience of close personal ties, with family, friends, lovers, the dead. There is an intense valorization of the world and of human life, together with a strong sense of the reconciliation of opposites—joy and sorrow, life and death, good and evil, divine and human, reality and illusion, whole and part, comic and tragic, time and timelessness. The sensation is not a timeless one as such, but an experience of time so full of significance that stillness and sweeping motion are the same thing. There is a sense of power combined with effortlessness. The poet or reader rises above the world, as it were, on the "viewless wings of poetry," and sees it all in its fullness and completeness, but without loss of the concreteness and clarity of its details. There is an awareness of one's own physical nature, of one's birth and death, and of a curious transcendence of them; and, often, a strong feeling of universal and particular love, and communal solidarity.

Of course not all these subjective sensations necessarily occur together in the experience of poetry, nor do they usually take their most intense form; but a poet or frequent reader of poetry will probably recognize most of them.

To this list, moreover, should be added a further property of metered poetry, which goes beyond the immediate experience of it: its memorability. Part of this property is undoubtedly a merely technical convenience: the knowledge of the number of syllables in a line and the rhyme, for instance, limits the number of words and phrases which are possible in a forgotten line and helps us to reconstruct it logically. But introspection will reveal a deeper quality to this memorability. Somehow the rhythm of the words is remembered even when the words themselves are lost to us; but the rhythm helps us to recover the mental state in which we first heard or read the poem, and then the gates of memory are opened and the words come to us at once.

Equipped with the general contemporary conception of brain-processing with which this essay began, with the temporal analysis of meter and its correlation to the hearing-system, and with the subjective reports of participants in the art, we may now begin to construct a plausible hypothesis of what goes on in the brain during the experience of poetry.

Here we can draw upon a relatively new and speculative field of scientific inquiry, which has been variously termed neurophysiology, biocybernetics, and biopsychology, and is associated with the names of such researchers as E. Bourguignon, E.D. Chapple, E. Gellhorn, A. Neher, and R. Ornstein. Barbara Lex's "The Neurobiology of Ritual Trance,"[19] in which she summarizes and synthesizes much of their work, provides many of the materials by which we may build an explanatory bridge between the observed characteristics of human verse and the new findings of the Munich group about the hearing mechanism. Although Lex is concerned with the whole spectrum of methods by which altered states of consciousness may be attained—alcohol, hypnotic suggestion, breathing techniques, smoking, music, dancing, drugs, fasting, meditation, sensory deprivation, photic driving, and auditory driving—and her focus is on ritual rather than the art of poetry, her general argument fits in well with my own findings.

Essentially her position is that the various techniques listed above, and generalized as "driving behaviors," are designed to add to the linear, analytic, and verbal resources of the left brain the more intuitive and holistic understanding of the right brain; to tune the central nervous system and alleviate accumulated stress; and to invoke to the aid of social solidarity and cultural values the powerful somatic and emotional forces mediated by the sympathetic and parasympathetic nervous systems, and the ergotropic and trophotropic responses they control.[20]

It has been known for many years that rhythmic photic and auditory stimulation can evoke epileptic symptoms in seizure-prone individuals, and can produce powerful involuntary reactions even in normal individuals. The rhythmic stimulus entrains and then amplifies natural brain rhythms, especially if it is tuned to an important frequency such as the ten cycle-per-second alpha wave. It seems plausible that the three-second poetic LINE is similarly tuned to the three-second cycle of the auditory (and subjective-temporal) present. The metrical and assonantal devices of verse, such as rhyme and stress, which create similarities between the LINES, emphasize the repetition. The curious subjective effects of metered verse—relaxation, a holistic sense of the world, and so on—are no doubt attributable to a very mild pseudo-trance state induced by the auditory driving effect of this repetition.

Auditory driving is known to affect the right brain much more powerfully than the left, and the fronto-limbic area more powerfully than the posterior cortical convexity. Thus, where ordinary unmetered prose comes to us in a "mono" mode, so to speak, affecting the left brain predominantly, metered language comes to us in a "stereo" mode—or even a quadraphonic one—simultaneously calling on the verbal resources of the left and the musical potentials of the right, the fronto-limbic sensitivity to rhythms and cycles, and the sensory-motor specializations of the posterior cortex.[21]

The accurate scansion of poetry involves a complex analysis of grammatical and lexical stress, which must be

continually integrated with a non-verbal right-brain understanding of metrical stress. The delightful way in
which the rhythm of the sentence, as a semantic unit,
counterpoints the rhythm of the meter in poetry, is thus
explained as the result of a co-operation between left and
right brain functions. The "stereo" effect of verse is not
merely one of simultaneous stimulation of different brain
areas, but also the result of a necessary integrative
collaboration and feedback between them. The linguistic
capacities of the left brain, which, as Levy says, provide a
temporal order for spatial information, are forced into a
conversation with the melodic capacities of the right,
which provide a spatial order for temporal information. It
may seem odd to characterize the appreciation of melody
as a spatial ability; but a closer examination of the
process will prove the point. The notes of a piece of music
appear in a temporal sequence, which must indeed be
perceived as such in the first place. But as musicians
know, what makes a tune a tune is the pattern that the
notes make when they are collected together in the
memory. A melody is a harmony smeared out in time,
and the capacity to reintegrate that smear into the
original harmony, which is the heart of melody recognition, is a rather exact paradigm of the spatial gestalt
capacity of the right brain, even if the "space" in this case
is what musicians call harmonic space. The left-brain
ability to take a spatial phenomenon such as a page of
type, ignore the right-brain tendency to reduce it all to a
grey textured pattern, and spin it out into a single
temporal thread of language, is perhaps the equivalent
capacity in the other hemisphere. The brain is a "Penelo-
pe" whose right hand weaves the shroud of meaning and
whose left hand disentangles the thread or clue of understanding.

The driving rhythm of the three-second LINE is not just
any rhythm. It is, as we have seen, tuned to the largest

limited unit of auditory time, its "specious present," within which causal sequences can be compared, and free decisions taken. A complete poem—which can be any length—is a duration, a realm of values, systematically divided into presents, which are the realm of action. It therefore summarizes our most sophisticated and most uniquely human integrations of time.

There is, perhaps, still another effect at work on the cortical level. The various divinatory practices of human-kind (another cultural universal, perhaps) all involve a common element: a process of very complex calculation which seems quite irrelevant to the kind of information sought by the diviner. A reader of the tarot will analyse elaborate combinations of cards, an *I Ching* reader will arrive at his hexagram through a difficult process of mathematical figuring, a reader of the horoscope will resort to remarkable computations of astronomical posi-tion and time. (The common use of the word "reader" in these contexts is suggestive.) The work of scanning metered verse, especially when combined with the activi-ty of recognizing allusions and symbolisms, and the combination of them into the correct patterns, seems analogous to these divinatory practices. The function of this demanding process of calculation may be to occupy the linear and rational faculties of the brain with a task which entirely distracts them from the matter to be decided—a diagnosis, a marriage, the future of an individ-ual. Once the "loud voice" of the reductive logical intelligence is thus stilled by distance, the quieter whis-pering of a holistic intuition, which can integrate much larger quantities of much poorer-quality information in more multifarious ways—though with a probability of accuracy which is correspondingly much lower—can then be heard. The technique is something like that of the experienced stargazer, who can sometimes make out a very faint star by focussing a little to one side of it, thereby bringing to bear on it an area of the retina which, though inferior in acuity, is more sensitive to light. The prophetic or divinatory powers traditionally attributed to poetry may be partly explained by the use of this technique. If the analogy is slightly unflattering to the work of some professional analytic critics of poetry—reducing their work, as it does, to the status of an elaborate decoy for the more literalistic proclivities of the brain—there is the compensation that it is, after all, a very necessary activity, indeed indispensable precisely because of its irrelevance.

On the cortical level, then, poetic meter serves a number of functions generally aimed at tuning up and enhancing the performance of the brain, by bringing to bear other faculties than the linguistic, which we can relate to the summary of healthy brain characteristics at the beginning of this paper. By ruling out certain rhythmic possibilities, meter satisfies the brain's procrustean demand for unambiguity and clear distinctions. By combining elements of repetition and isochrony on one hand with variation on the other, it nicely fulfills the brain's habituative need for controlled novelty. By giving the brain a system of rhythmic organization as well as a circumscribed set of semantic and syntactical possibilities, it encourages the brain in its synthetic and predictive activity of hypothesis-construction, and raises expectations which are pleasingly satisfied at once. In its content poetry has often had a strongly prophetic character, an obvious indication of its predictive function; and the mythic elements of poetry afford more subtle models of the future by providing guides to conduct. Poetry presents to the brain a system which is temporally and rhythmically hierarchical, as well as linguistically so, and therefore matched to the hierarchical organization of the brain itself. It does much of the work that the brain must usually do for itself, in organizing information into

rhythmic pulses, integrating different types of information—rhythmic, grammatical, lexical, acoustic—into
easily assimilable parcels and labeling their contents as
belonging together. Like intravenous nourishment, the
information enters our system instantly, without a
lengthy process of digestion. The pleasure of metered
verse evidently comes from its ability to stimulate the
brain's capacities of self-reward, and the traditional concern of verse with the deepest human values—truth,
goodness, and beauty—is clearly associated with its involvement with the brain's own motivational system.
Poetry seems to be a device the brain can use in reflexively calibrating itself, turning its software into hardware
and its hardware into software. And, accordingly, poetry
is traditionally concerned, on its semantic level, with
consciousness and conscience. As a quintessentially cultural activity, poetry has been central to social learning
and the synchronization of social activities (the sea-
shanty and work-song are only the crudest and most
obvious examples). Poetry enforces cooperation between
left-brain temporal organization and right-brain spatial
organization and helps to bring about that integrated
stereoscopic view that we call true understanding. And
poetry is, *par excellence*, "kalogenetic"—productive of
beauty, of elegance, of coherence, and of predictively
powerful models of the world.

It might be argued—and this is a traditional charge
against poetry—that in doing all these things poetry
deceives, presenting an experience which, because it is so
perfectly designed for the human brain, gives a false
impression of reality and separates one from the harsh
world of actuality. Much modern aesthetic theory is in
fact devoted to reversing this situation, and to making
poetry—and art in general—so disharmonious with one's
natural proclivities that it shocks one into awareness of
the stark realities. Clearly a poetry which was too merely

harmonious would be insipid—for it would disappoint
the brain's habituative desire for novelty. But mere random change and the continuous disappointment of expectations is itself insipid; one is as capable of becoming
habituated to meaningless flux as to mindless regularity.

Modernist aesthetic theory may be ignoring the following possibility: that our species' special adaptation
may in fact be to expect more order and meaning in the
world than it can deliver; and that those expectations
may constitute, paradoxically, an excellent survival strategy. Humans are strongly motivated to restore the equi-
librium between reality and our expectations by altering
reality so as to validate our models of it—to "make the
world a better place." The modernist attack on beauty in
art would therefore constitute an attack on our very
nature; and the modernist and post-modernist criticism
of moral and philosophical idealism likewise flies in the
face of the apparent facts about human neural organization. What William James called "the will to believe" is
written in our genes; teleology is the best policy; and
paradoxically, it is utopian to attempt to do battle against
our natural idealism. Much more sensible to adjust
reality to the ideal.

But this discussion of the effects of metered verse on
the human brain has ignored, so far, the subcortical levels
of brain activity. Substitute as *pars pro toto*, "metered
verse" for "ritual" in the following summary by Barbara
Lex:

> The *raison d'être* of rituals is the readjustment of
> dysphasic biological and social rhythms by manipula-
> tion of neurophysiological structures under controlled
> conditions. Rituals properly executed promote a feel-
> ing of well-being and relief, not only because prolonged
> or intense stresses are alleviated, but also because the

driving techniques employed in rituals are designed to sensitize and "tune" the nervous system and thereby lessen inhibition of the right hemisphere and permit temporary right-hemisphere dominance, as well as mixed trophotropic-ergotropic excitation, to achieve synchronization of cortical rhythms in both hemispheres and evoke trophotropic rebound.[22]

Lex maintains that the "driving" techniques of rhythmic dances, chants, and so on can produce a simultaneous stimulation of both the ergotropic (arousal) and the trophotropic (rest) systems of the lower nervous system, producing subjective effects which she characterizes as follows: trance, ecstasy, meditative and dream-like states, possession, the "exhilaration accompanying risk taking," a sense of community, sacredness, a "process of reviving the memory of a repressed unpleasant experience and expressing in speech and actions the emotions related to it, thereby relieving the personality of its influence," alternate laughing and crying, mystical experience and religious conversion, experiences of unity, holism, and solidarity. Laughlin and d'Aquili add to these effects a sense of union with a greater power, an awareness that death is not to be feared, a feeling of harmony with the universe, and a mystical *"conjunctio oppositorum"* or unity of opposites. This list closely resembles our earlier enumeration of the experience of good metered verse as described by literary people.

If Lex is right one can add to the more specifically cortical effects of metered verse the more generalized functions of a major ritual driving technique: the promotion of biophysiological stress-reduction (peace) and social solidarity (love). Meter clearly synchronizes not only speaker with hearer, but hearers with each other, so that

each person's three-second present is in phase with
the others and a rhythmic community, which can become a "performative community," is generated.

Laughlin and d'Aquili connect the mythical mode of
narrative with the driving techniques of ritual, pointing
out that mythical thought expresses the "cognitive imperative," as they call it, or the desire for an elegant and
meaningful explanation of the world;[23] and McManus
argues that such practices are essential in the full development and education of children.[24] (Again we might
point out that the modernist praise of mythical thought
is misplaced; for it values the irrational element it
discerns in myth, whereas true mythical thought, as
Lévi-Strauss has shown, is deeply rational and has much
in common with scientific hypothesis.)

The theory of the state-boundedness of memory might
also explain the remarkable memorability of poetry. If
meter evokes a peculiar brain state, and if each meter and
each use of meter with its unique variations carries its
own mood or brain-state signature, then it is not surprising that we can recall poetry so readily. The meter itself
can evoke the brain-state in which we first heard the
poem, and therefore make the verbal details immediately
accessible to recall. Homer said that the muses were the
daughters of memory, and this may be what he meant. By
contrast, the modernist critic Chatman sneeringly dis-
misses the mnemonic function of metered poetry as
being in common with that of advertising jingles. But if
advertising jingles are left holding the field of human
emotional persuasion, poetry has surely lost the battle—
or the advertising jingles have become the only true
poetry.

To sum up the general argument of this paper: Metered
poetry is a cultural universal, and its salient feature, the
three-second LINE, is tuned to the three-second present

moment of the auditory information-processing system. By means of metrical variation the musical and pictorial powers of the right-brain are enlisted by meter to cooperate with the linguistic powers of the left, and by auditory driving effects the lower levels of the nervous system are stimulated in such a way as to reinforce the cognitive functions of the poem, to improve the memory, and to promote physiological and social harmony. Metered poetry may play an important part in developing our more subtle understandings of time, and may thus act as a technique to concentrate and reinforce our uniquely human tendency to make sense of the world in terms of values like truth, beauty, and goodness. Meter breaks the confinement of linguistic expression and appreciation within two small regions of the left temporal lobe and brings to bear the energies of the whole brain.[25]

The consequences of this new understanding of poetic meter are very wide-ranging. This understanding would endorse the classical conception of poetry, as designed to "instruct by delighting," as Philip Sidney put it.[26] It would suggest strongly that free verse, when uncoupled from any kind of metrical regularity, is likely to forgo the benefits of bringing the whole brain to bear. It would also predict that free verse would tend to become associated with views of the world in which the tense-structure has become very rudimentary and the more complex values, being time-dependent, have disappeared. A bureaucratic social system, requiring specialists rather than generalists, would tend to discourage reinforcement techniques such as metered verse, because such techniques put the whole brain to use and encourage world views that might transcend the limited values of the bureaucratic system; and by the same token it would encourage activities like free verse, which are highly specialized both neurologically and culturally. Prose, both because of its own syntactical rhythms and because of its traditional liberty of topic and vocabulary, is less highly specialized; though it is significant that bureaucratic prose tends toward being arhythmic and toward specialized vocabulary. The effect of free verse is to break down the syntactical rhythms of prose without replacing them by meter, and the tendency of free verse has been toward a narrow range of vocabulary, topic, and genre—mostly lyric descriptions of private and personal impressions. Thus free verse, like existentialist philosophy, is nicely adapted to the needs of the bureaucratic and even the totalitarian state, because of its confinement of human concern within narrow specialized limits where it will not be politically threatening.

The implications for education are very important. If we wish to develop the full powers of the minds of the young, early and continuous exposure to the best metered verse would be essential; for the higher human values, the cognitive abilities of generalization and pattern-recognition, the positive emotions such as love and peacefulness, and even a sophisticated sense of time and timing, are all developed by poetry. Furthermore, our ethnocentric bias may be partly overcome by the study of poetry in other languages and the recognition of the underlying universals in poetic meter. Indeed, the pernicious custom of translating foreign metered verse originals into free verse may already have done some harm; it involves an essentially arrogant assumption of western modernist superiority over the general "vulgar" human love of regular verse.

It may well be that the rise of utilitarian education for the working and middle classes, together with a loss of traditional folk poetry, had a lot to do with the success of political and economic tyranny in our times. The masses, starved of the beautiful and complex rhythms of poetry, were only too susceptible to the brutal and simplistic rhythms of the totalitarian slogan or advertising jingle. An education in verse will tend to produce citizens capable of using their full brains coherently, able to unite rational thought and calculation with values and commitment.

NOTES

1. This body of theory is developed in J.T. Fraser's *Of Time, Passion and Knowledge* (Braziller, 1975), and in J.T. Fraser *et al.*, eds., *The Study of Time*, Vols. I, II, and III (Springer-Verlag, 1972, 1975, 1978).
2. The following summary of characteristic human information processing strategies owes much to these sources of information: The proceedings of the Werner Reimers Stiftung *Biological Aspects of Aesthetics Group*;

   C.D. Laughlin, Jr., and E.G. d'Aquili, *Biogenetic Structural Analysis* (Columbia University Press, 1974);

   E.G. d'Aquili, C.D. Laughlin, Jr. and J. McManus, eds., *The Spectrum of Ritual: A Biogenetic Structural Analysis* (Columbia University Press, 1979);

   D.E. Berlyne and K.B. Madsen, eds., *Pleasure, Reward, and Preference: Their Nature, Determinants, and Role in Behavior* (Academic Press, 1973);

   A. Routtenberg, ed., *Biology of Reinforcement: Facets of Brain Stimulation Reward* (Academic Press, 1980);

   J. Olds, *Drives and Reinforcements: Behavioral Studies of Hypothalmic Functions* (Ravens Press, 1977); and

   C. Blakemore, *Mechanics of the Mind* (Cambridge University Press, 1977).

3. E. Pöppel, "Erlebte Zeit—und die Zeit überhaupt," paper given at the Werner Reimers Stiftung "Biological Aspects of Aesthetics" conference, January 1982.
4. Private communications, Ingo Rentschler, 1981 and 1982.
5. "Biological Aspects of Aesthetics" conference, January 1982.
6. F. Turner, "Verbal Creativity and the Meter of Love-Poetry," paper given at the "Biological Aspects of Aesthetics" conference, September, 1980.
7. On cultural universals, see I. Eibl-Eibesfeldt, *Ethology* (Holt, Rinehart, 1970).
8. J. Rothenburg, *Technicians of the Sacred* (Doubleday-Anchor, 1968).
9. W.K. Wimsatt, *Versification: Major Language Types* (New York University Press, 1972).
10. Presented at the "Biological Aspects of Aesthetics" conference, April, 1981.
11. For instance, in Yanomami contract-chants and Western advertising jingles.
12. W.K. Wimsatt, *op. cit.*
13. This is a narrative meter, whose actual pauses do not necessarily fall upon the line-endings. In Aeschylus' *Agamemnon*, for example, an eleven-line sample contained fifteen pauses, and lasted forty-eight seconds. Thus in practice the LINE-length is about three seconds.
14. Probably reflects the statistical effect of lines with a strong caesura.
15. Charles Olson's *Projective Verse* (New York: Totem Press, 1959), is a good example of such free-verse theories.
16. W.K. Wimsatt, *op. cit.*
17. There is an interesting account of various critical theories of meter in the introductory chapter of S. Chatman's *A Theory of Meter* (Mouton, 1965); but it is flawed by a bias against the possibility of biological foundations for metrical usage.
18. Private communication, Ingo Rentschler, 1981.
19. In E.G. d'Aquili, C.D. Laughlin, and J. McManus, eds., *op. cit.*
20. "Ergotrophic" refers to the whole pattern of connected behaviors and states that characterize the aroused state of the body, including an increased heart rate and blood flow to the skeletal muscles, wakefulness, alertness, and a hormone balance consistent with "fight or flight" behavior.
"Trophotropic" refers to the corresponding system of rest, body

maintenance, and relaxation: decreased heart rate, a flow of blood to the internal organs, and increase in the activity of the digestive process, drowsiness, and a hormone balance consistent with sleep, inactivity, or trance.

21. John Frederick Nims makes exactly this point in his *Western Wind: An Introduction to Poetry* (Random House, 1983, p.258). See also K.H. Pribram, "A Review of Theory in Physiological Psychology," *Brain and Behavior*, Vol.1 (Penguin 1969).

22. D'Aquili, Laughlin, McManus, *op. cit.*

23. D'Aquili, Laughlin, McManus, *op. cit.*, ch. 5.

24. D'Aquili, Laughlin, McManus, *op. cit.*, ch. 6.

25. Charles O. Hartmann, in his *Free Verse: An Essay on Prosody* (Princeton University Press, 1980), like many free-verse theorists, argues against the isochronic theory of meter. But his strictures apply to the lengths of syllables and feet, not to the LINE; and part of his argument is based on the fact that much free verse does not fit any temporal schema. This would not be a problem for our argument, which does not consider such free verse to be poetry in the strict sense. His argument attempts to save free verse, and therefore defines verse in a hopelessly vague way; ours is content to abandon it *as verse* unless it consciously or unconsciously employs the human and universal grammar of meter. It may be an admirable kind of word play, and it might even be argued that it is a new art-form of our century. But it is not poetry; and if this sounds dogmatic, it should be remembered that dogmatism is only bad when it is wrong.

26. In *A Defense of Poetry*.

INTERCHAPTER III

At various times in history poets and artists have taken to themselves that body of conceptions and practices which I have characterized as natural classicism. The epic is the quintessential natural classical genre. Its poets have either had immediate access to an oral tradition which already embodied the classical psychic technologies and subject matters, as in the case of the Gilgamesh epic, the Heike, the Ramayana, and the epics of Homer; or have reached out to the human and natural sciences for an appropriate ontological conception of their work, and thus rediscovered a natural classicism of their own: among these we may place Virgil, Dante, and Milton.

Whole groups of writers, dramatists, philosophers, artists, and scientists have sometimes arisen, energized by natural classical principles: the paradigm case is obviously classical Athens, but we may identify such groups as the circle of Tu Fu and Li Po in China, Renaissance Florence, the circle of Wordsworth and Coleridge, the circle of Goethe, the American Renaissance that surrounded Emerson, and the artistic ferment that marked the birth of the Kabuki theater in Japan. Alas, we cannot record those unnamed shamans and spirit doctors of the non-literate cultures of the world who advanced our understanding and skill in those psychic technologies, but some of the greatest were caught in writing, and they include the sages of the Upanishads, Buddha, and Jesus.

In such periods the artists, sages, or shamans seem to have the confidence to rise to a conception of their work as performative fiat. Their arts hark back to their roots in performance, ritual, and the oral tradition; the great Romantics to the ballad, the tale, and the prophetic tradition; the Greek and Elizabethan dramatists to the ritual theater; the illuminati of the American Renaissance—Thoreau, Melville, Whitman, and the others—to traditional rituals and forms of utterance. They share a notion of art as a new creation at the leading edge of being, where being abuts on nothingness, and of the artist as a trailblazer into the undetermined, into the realm of those strange verb tenses: the conditional, the subjunctive, the future itself (which, on examination, is no less odd than the others). Each such period makes new discoveries in the ancient tradition of mnemonic, rhythmic, narrative, and other psychic technologies.

What kind of aspiration and conversation makes such an age work? How would one go about making a Renaissance? I have chosen to examine two such periods closely. One is that of the intellectual circle of William Shakespeare, who is for me the greatest natural classicist of all. The School of Night came together at the last moment in Western culture when the matter of science and the matter of the arts and humanities could still be considered the same. The last, that is, until the present decades of our own century. As we shall see, there is a special irony in the achievements of this group of artists, philosophers, and scientists: they helped to bring about that very alienation whose dangers it was their glory to have discovered and, however briefly, transcended.

The School of Night

Fifteen-ninety-three was a plague year in England. A plague makes nothing matter: the black noise of apparently random and horrible death amid blooming health and plenty drowns out the subtler vibrations of moral and political significance.

> They come, they goe, they trot, they daunce: but no speech of death. All that is good sport. But if she [that is, Death] be once come and, on a sudden and openly, surprise either them, their wives, their children, or their friends, what torments, what out-cries, what rage, and what despaire doth then overwhelm them? . . . At the stumbling of a horse, at the fall of a stone, at the least prick with a pinne, let us presently ruminate, and say with our selves, What if it were death it self?[1]

England itself was sick: the euphoria of 1588 at the defeat of the Spanish Armada had soured by 1593; Philip Sidney, the stellar fire of English civilization, had died at the battle of Zutphen; Raleigh was in disgrace; Marlowe's *Doctor Faustus*, with its odor of brimstone and despair, was touring the provinces. At a performance of the play in Exeter the actors noticed there was one devil too many in the damnation scene. They closed the show and left the place in terror, and the actor Alleyn wore a cross thereafter when he played Faust.

In London, if we can trust Jonson's portrait in *The Alchemist*, the plague year had a mood of manic charivari, of picaresque atrocity, unbridled lust and ingenious crime. Law was ridiculed or in abeyance. The hero was the conny-catcher, the spy, the con-man, the Felix Krull. That year the trial of Christopher Marlowe for atheism took place, marked by the treachery of the playwright Thomas Kyd to his erstwhile roommate and the lurid half-truths of the informer Richard Baines. Marlowe was not convicted because he was murdered first, in one of those tavern brawls he got into, not unlike Shakespeare's Mercutio:

> Benvolio: . . . For now, these hot days, is the mad blood stirring. Mercutio: Thou art like one of these fellows that, when he enters the confines of a tavern, claps me his sword upon the table, and says "God send me no need of thee!" and by the operation of the second cup draws him on the drawer, when indeed there is no need.[2]

As Touchstone says, "it strikes a man as dead as a great reckoning in a little room."[3] Robert Green, the writer of *The Art of Conny-Catching*,[4] had himself died in poverty and bitterness the year before, warning his friend Marlowe against the consequences of atheism.[5]

Many of the great hopes of the previous decade had come to nothing. The fantasy of wealth from the New World had fired the imagination of the age:

> And cheerfully at Sea
> Successe you still intice
> To get the Pearle and Gold,
> And ours to hold,
> VIRGINIA
> Earth's onely Paradise . . .[6]

To Faustus, if he is resolute, his magic will bring

> . . . from America the Golden Fleece,
> That yearely stuffes old Phillip's treasury.[7]

Sir Epicure Mammon, that plague year, waits in expectation for the alchemist Subtle to produce "the flower of the sun,/ The perfect ruby, which we call elixir":[8]

> Now, you set your foot on shore
> In *novo orbe*; Here's the rich *Peru:*
> And there within, sir, are the golden mines,
> Great SALOMON's *Ophir!*[9]

But the American elixir had turned out to be a fraud. Raleigh's Virginia expedition had perished on the shoals and shores of Hatteras, and what gold had entered the

European economy had fueled rampant inflation. We can imagine it in modern terms: the revulsion against the space-program in the seventies, perhaps even the inflationary interbellum Germany of George Grosz and Thomas Mann. The excitement of a new world has turned into a fever and thence into a sickness.

Perhaps we can glimpse the same confrontation with the abyss in the religious and philosophical sphere. However terrifying, the seizure of religious power by Henry VIII and Elizabeth must have felt like an intoxicating liberation to those who thought about such things: they had taken control over their own spiritual lives, the human arrangements of law and state were, all along, the earthly embodiment of the laws of the cosmos, there was a divine stamp upon social intercourse.[10] The minor loss of the rituals of the old church had been more than compensated for by the magnificent spectacle of court and theater; the loss of the cult of the Virgin Mary was replaced by the cult of the Virgin Elizabeth; the translation of the Bible into English did not demystify the Word of God but gave it greater dignity, so splendid was the English of the translation.

But after all, what was this human world but a quintessence of dust? Man does not live by words alone; he must be nourished by the Eucharistic bread of heaven. The theater is not a church. The queen is aging; her pageantry and painting can no longer conceal it. Perhaps the safest thing to do with the Word of God is to make it into an iron rule for life, as the Puritans did, and so overcome the uncertainty of this new world.

Even in the sciences the boundaries of the world have cracked, giving a glimpse of a void beyond. No use covering up one's eyes with one's hands like Michelangelo's damned soul: the Renaissance pride of knowledge makes one peer between one's fingers:

> Let not light see my black and deep desires;
> The eye wink at the hand; yet let that be
> Which the eye fears, when it is done, to see.[11]

Thus the deicide Macbeth. The optical research that produced the telescope was already in progress; the many comets of the time were being carefully observed and mathematically recorded. The new philosophers were prying into the privates of God.

It was in this context that a remarkable gathering came together around Walter Raleigh, exiled from the court and living in the pleasant country estate of Sherborne in Dorset.[12] There, many young gentlemen and intellectuals flocked to him, to "fleet the time carelessly, as they did in the golden world."[13] Shakespeare's court of Aragon in scholarly retirement is surely a portrait of them; and so perhaps is the exiled duke and his retinue in *As You Like It*. They called themselves The School of Night and affected black apparel, like Jaques' melancholy garb or Hamlet's "suits of sables."[14] Melancholy, with its fine edge of madness, genius, and suicidal boldness of speculation, was their humor.

Who were they? First, of course, Raleigh himself. Raleigh wore black velvet, with a myriad of pearls sewn on loosely so that in a crowd they would fall and roll among the throng, to be fought over as he passed on, with his gold earring, his princely perfume. Raleigh's heart, so his myth went, was broken by the Queen. She called him "Water," making fun of his name, and he, in his epic love-poem to her, called himself "Ocean" and her the queen of night, Cynthia, the moon, who controlled the wild tides. The Queen had flown into a jealous rage when she found out about his secret marriage to Elizabeth Throckmorton, and had exiled him from court. His mood ranged from the elegiac to the bitter:

Like truthless dreams, so are my joys expired,
And past return are all my dandled days,
My love misled, and fancy quite retired;
Of all which past, the sorrow only stays.
My lost delights, now clean from sight of land,
Have left me all alone in unknown ways;
My mind to woe, my life to fortune's hand;
Of all which passed the sorrow only stays. . . .[16]

and again:

Go, soul, the body's guest,
Upon a thankless arrant;
Fear not to touch the best;
The truth shall be thy warrant:
Go, since I needs must die,
And give the world the lie.

Say to the court, it glows
And shines like rotten wood;
Say to the church, it shows
What's good, and doth no good:
If church and court reply
Then give them both the lie.[17]

   Raleigh knew well the void that lies behind the grand
theater of the world: "Who was it," he asks in his *History
of the World*," that appointed the earth to keep the
centre, and gave order that it should hang in the air?" If
the Earth is no sure foundation, then we all "hang in the
air" together; or to change the metaphor, "all the world's
a stage, and all the men and women merely players."[18]
Shakespeare's melancholy Jaques, who speaks this fa-

mous speech, is echoing or echoed by a poem of Raleigh's:

> What is our life? The play of passion,
> Our mirth? The music of division:
> Our mother's wombs the tiring-houses be,
> Where we are dressed for life's short comedy.
> The earth's the stage; Heaven the spectator is,
> Who sits and views whosoe'er doth act amiss;
> Our graves that hide us from the scorching sun
> Are like drawn curtains when the play is done.
> Thus playing post we to our latest rest . . .

And then the last line, that only Raleigh could have
written:

> And then we die in earnest, not in jest.[19]

The origin of this poem was probably the wonderful *Fable
About Man* by Juan Vives,[20] the Spanish Renaissance
philosopher, which in turn derives from ideas in Pico
della Mirandola's *Oration on the Dignity of Man*. In
Vives' fable, the gods are celebrating Juno's birthday. Like
Shakespeare's Prospero, Jupiter stages a masque for their
entertainment. The theater that he creates is the world,
the "great globe itself." The actors are the living crea-
tures that grow and crawl upon its face. Lastly Jupiter
creates Man, costuming him in the excellent mask and
costume of head, body, limbs, senses. Man is the greatest
actor of all, the finest mimic. He mimics plants and
animals with brilliant verisimilitude; then he retires, and
the curtain is drawn back to reveal him as a rational
social creature, prudent, just, faithful, human, kindly,
and friendly, at home in civil society. Next, he robes
himself more splendidly still, and presents the gods
themselves in all their beauty and wisdom. At last he

impersonates Jupiter himself, so well that none of the
gods can tell the difference between the real and the
counterfeit. Whereupon Man is seated at the divine
banquet, and crowned the brother of the gods.

Only we die in earnest, that's no jest. Well, said
Raleigh, let us play out the play nevertheless. His whole
life became an exercise in the Gay Science of the magnificent gesture. If life is a game, then is it not noble to play it
as well as, or better than, something more serious and
thereby put the gods to shame? Perhaps, as with Shakespeare's Antony, that fascinating queen had corrupted
the brave soldier. Raleigh's loose pearls are reminiscent
of the "crowns and crownets" of Antony, which are like
"plates dropped from his pocket";[21] Raleigh's sea-battles
remind us of Antony's; his bounty likewise; like Antony,
Raleigh botched a suicide; and like Antony, Raleigh
began his dying speech twice, in order to get the full
attention of his audience.

In any case, Raleigh played the game with magnificent
gallantry. In his role of soldier he is seen storming the
land and sea defenses of Cadiz against absurd odds, he and
Essex striving which could show the craziest streak of
courage, sacking the city, carrying off its great library
among the spoils, to be the nucleus of the Bodleian
Library. There Raleigh got the terrible splinter-wound
from which he limped the rest of his life.[22] Or again at
Fayal in the Azores, storming ashore at a disadvantage,
for he could have landed elsewhere in greater safety. As
he says in his *History of the World*:

> The truth is, that I could have landed my men
> with more ease than I did, yea, without finding
> any resistance, if I would have rowed to another
> place; yea, even there where I landed, if I would
> have taken more company to help me. But,
> without fearing any imputation of rashness, I

> may say that I had more regard of reputation in
> that business than of safety. For I thought it to
> belong unto the honour of our prince and
> nation that a few islanders should not think
> any advantage great enough against a fleet set
> forth by Queen Elizabeth . . .[23]

It was Raleigh's ambition not only to grace the stage of
his world but to have changed the stage itself. He pushed
out the boundaries of the world with his expeditions to
Virginia, the Orinoco, Guyana; he sought the legendary
Eldorado, and though he brought back little gold, he
changed the economics and ecology of the world by
introducing to Europe the tomato, the potato, and tobacco. Like Othello, he brought back tales of monsters and
"Anthropophagi, and men whose heads do grow beneath
their shoulders."[24] He trafficked not only with the void
beyond the world of maps but the void of the future, and
changed both into a setting for his grand gestures.

But there was nothing lightweight about him: he was
an imagemaker, but his images grew "to something of
great constancy,/ But howsoever strange and admirable."[25] He knew the foremost scientists, scholars, naviga-
tors, and mathematicians of his time, and he contributed
seriously in a number of academic fields. His *History of
the World* was, for some time, definitive. It is typical of
him to have embarked not just on a history of England,
but of the whole world:

> I confess that it had better sorted with my
> disability, the better part of whose times are
> run out in other travails, to have set together
> (as I could) the unjointed and scattered frame of
> our English affairs than of the universal; in
> whom, had there been no other defect (who am
> all defect) than the time of day, it were enough;

the day of a tempestuous life drawn on to the
very evening ere I began. But those inmost and
soul-piercing wounds which are ever aching
while uncured, with the desire to satisfy those
few friends which I have tried by the fire of
adversity—the former enforcing, the latter
persuading—have caused me to make my
thoughts legible, and myself the subject of
every opinion, wise or weak.[26]

The point of view one must adopt if one wishes to
discuss the whole world is necessarily outside it. Like
Descartes, Raleigh embarked on a program of systematic
skepticism. There are stories of his refuting divines who
fell back on invisible essences when the conversation
turned to God or the soul.[27] Raleigh does not deny the
existence of either, but he refuses to allow his interlocu-
tor to claim that something which is an artifact of verbal
definitions had extra-verbal authority. The soul, he felt,
was created, as Vives' actor creates his part, but is no less
real for that. Whether he felt the same way about God we
do not know.

Raleigh was the Renaissance Man *par excellence*, "the
courtier's, soldier's, scholar's, eye, tongue, sword," and
he collected around him an astonishing variety of genius.
Christopher Marlowe was certainly one of his circle. The
unsavory informer Richard Baines, who testified in Marlowe's trial for atheism, links Marlowe with Raleigh
repeatedly, relying on the latter's disgrace with the
Queen to aim so high in his slanders. Baines' evidence
gives a fascinating if unreliable record of the conversation
of the School of Night. Marlowe, Baines maintained, had
stated that "Moyses kept the Jews 40 years in the wilderness . . . to thintent that those who were privy to most
of his subtilties might perish and so an everlasting

superstition Remain in the hartes of the people." Critics usually take this, if Marlowe indeed said it, to be an angry young intellectual's usual outrageousness, to upset the proper citizen; but if we look closer, and in the context of Marlowe's undoubted learning and his political opinions as shown in Tamburlaine, a more interesting possibility arises. What Marlowe must have been talking about was the Noble Lie of Plato's Republic: the necessary fiction that underlies any society, the illusion that protects the vulgar from the terror and chaos of their own freedom. Other elements of Baines' testimony confirm this hypothesis: "Moyses, being brought up in all the artes of the Egiptians," found it easy "to abuse the Jews, being a rude and grosse people." Marlowe (probably through Giordano Bruno) had come across the neoplatonic tradition that the chimerical Egyptian sage Hermes Trismegistus was of equal antiquity with Moses.[28] Further, Marlowe said (according to Baines) that the Jews were right to crucify Jesus: naturally one should defend the fiction upon which all one's values must rest. Since we must play a game of life, let it at least be a good one. The Catholics had a better claim than the Protestants to God and good religion because their pomp and ritual were better. Marlowe, said Baines, proposed to write a new religion—its Greek, at any rate, would be better than that of the New Testament.

But there is a terror in the nakedness of such a mind. Having no God to mediate the ferocity of its aspiration, it must contemplate and prey upon itself, until the veils of habit, tradition, and expectation are torn away and the soul confronts the essential zero at its core. But the fierce spirit presses on:

> All things that move between the quiet poles
> Shall be at my command. Emperors and Kings
> Are but obey'd in their several Provinces:

> Nor can they raise the winde or read the cloude:
> But his dominion that exceeds in this
> Stretcheth as farre as doth the mind of man:
> A sound Magitian is a Demi-god:
> Here, tire my braines to get a Deity.[29]

All that might frighten him is but a tissue of words:

> This word Damnation terrifies not me
> For I confound hell in *Elizium*.[30]

But the answer is that

> Hell hath no limits, nor is circumscrib'd,
> In one selfe place; but where we are is hell,
> And where hell is there must we ever be. . . .[31]

Shakespeare's Hamlet stares into the same darkness:

> I could be bounded in a nutshell and count
> myself a king of infinite space, were it not that I
> have bad dreams.[32]
> There is nothing either good or bad but think-
> ing makes it so.[33]

That "nothing," the "not to be" which Hamlet poises against "to be," is the fascination, the terror that ravishes the minds of these Renaissance men. First it is the realm of possibility, the void that Lucretius posits as the necessary space for new things to happen in. But it becomes a sort of black hole that sucks the self into itself in a feverish vortex of reflection, until the self yearns to be rid of itself:

> All beasts are happy, for when they die,
> Their soules are soon dissolv'd in elements,

But mine must live still to be plagu'd in hell.
Curst be my parents that ingend'red me;
No *Faustus*, curse thyself, curse *Lucifere*,
That hath depriv'd thee of the joies of heaven.
It strikes, it strikes; now body turne to aire,
Or *Lucifer* will beare thee quicke to hell.
O soule be chang'd into little water drops
And fall into the Ocean, ne're be found.
My God, my God, looke not so fierce on me . . .[34]

Milton's fallen angels will inhabit that same mental space:

The mind is its own place, and in itself
Can make a Heav'n of Hell, a Hell of Heav'n.
What matter where, if I be still the same,
And what I should be, all but less than hee
Whom Thunder hath made greater? Here at least
We shall be free . . .[35]

. . . for who would lose
Though full of pain, this intellectual being,
Those thoughts that wander through Eternity,
To perish rather, swallow'd up and lost
In the wide womb of uncreated night,
Devoid of sense and motion?[36]

But the paradox is that the "intellectual being," to be what it is, must have a frontier with the void. Its own corrosive skepticism, like Descartes' doubt of all things sensory, must burn itself to the quick. And the burning is both a torment and a delight, a ravishment.

All the same, the world seen from such a vantage-point —the All seen from the only point of view outside it, that it, Nothing—becomes valueless in turn, and we are left with the dark charivari of Wagner and the devils, unnat-

ural grapes in winter, delicious, soul-stealing sexuality
without heart or issue—a theater-world of illusion and
sensation without substance. One of the things they
talked about, that plague year in Sherborne, was what
kind of value can be found or created in such a world. If
we are masks, can masks love each other? If Vives' fable
of Man the protean actor is accurate, can we act Goodness and Truth and really make them come to be? To do
that would be a godlike work enough—to claim from the
wilderness of the void, "clean from sight of land," a new
world. Shakespeare, I believe, was trying to answer these
questions in *Othello*, *Macbeth*, *Antony and Cleopatra*,
and *The Tempest*.

Who were the others in the School of Night? John
Florio was one: Florio was the translator of Montaigne,
and a friend of Giordano Bruno, Richard Hakluyt, and
Shakespeare's patron the Earl of Southampton. Giordano
Bruno came to England in 1583 and lived at the house of
his patron, Mauvissière the French ambassador. Bruno's
presence may in fact have catalyzed the formation of the
School of Night. To those memorable dinners at the
French Embassy came Walter Raleigh, Christopher Marlowe, Philip Sidney, and Fulke Greville; Florio, Bruno,
and Mauvissière played host. The conversation, according to Bruno's *Cena de le ceneri*, dwelt on the new
Copernican system of astronomy and its philosophical
implications.[37] Florio's Montaigne was on Shakespeare's
shelves, we know, for there is a copy with his hooked-S
signature in it. Another member was Florio's publisher,
Edward Blount, one of the "stationers in Paules
churcheyard" who were implicated with Marlowe in
Thomas Kyd's accusations of atheism.[38] Blount was also
the publisher of Shakespeare's First Folio. Matthew
Roydon the poet and William Warner, a scientist who
probably anticipated Harvey in his discovery of the
circulation of the blood,[39] were associates of Marlowe and

also of other members of the School of Night. The wizard John Dee, whose magical entertainment of the emperor Rudolf II at his court at Prague in the late eighties probably formed the basis of the corresponding scene in *Doctor Faustus*, was also closely connected with the group. Although Dee himself published little, the work of his disciple Robert Fludd gives us a good idea of the nature of his thought. Fludd developed a remarkable memory system called the *Theatrum Mundi*, the Theater of the World. Frances Yates believes that the architecture of the Globe Theatre was partly inspired by this system.[40] George Chapman, the translator of Homer, was another member of the School. Some have speculated that Chapman was Shakespeare's "rival poet," though others, notably A. L. Rowse, believe Marlowe himself better fits the part. In either case, the rivalry might explain the peculiar relationship of Shakespeare to the group, one of close interest, admiration, and intimate knowledge, but also a certain personal distance and even hostility. Chapman's close relationship with Marlowe is attested to by his completing of Marlowe's *Hero and Leander*, which had been interrupted by Marlowe's death.

Through Raleigh, who was his patron, Edmund Spenser himself must have come to know other members of the group. Muriel Rukeyser believes that there had been an earlier gathering of some elements of the School at the Abbey of Molanna in County Cork, Ireland, during Raleigh's Irish sojourn in the late eighties.[41] In the *Mutabilitie Cantos* of Spenser a philosophy of change and appearance is adumbrated which accords closely with the preoccupations of the School of Night. More interesting still, the astronomical researches of the School are reflected in these cantos, and the philosophical thesis of the poem is illustrated by a myth in which the river-nymph Molanna betrays the natural mysteries of Diana's nakedness to the curiosity of a faun. If the abbey of Molanna

was the site of philosophic, scientific, and astronomical
researches and discussions, the myth, translated, might
well describe the School of Night. If Diana is taken to be
the moon, there is a still more exciting possibility. One
member of the School of Night, the actual proprietor of
the abbey of Molanna, was a great astronomer who is
known to have observed the craters of the Moon. To this
subject I shall return.

Spenser's *Faerie Queene* reflects another interest of the
School: the new-found-land of America. Fairyland is,
according to the second canto of the Second Book, compared with the "Indian Peru," the lands about the Ama-
zon, and "fruitfullest Virginia" itself. In a sense, the
fairies are Californians. (California was named for a
fabulous country in a Spanish romance.)

Philip Sidney's premature death was deeply mourned
by the School of Night. Almost all its poets contributed
to the volume of elegies that was put together in his
honor, *The Phoenix Nest*. After Philip's death his brother
Robert Sidney kept up the association. It is not inconsis-
tent with the evidence to suggest that *The Defence of
Poetry* is one of the early fruits of the intellectual climate
fostered by the School. But whereas Marlowe's drama and
Raleigh's verse show a dark preoccupation with the void
that is opened up when the mind of man contemplates
and thus exceeds his own nature, Sidney's handling of
similar ideas is delightfully sunny and wholesome. *The
Defense of Poetry* is one of the exemplary texts of natural
classicism. Sidney argues that the creative activities of
the human mind are not opposed to nature, nor merely
subordinate to it, but are instead its continuation and
apotheosis:

> Only the poet, disdaining to be tied to any such
> subjection, lifted up with the vigor of his own
> invention, doth grow, in effect, into another

nature, in making things either better than
nature bringeth forth, or quite anew - forms
such as never were in nature, as the heroes,
demi-gods, cyclops, chimeras, furies, and such
like; so as he goeth hand in hand with Nature,
not enclosed within the narrow warrant of her
gifts, but freely ranging within the zodiac of his
own wit. Nature never set forth the earth in so
rich tapestry as divers poets have done; neither
with so pleasant rivers, fruitful trees, sweet-
smelling flowers, nor whatsoever else may
make the too-much-loved earth more lovely;
her world is brazen, the poets only deliver a
golden.[42]

Indeed, for Sidney, the artistic imagination was a gift
inherited from before the fall of man, and its powers, by
which man shares in the creative work of God, are
supremely natural to him. Likewise, his essay does not
present the artistic imagination as divorced from the
world of the natural and human sciences, but rather as
their culmination and purpose. I believe that Shakespeare
has Sidney's theory in mind when he writes in *A Midsummer Night's Dream:*

The poet's eye, in a fine frenzy rolling
Doth glance from heaven to earth, from earth to
heaven,
And as imagination bodies forth
The forms of things unknown, the poet's pen
Turns them to shapes, and gives to airy nothing
A local habitation and a name.[65]

Also in the School were the discoverer of San Francisco
Bay, Raleigh's friend and kinsman Francis Drake, his
half-brother Humphrey Gilbert, and his close associate

Richard Hakluyt.[43] I do not mean to imply that the School
of Night was a sort of club with rules and membership-
cards. It was more like a loose network, changing and
adding to itself as time passed, conducting ideas very
rapidly across its membership and, though a nucleus is
clearly identifiable, without a clear boundary line. We
have in the School of Night a living demonstration of the
actual workings of a *Zeitgeist* or "climate of thought"; a
civilization is not an impersonal force but a network of
conversations in which ideas are generated and developed. There is no "program" except the program that the
conversation itself creates; and people join and drop out
of the conversation in no systematic way. Henry Percy,
the Earl of Northumberland, for instance, became in later
years a central figure in the group, taking over the role of
prime financial patron from the impoverished Sir Walter
Raleigh; but in 1593 he was a relative newcomer. Later
the main meeting-place of the School was Northumberland's London seat, Sion House, across the Thames from
Kew Gardens; and here his circle, which included the
Earl of Derby, Ben Jonson, the poets Goodge and Peele,
the astronomer Robert Hughes, and others, merged with
Raleigh's. Northumberland was nicknamed "The Wizard
Earl," and was the patron of a number of poets, scholars,
scientists and mathematicians.

Nicholas Hilliard's miniature portrait of Northumberland repeats a theme which is becoming familiar.[44] He is
lying in a garden; on his face is an expression of meditation and melancholy; above him in the sky is an odd
emblem, a balance-scale whose yoke or fulcrum is so
close to one end of the balance-beam that the cannon-ball
or globe on the nearer end is exactly balanced by the
feather on the other. Written alongside is the motto:
tanti, meaning "so much" and "so little." The great
weight in one scale, if the leverage is correct, can be
sustained by the featherweight in the other. Archimedes

had claimed to be able to move the world if he were given a fixed place for a fulcrum. The emblem and motto develop Archimedes' idea in a way peculiar to the School of Night. Does the emblem mean that the world is equal to nothing? Or that it is supported by nothing? Or that so great is human thought that though it have but a feather's weight in the physical realm, yet by the contrivance of a machine it can move the world? From what bird came the feather? The mind or imagination of man was likened to a bird in a metaphor standard to the great Renaissance humanists. The fulcrum is a sort of equal-sign; the length of the beam on either side can be compared to a numerical multiplier; the weights are the multiplicands. What does the equation mean?

Walter Raleigh once astonished the Queen by claiming to be able to weigh tobacco-smoke. When challenged, he weighed a pipe of tobacco, smoked it, weighed it again, and subtracted the second figure from the first. There is a power of thought behind this trick which, two hundred years before the oxygen-phlogiston controversy, has already seized the importance of the competing principles involved. The apparently insuperable problem of weighing smoke has yielded to the leverage of a mental algebra that, by reversing the problem, solves it easily. The terms of the solution are opposite to the terms of the problem, just as the force exerted at one end of a lever is opposite to the force experienced by the mass at the other.

The generalization of the lever-idea in the Renaissance has been noted by Frances Yates. The frontispiece of Robert Fludd's *Technical History of the Macrocosm*, which Yates reproduces in her book *The Theatre of the World*, depicts a wheel, whose hub is an ape, emblematic of Man's mimetic powers.[45] The spokes divide a series of representations of human technical activities: surveying, lifting by pulleys, chronometry, architecture, navigation, astronomy, music, and so on. Pulleys, like hydraulic screws, are relatively simple extensions of the lever concept: both translate distance into mass and vice versa in the same way as does a lever. More subtly, the translation is effected in terms of strict ratios: a single block-and-tackle lifts twice the weight half the distance, a screw of a given periodicity will lift twice the water half as fast as a screw of half that periodicity, and so on. In light of the principles of ratio and proportion, the relevance of the other technical activities becomes clear: musical notes consist of periodicities in integral ratios to each other; surveying, navigation, architecture, and astronomy use the trigonometrical proportions of the sides of triangles—parallax is a sort of mental leverage and an angle is a spatial ratio; and chronometers, besides using the differential proportions of cogged wheels and levers, indicate the rational relation of various periodicities in the cosmos: terrestrial, lunar, solar, and sidereal. Moreover the lenses used in telescopes and theodolites, which were being developed by the School of Night during this period, display similar rational relations between their refractive indexes, radii of curvature, magnification and focal length.

Fludd himself was probably on personal terms with several members of the School in its later years. If we generalize his principles once more, we are very close to the ideas we have already detected as characteristic of the School of Night. The principle of the lever, whereby a lesser weight balances a greater across a fulcrum by means of a proportionate difference in the length of the beam ends, can be extended and abstracted in a very suggestive way. In theory, for instance, an infinite weight could be properly balanced by an infinitesimal one if the scales are properly biassed: the world against a feather. The weightless thoughts of man can effectively control the massive universe itself, if correct principles of rational transformation—proper levers, pulleys, lenses, clocks, quadrants—can be found. The microcosm can not only reflect, but control, the macrocosm. With correct mnemonic technology, the whole universe can be stored in one man's memory: here the levers are the "commonplaces," the *topoi* of the "memory theater" system of recall. Modern science tells us that the information storage capacity of the human brain is many orders of magnitude greater than the amount of information in the physical universe, so the idea is in principle quite sound.

The theater itself can balance the great stage of the world in the same way. Outside Shakespeare's Globe Theatre hung an emblem of Hercules, earning the status of a god by carrying on his shoulders the globe of the world. If our dramatic technology is sophisticated enough, the empty space inside the theater, populated only by weightless thoughts and imaginings, "airy nothings," "the forms of things unknown," can influence the universe itself outside its walls. The fulcrum is the trope, the transforming leverage of metaphorical language. Artistic mimesis is in this sense an originating and creative force; not a passive copying but an active seizing of control over the world.

Again we are presented with the vertiginous idea of the whole universe in one pan of the scales, and nothing in the other: with the implication that if we can inhabit that nothingness, colonize it with plantations, so to speak, we shall gain magical control over the world. Even the difference between man and God becomes trivial if the lever which weighs them is properly adjusted. And this leaves us in the same loneliness as God's own loneliness, with no superordinately responsible guardian between us and the absolutely arbitrary.

If the weights at either end of a lever correspond in algebra to the quantities on either side of an equation, and the lengths of the balance-beam ends to the multiplicands, to what does the fulcrum correspond? The answer, of course, is the equals sign, which divides and connects the two sides of the equation. We may fruitfully think of the equals sign as a transformation of the double colon used to indicate the isomorphism of a pair of ratios, as in $2 : 3 :: 4 : 6$. The double colon becomes a pair of lines (=) in a delightfully appropriate geometrical development from zero-dimensional point to one-dimensional line, just as the single colon, transformed to a single line, and rotated 90°, becomes the line between the numerator and denominator of a fraction. Thus $\frac{2}{3} = \frac{4}{6}$. This development from point to line reminds us of that wonderful finesse whereby the calculus enables us to treat continuities as assemblies of infinitesimals.

And who devised the modern equal sign? The fulcrum of this essay lies in the answer to this question. The great Arabic mathematicians had invented practical algebra (al-jabr : "the art of bone-setting"); but between them and the theoretical elegance of Newton, Leibniz, and Descartes lies a mysterious gap. The finesse, or *Aufhebung*, whereby fractions are cancelled, becomes, when generalized, the spirit of modern mathematics. It is usually believed that the French mathematician Ferdinand Vieta must take most of the credit for universalizing the useful techniques of the Arabs into a fully-fledged body of theory. But there is strong evidence to suggest that much of the credit must go to the English mathematician Thomas Hariot.[46] Hariot's disciple Nathaniel Torporley had indeed been Vieta's secretary; Vieta and Hariot clearly knew each other's work; in a period of scientific breakthrough we know that discoveries are often made simultaneously and independently (as of course with the discovery of calculus in the next generation). But whoever first used the equals sign, we do know that Hariot was the first to use its immediate derivatives, the signs for "greater than" and "less than," $>$ and $<$, which show a theoretical interest in and understanding of the meaning of the equals sign. To Hariot we can assign the mathematical fulcrum. He was said to be "the first that squared the area of a spherical triangle" and, it was claimed, he could "make the sign of any arch on demand," that is, provide the formula of any curve. Hariot was beating on the frontiers of the calculus.

Most important of all, and perhaps Hariot's greatest contribution to mathematics, was his systematic practice of "bringing the whole equation over to one side and making it equal to nothing," that is, the fundamental operation, the *sine qua non*, the "to be or not to be," of any modern algebra.[47] And here we surely recognize our theme once more.

For Thomas Hariot was the nucleus of the School of Night, perhaps its greatest generator of ideas. He was probably Raleigh's closest friend. In his will Raleigh left him all the "blacke suites of apparell" he possessed, together with a generous pension; there exists in the British Museum a paper written in Hariot's handwriting containing notes on Raleigh's magnificent speech on the scaffold; when Raleigh tried suicide in the tower after his first arrest for treason, Hariot attended him; Raleigh gave the Irish estate of Molanna, once a monastery, to Hariot for his own.[48] For indeed, Hariot was that astronomer who laid bare the glories of Diana.

Hariot was even suspected, with Raleigh, of having been involved in the Gunpowder Plot; so great was King James' fear of Hariot that one of his accusations against Raleigh was that Raleigh had made Hariot cast the horoscope of the king.[49] Countless other documents connect them; their association lasted over thirty-six years, from 1581 or thereabouts, when Raleigh took Hariot into service, until Raleigh's death in 1618.

Perhaps it was the context of wild adventure surrounding their early association that cemented their friendship. Hariot had attended Oriel College, where he made the

acquaintance of Robert Hughes (they graduated the same
year, 1579). Hariot already had the reputation of a brilliant mathematician and scholar. Raleigh probably hired
him as a tutor in the expanding science of navigation (in
those years Raleigh also consulted Drake, Hakluyt, and
Humphrey Gilbert on the same subject). Hariot may even
have been an observer on the Amadas-Barlow voyage of
1584. In any case, Raleigh entrusted to Hariot the scientific mission of the first Virginia Expedition of 1585.[50]

On that expedition the astonishing breadth of Hariot's
genius began to show itself. He mapped the coastline of
the Hatteras peninsula, the Albermarle and Pamlico
Sounds, and the shoals and island to the north and south.
He recorded the new species of animals and plants that
abounded in the New World, and gave them names; he
wrote down the customs, history, and politics of the local
Indians; he even made the first transcript of a North
American Indian language, Carolina Algonquian, developing a system of English orthography for the purpose,
and taking note of the interesting linguistic implications
of its dialectal variations. He made friends with two
Indians, Manteo and Wanchese. During the voyage he
observed comets and eclipses, and developed an improved version of the cross-staff, the navigational fore-
runner of the sextant. As geographer, cartographer,
biologist, anthropologist, linguist, and astronomer he
brought back out of the wreck of the colony not gold but
the intangible riches that accrue from traffic with the
unknown and the nonexistent. He had had his first brush
with the Nothing, the unnamed, and his eyes were
opened. Perhaps the experimental, improvisational, and
opportunistic spirit of American civilization derive mys-
teriously from that moment when Thomas Hariot first
set foot upon those printless sands.

When Hariot returned he wrote, at Raleigh's request, a
sketch of his discoveries, entitled *A Brief and True*

Report of the New Found Land of Virginia. Michael Drayton, another member of the School of Night, was inspired by this document to compose the ode "To the Virginian Voyage" I have already quoted. (In his "Of Poets and Poesy" Drayton pays lavish tribute to his fellow-poets in the School of Night—Spenser, Warner, Marlowe, and Chapman—as well as to Sidney, Shakespeare, Jonson, and others.) Hariot's American experience had released a flood of questions and philosophical speculations. It was in this period that Hariot met Marlowe. We know this because one of the gravest charges against Marlowe was his consorting with the reputed magician Hariot. Marlowe, said Richard Baines, had dismissed Moses as "a jugler, and . . . one Heriots [sic] being Sir W. Raleighs' man can do more than he."[51] Hariot had "read the Atheist lecture" to Raleigh.[52] Raleigh's "School of Atheism" as Father Parson termed it in his *Responsio ad Elizabetha Edictum* of 1592, was centered, he claimed, upon Hariot. Aubrey deplores Hariot's influence on Raleigh and Northumberland, claiming that Raleigh's *History of the World* also bears the taint of Hariot's "deism." Antony à Wood, conceding Hariot's great skill in mathematics, says that Hariot "had strange thoughts of the Scriptures and always undervalued the old story of the Creation of the World, and could never believe that trite position, *ex nihilo nihil fit.*"[53] It was only his powerful protectors, evidently, that kept Hariot from the stake, or worse. Dee's library at Mortlake had been burned by an angry, terrified populace, and Dee's reputation was if anything rather less lurid than Hariot's. Giordano Bruno, on his way from the Thames landing stages to the French ambassador's mansion for dinner with the School of Night, had nearly been lynched.[54] Hariot complained in a letter to Johannes Kepler that it was impossible to express one's views freely in public.[55] Raleigh's estate at Sherborne, where the School gathered in exile from the

Queen's displeasure and the Plague, quickly gained the reputation of a place of black arts and witchcraft.[56] Raleigh and Northumberland were finally beheaded for their views; Hariot was imprisoned; Giordano Bruno was burnt at the stake; Spenser was exiled; Marlowe was saved from the gallows by the thrust of a dagger.

But even in the fear and calumny we can see a grain of truth, I think. What Hariot had actually said about the Creation of the world was more subtle than Wood's quotation: It was that in a sense the two statements *ex nihilo nihil fit* (out of nothing nothing is made) and *omnia fint ex nihilo* (out of nothing everything is made) could both be true and did not contradict each other.[57] Now the Aristotelian idea that "nothing can come from nothing," as King Lear puts it, is surely opposed to the Biblical account of the creation of the world out of nothing. Antony à Wood is obviously confused, or his Latin has deserted him. Hariot would have been quite orthodox in denying the impossibility of creation *ex nihilo*. But what he really maintained was a very mysterious paradox: that both nothing, and everything, are made out of nothing. Obviously our theme, of the world and nothing balanced across the fulcrum (or yoke, or *jugum*, or *yoga*) of the scales, has recurred, more clearly still.

How can we resolve the paradox? Perhaps one way is suggested by Marlowe's claim (according to Kyd) that he had as much right to strike coins as did the Queen.[58] That is, perhaps the world has the same sort of reality as the value of a coin: a conventional reality, for it is "only" convention that distinguishes between a counterfeit coin and a genuine one. If the universe is indeed the result of a fiat, a spoken word, then it is obviously of the same order of being as a conventional entity, such as a law, a game, a contract, a marriage, or a fiction. Like Moses' "subtilties," the universe itself is a Noble Lie. "All the world's a stage"; the "great globe itself, yea, all which it inherit, shall dissolve, and like this insubstantial pageant faded, leave not a rack behind. We are such stuff as dreams are made on . . ." Vives' fable comes back to us again.

So the world is like language: a self-maintaining, self-validating conventional reality. Indeed, it *is* language: or, one might say, language *is* it. The act of translation, then, is not merely an epistemological operation, but an ontological one as well. We know already of Hariot's fascination with the nature of translation: his friendship with the Amerindian princes Wanchese and Manteo, his naming the unnamed-in-English, his linguistic and orthographic investigations. Now, through Walter Raleigh, Hariot met the translators John Florio and George Chapman and became closely involved with the issue of translation in general, and the translation of Homer's *Iliad* and *Odyssey* in particular. In Chapman's dedication of his Homer he thanks his helpers (including Robert Hughes, another member of the School of Night); but his chief praise and gratitude are saved for Thomas Hariot, whose learning was essential to the whole enterprise.[59] Muriel Rukeyser thinks that Keats noticed Hariot's name in Chapman's dedication, and that Keats has Hariot in mind in his magnificent "On First Looking into Chapman's Homer". Hariot is both the "watcher of the skies" and the explorer who looks on the new ocean "with a wild surmise."[60]

One of the reasons for the present obscurity of Hariot was that his executor and former mathematical associate Nathaniel Torporley failed to publish most of the work Hariot left behind. Further, Torporley, afraid of King James and the new atmosphere of superstitious terror and suppression of magic that James fostered, betrayed his dead friend by turning on him in print and attacking him for his atomist opinions. Worse, he sat on Hariot's most important work and thus condemned it to obscurity. Hariot (like Shakespeare, as one critic notes) was careless in his lifetime of his own literary posterity and never bothered to publish his major work.

What was the atomism Torporley condemned? Why was it abhorrent to the orthodox? Is there a connection with Hariot's other speculations and discoveries? The masterwork of classical Democritean atomism was the *De Rerum Natura* of Lucretius. Hariot and his School undoubtedly knew it well. (So did Shakespeare; he quotes from it continually.) For Lucretius the world is made up of indivisible particles, just as a discourse in a language is made up of the individual letters of the alphabet. The atoms could be combined into various levels of organization, as letters are combined into words, sentences, discourses and so on. The idea of the world as language is one we have already encountered. But Lucretius went further. If the world were made *only* of atoms, he argued, there could be no motion: the world would be a fixed block, like Parmenides' One. But motion obviously occurs, and all changes are a kind of motion. Motion must have space in which to occur; there must be something other than atoms. But there is nothing other than atoms, therefore the universe must be partly composed of void; the atoms float within a void, and the density or rarefaction of matter is a function of how much void it contains. Of course we have here the embryo of modern physical chemistry.

Hariot took this line of thought much further. Armed with the Renaissance theory of optics originally proposed by Alhazen, that light does not proceed from the eyes to the object of vision, but is reflected from the object of vision to the eyes, Hariot began an investigation of the atomic structure of matter in terms of its optical characteristics.[61] There exists a long correspondence between him and Johannes Kepler on the optical properties of various transparent substances, their refractive indexes, relative densities, and so on.[62] This line of research now

joined up with Hariot's practical knowledge of lenses as a
navigator and sailor, and with his expertise in surveying
and trigonometry. Even on the Virginia voyage, as early
as 1585, he had astonished the Indians with his burning-
glass and his "perspective glasses." The combination of
his practical with his theoretical knowledge resulted,
probably before 1600, in the invention of the telescope, or
the "perspective truncke," as he called it. Whether his
invention preceded Galileo's is not clear, but he must
certainly now share the credit. In the next few years he
observed the craters of the moon, the moons of Jupiter,
the sunspots, and the horns of Venus, and predicted
comets and eclipses. In his correspondence with Kepler
he speculated on the structure of the whole universe; he
was especially interested in how the universe would look
from the point of view of one of the "fixed stars," which
were then thought to lie at the very edge of the universe.
Stripped of their merely technical naïveté, his questions
are identical to the questions asked by modern relativis-
tic cosmologists: Is the universe homogeneous in space
and time, or only in one of them, or in neither?

These questions bring us back to the problem of why
Hariot's atomism was so egregious an object of disapprov-
al to Torporley. The problem is that in the atomic theory
atoms are immortal, uncreated, and responsible for the
nature and existence of the world. These properties were
for orthodox theology rightfully attributed to God alone.
So the theory of the optical characteristics of matter
which made the telescope possible, was equally as opposed to the orthodox world-picture as was the disruption
of the orthodox heavens that the telescope revealed. The
seeds of the quantum theory and relativity had been
planted in the womb of European thought.

A modern reader, with his habits of reliance on training and specialization, is inclined not to take seriously
the work of someone who crossed the boundaries be-

tween the literary, the philosophical, and the scientific, and between the worlds of language, thought, and action, as much as Hariot did. But he is at least consistent, and his work bore fruit. As Hariot himself scrawled on a margin, adapting an old proverb:

> A man of wordes and not of deedes
> Is like a garden full of weedes:
> A man of deedes and not of wordes
> Is like a privie full of tourdes.[63]

The Rabelaisian freedom is quite characteristic.

If we can come back once more to the question we have asked several times in this essay, "What did the School of Night talk about?", I think we now have a good idea of the answer. They talked about Nothing. Or, more accurately, about Everything and Nothing. From Raleigh came the shocking, magnificent vision of the world as a stage and human life as a self-maintaining fiction or game we play out, like Drake's bowls, in the face of the abyss. From Marlowe came the idea of men as gods, and the mood of euphoria, fatal intoxication, terror, loneliness, and charivari that the god-man must endure as his mind plummets the dark. From Bruno came the continental astronomy and a mystical theology of nature. Through Florio came the introspective spirals of Montaigne; and from both Chapman and Florio came a preoccupation with the nature of language. From Spenser came a vision of the alternative universe of the imagination; from Hakluyt, Gilbert, and Drake came accounts of the edge of the known world. Dee, Warner, and Hughes supplied technical and scientific theory; Jonson provided the perspective of the theater; and the great Earl of Northumberland gave brilliant patronage and political protection. At the center was Hariot, who brought, as I have tried to show, the single, sinuous twist of thought that held them all together—the seeing of everything in the context of nothing; the recognition of the edge that the world shares with the void, which is the only chance for creation, novelty, and freedom.

And outside the School, linked to it by many subtle threads of personal involvement, philosophical influence, and artistic rivalry, was Shakespeare.

In the nocturnal world of *A Midsummer Night's Dream*, we find, as we do at Sherborne in that plague year of 1593, the lunatic, the lover, and the poet. The lovers are in exile from the court, like Raleigh himself. The fairies perhaps come partly from Spenser. The lunar imagery is typical of the School of Night. The philosophy of the imagination, in which the "poet's eye" glances from Earth to heaven and back, that is, from the known or existent to the unknown or nonexistent and back, and "bodies forth" the "forms of things unknown," giving to "airy nothing" a "local habitation and a name," is one we recognize as characteristic of the School.

But suppose, taking the world to be a stage, we find, as Hamlet does, fratricide and incest under the surface of convention? The glance from Earth to heaven becomes the question "to be or not to be?" To stand outside both is to have no basis for choosing either, and the mind is left terribly alone. Worse, there are evil fictions—those of Iago and Edmund. That "airy nothing" can become the terrible "nothing" of Iago's lies or the worse "nothing" of *King Lear*.

Shakespeare's deepest discussion of Nothing is *King Lear*. When the King's crown is broken in two it is both All and Nothing that are broken: the circle stands for the globe (and the Globe) and for the zero. What is left is only numbers, eggshells, pea pods, parings, oyster-shells, empty eye-sockets. The soft life that the whole-hole protects is spilt, and lies naked to the storm. The evil fictions of Edmund, once the groundedness of sacred tradition is exposed as a game, are triumphant. But both Lear and Edmund are wrong in believing the naturalist position that "nothing can come from nothing." There can be good fictions, fictions which do not distort an existing system, as Edmund's do, but generate a new system. By a "noble lie" Edgar convinces Gloster that his life is a miracle and that the "clear gods" are to be thanked; and he puts on the armor of a Divine Justice which will not come except through his own reinvention of it.

The problem of evil fictions intensifies in *Macbeth*, where imagination becomes a fever and a sickness, and confusion "makes his masterpiece." Macbeth is an originator; Edmund is merely a distorter. We may become more than human by creating and inhabiting such a fiction as Macbeth's, but we are damned by it to an inhuman world of dream, "told by an idiot, signifying nothing." Macbeth is Tamburlaine and Faust.

But suppose we take the question out of the Christian era, back to just before the birth of Christ—to the world of Antony and Cleopatra. Now Cleopatra is a "Great Fairy" who cannot be condemned by a Christian morality that has not yet come into existence. As with Titania, the moral laws do not hold for her, the "holy priests Bless her when she is riggish." Even though, like Elizabeth's, the "mortal moon" of Cleopatra must endure its eclipse and her proud lover be vanquished by a cold young king, nevertheless in the last days of their reign Antony and Cleopatra can create together a splendid fiction of love at the "darkling" "shore of the world." That ungrounded reality, the All that faces Nothingness, triumphs over Caesar, who is the slave to natural groundedness.

But in *The Tempest*, islanded off from history, the Magician-Artist-Scientist-Philosopher is free within his magical theater to revise the moral rules of the world for the better. Surrounded by the nothingness of the sea,

"rounded" with "a sleep," uncoupled from the responsi-
bilities of the old world, a new paradise is brought into
being by Prospero. In it Miranda, his Eve, and Ferdinand,
his Adam, can reenact the story of the Fall without its
evil consequences. Creativity and change need not be
necessarily evil. Prospero's prohibitions, unlike Jehovah's, are meant to be broken. Sexuality is not, as in
Genesis, permitted in Paradise and cursed after the expul-
sion from Paradise, but marvellously transformed into a
reward for that disobedience and generosity by which the
young seize to themselves their freedom from their
parents. Prospero, instead of making toil into the punishment of disobedience, as Jehovah did, transforms it into
the trial of love, and gives us the beautiful spectacle of
Miranda helping Ferdinand pile up logs. Most important
of all, Shakespeare grounds his new ethics neither on
brute nature (you cannot trust Caliban) nor on the inborn
essential soul (you cannot trust the souls of Antonio and
Sebastian), but rather on a natural act of art, a cultural
chess-game in which the game itself establishes the
spiritual identity of its players. Miranda's ethics are
naturally classical. The climactic moment of revelation
that sums up Shakespeare's life of art is the drawing aside
of the curtain to reveal Ferdinand and Miranda at chess.
The brave new world, the moral America, is, like a game,
ungrounded, for it needs no ground. Humanity here
generates its own values; it writes its own constitution. It
is precisely this power which is guaranteed by our true
nature. Prospero is a juggler, like Marlowe's Moses, but
he sets his children free not only physically but spiritual-
ly too. He breaks his staff and drowns his book, freely
renouncing the authority that his children have claimed
as their birthright. His noble lie does not conceal the fact
that it is "only" a fiction, an "insubstantial pageant"
which, having served its purpose, can dissolve, solemn
temples and all, and "leave not a rack behind."[64] The best

posterity is the freedom and self-command of one's descendants. Perhaps (and this is mystical) Shakespeare intended to let his plays perish without being put into a book.

It is here, in *The Tempest*, that we find the last words of that debate on Nothing that began in the French ambassador's house in 1583, continued across the Atlantic, into Virginia, through Hariot's abbey of Molanna in Ireland, through the plague years at Sherborne, to its darkest moments at Sion House and the Tower of London in the time of the Gunpowder Plot. Suppose, went the debate, the world were founded on nothing? Where is the edge of the world? Would not the boundary between all and nothing constitute a fulcrum whereby we could get tremendous leverage on the world—even if that boundary existed in all matter, depending on its density or rarefaction? Suppose the soul itself were not so much an entity, a being, as a reflexive process at the boundary of being (or even a systematic absence whose suction galvanizes the world into action?) like desire, for instance, which, as does a lack, disappears when it is fulfilled? If we are masks, can masks love each other? Why not? Is there a fertility not only of the order of nature but also of the order of art? What is justice, if the soul is artificial? If the world is unfounded, like a game or a language - that is, if it is conventional by nature - what constitutes a new move or a new utterance in that game or language? What is translation if language is no less real than the world? Can we change the rules? Should we change the rules?

These questions, in historical fact, led to modern algebra, astronomy, optics, political theory, moral philosophy, psychology, and aesthetics, and constituted the beginning of the modernist world view. Modernism is one set of answers to them. Tragically, but of necessity, those answers resulted in the overthrow of the old Western idea of nature as a stable hierarchy of being, by which meaning and value were systematically generated. When we found that we could transcend nature, we began to consider ourselves exempt from the syntactical rules of our own nature—those very rules that had enabled us to transcend nature in the first place. It is only in the last few years that we have begun to glimpse the possibility of another set of answers, one which neither reduces nature to our passive victim, as did the Enlightenment and the Industrial Revolution, nor elevates it into a comprehensive answer in itself, as did the Romantics. The theory of evolution has provided us with the means to reconstruct the great chain of being, but without its ancient rigidity. We have begun to see our capacity to transcend nature as the result of obedience to the rules of our nature, and as a process which continues nature's own project.

Nevertheless, in that moment before the ideas of Natural Law and the Great Chain of Being had dissolved, yet after empirical science had already begun to make us masters of nature, there was a chance for the creative energies of natural classicism to be released:

> Yet nature is made better by no mean
> But nature makes that mean; so, o'er that art
> Which you say adds to nature, is an art
> That nature makes. You see, sweet maid, we marry
> A gentler scion to the wildest stock,
> And make conceive a bark of baser kind
> By bud of nobler race. This is an art
> Which does mend nature,—change it rather; but
> The art itself is nature.[65]

NOTES

1. John Florio, trans., *The Essays of Montaigne* (Modern Library, 1933, pp. 52–3).
2. *Romeo and Juliet*, III. i. 4. All quotations from Shakespeare are taken from the Riverside Edition, ed. Evans *et al.*, 1974.
3. *As You Like It*, III. iii. 14.
4. Robert Greene, *A Notable Discovery of Coosenage* (1891) ed. G.B. Harrison (London: The Bodley Head Quartos, 1923).
5. Robert Greene, *Greens Groats-worthe of Witte* (1592), ed. G.B. Harrison (London: The Bodley Head Quartos, 1923).
6. Michael Drayton, "To the Virginian Voyage," *The Works of Michael Drayton* (Oxford University Press, 1932).
7. Christopher Marlowe, *Doctor Faustus*, Vol. II, p. 363. I.i. 159, *The Complete Works of Christopher Marlowe*, Fredson Bowers, ed. (Cambridge University Press, 1973).
8. Ben Jonson, *The Alchemist*, II. i. 47, in C.H. Herford and Perry Simpson: *Ben Jonson*, Vol. V.
9. *The Alchemist*, II. i. 1.
10. As adumbrated in Richard Hooker, *Of the Laws of Ecclesiastical Polity*, Books I-V (New York: Everyman, 1907).
11. *Macbeth*, I. iv. 51.
12. The Cerne Abbas Commission, which was set up to hear evidence on a "set of atheists" reputed to be meeting under

Raleigh's patronage at Sherborne, gives amusing glimpses of the local reputation of the group. For accounts of the commission's findings see Muriel Bradbook, *The School of Night* (Cambridge University Press, 1936, pp. 13–22) and Muriel Rukeyser, *The Traces of Thomas Hariot* (New York: Random House, 1970, pp. 135–9).

13. *As You Like It*, I. i. 118.
14. *Hamlet*, III. ii. 130.
15. See Stephen J. Greenblatt, *Sir Walter Raleigh: The Renaissance Man and His Roles* (New Haven: Yale University Press, 1973).
16. J. Hannah, D.C.L., ed., *The Poems of Sir Walter Raleigh* (George Bell and Sons, 1891, p. 13).
17. "The Lie," Hannah, *op. cit.*, p.23.
18. *As You Like It*, II. vii. 139.
19. Hannah, p.29.
20. Juan Vives, *Fabula de Homine* (1518), Nancy Lenkeith, trans., *The Renaissance Philosophy of Man*, Ernst Cassirer, *et al.*, eds. (University of Chicago Press, 1956).
21. Antony and Cleopatra, V. ii. 91.
22. In "A Relation of the Cadiz Action," in *The Works of Sir Walter Raleigh, Kt.* (Oxford University Press, 1829, pp.673–4).
23. G.E. Hadow, ed., *Sir Walter Raleigh: Selections* (Oxford University Press, 1926 and (1917), p.111).
24. *Othello*, I. iii. 144.
25. *A Midsummer Night's Dream*, V. i. 26.
26. *The Works of Sir Walter Raleigh*, Vol. II, p.26.
27. See the Cerne Abbas testimony, note 12.
28. On Baines' testimony, see Muriel Bradbrook, *The School of Night*, pp. 12–18; Muriel Rukeyser, *The Traces of Thomas Hariot*, pp. 126–128.
29. *Doctor Faustus*, I. i. 83, *The Complete Works of Christopher Marlowe*, Fredson Bowers, ed. (Cambridge University Press, 1973).
30. *Doctor Faustus*, I. iii. 286.
31. *Doctor Faustus*, II. i. 510.
32. *Hamlet*, II. ii. 254.
33. *Hamlet*, II. ii. 249.
34. *Doctor Faustus*, V. ii. 1969.
35. *Paradise Lost*, I. 254, *John Milton: Paradise Lost*, Merritt Y. Hughes, ed. (Odyssey, 1935).
36. *Paradise Lost*, II. 146.

37. For a graphic account of this meeting, see Frances Yates, *John Florio* (Cambridge University Press, 1934, pp. 92–7).
38. Rukeyser, *op. cit.*, p. 128.
39. Rukeyser, *op. cit.*, p. 75.
40. See Frances Yates, *The Theatre of the World* (Chicago: University of Chicago Press, 1969).
41. Rukeyser, *op. cit.*, pp. 89–93.
42. Philip Sidney, *The Defense of Poetry.*
43. Rukeyser, *op. cit.*, p. 77.
44 On Northumberland and his portrait by Hilliard see Rukeyser, *op. cit.*, pp. 78–81, and passim.
45. Frances Yates, *The Theatre of the World*, plate 4.
46. E.G. John Wallis, *A Treatise of Algebra* (London: R. Davis, 1685, p. 198); Eric Temple Bell, *The Development of Mathematics* (New York: McGraw-Hill, 1940, p. 158); and John M. Ingram, *Christopher Marlowe and His Associates* (London: Grant Richards, 1904, p. 188).
47. John Wallis, op. cit., p. 198.
48. Rukeyser, *op. cit.*, pp. 89–93.
49. Rukeyser, *op. cit.*, pp. 194–5.
50. See Henry Stevens of Vermont, *Thomas Hariot, the Mathematician, the Philosopher, and the Scholar*, privately printed, London 1900, also John Shirley, ed., *Thomas Hariot, Renaissance Scientist: A Brief and True Report of the New Found Land of Virginia* (New York: History Book Club, 1951): and Rukeyser, *op. cit.*, pp. 17–48.
51. Rukeyser, *op. cit.*, p. 127.
52. Muriel Bradbrook, *The School of Night* (Cambridge University Press, 1936, p. 12).
53. Ingram, *op, cit.*, p. 193.
54. Philip Henderson, *Christopher Marlowe* (London: Longmans, 1952, pp. 44–5). See also Bruno's *Cena de le Ceneri.*
55. Ingram, *op. cit.* p. 192.
56. The Cerne Abbas Inquiry of 1594 was set up to investigate the reports of witchcraft.
57. Rukeyser, *op. cit.*, p. 208.
58. Henderson, *op. cit.*, p. 64.
59. Bradbrook, *op. cit.*, pp. 25, 143–5.
60. Rukeyser, *op. cit.*, pp. 148–9.
61. Rukeyser, *op. cit.*, pp. 178–81.
62. Rukeyser, *op. cit.*, pp. 118–21, 162–4, 178–82.

63. Rukeyser, *op. cit.*, p. 269.
64. *The Tempest*, IV. i. 155.
65. Shakespeare, *The Winter's Tale*, IV. iii. 89.

INTERCHAPTER IV

The next essay, in an anecdotal fashion, sketches the outlines of how a practical criticism and pedagogy might develop from natural classical principles. This book is not intended as an exhaustive treatise or handbook of natural classical criticism: such works will perhaps follow, and it is to be hoped that they will remember to practice what they preach and not depart too far from the vital sources of human interest in the direction of meticulous reproducible method. But this book would be incomplete without at least an indication of the opportunities offered to academic literary criticism by the natural classical perspective, and the critical problems it might help to solve. When reading itself is conceived of as a performance, the reader is at once taken up into the drama of the literary work, which surrounds one as does one's family and social matrix, and which calls out from the reader the practiced and subtle capacities of narrative by which one makes sense of one's life. And in this perspective literature is once more freed to be moral, insulated alike from the risk of evil consequences and the danger of censorship, by the subtle semipermeable membrane that separates performer from role.

Reading as Performance

Recently, as a result of my experience working with Bernard Beckerman's Folger Institute Symposium on Shakespeare in performance, I added a performance component to my year course on Shakespeare. My students directed, cast, acted in, and staged various scenes from Shakespeare, and I adapted my lectures so as to use these scenes as illustrations and cases for analysis.

I had been giving special attention to the character and role of Viola in *Twelfth Night*. The line I took was that her exposure to the realities of death and survival, her disguise (and its consequence, that her behavior must constantly be deliberate and self-examined), her crossing of the barrier of sexual roles, and the more mysterious archetypes of her twinship or döppelgängerhood and the Providential Rescue from the Sea—all of these gave her a peculiar transforming power in Illyria, making of her a touchstone for the genuineness of motive, a driving force in the plot, and giving her a point of view somewhat privileged by its detached overview of the human condition. Even when she falls in love she is capable of a wry objectivity about her own emotions, and this, I argued, was a large part of her charm.

Such a Viola as this can, I believe, be acted; in fact it seemed to me that a good classroom interpretation, if it is reasonably coherent and imaginatively appealing, is a kind of performance of the part in itself.

But then my students staged Act II, scene iv—the one that begins with Orsino calling for "that old and antique song we heard last night," and continues between him and Viola in her disguise as Cesario ("Women are as roses, whose fair flow'r / Being once displayed, doth fall that very hour;" ". . . with a green and yellow melancholy / She sate like Patience on a monument / Smiling at grief"); where Viola essentially declares her love for Orsino without his suspecting that is what she is doing.

The Viola they came up with was quite different from the one I had lectured about. Part of the change was no doubt due to the physical presence of the actors. Viola was played by one of those quiet, small, intense, intelligent, rather mousy young women who really come alive on stage, where their vulnerability is protected by the disguise of pretence. Orsino was played by a big, kind, gentle jock, a rather old-fashioned boy whose chivalry made it inconceivable to him that a woman should take the lead. The student director of the scene, interested in the Shakespearean relationship between master and servant, emphasized to both actors that Viola *is* only a servant and that much of her motivation is a good servant's loyalty to a master, and Orsino is a kind master interested in the welfare of his followers. Add to all this that the actress playing Viola had decided to really go to town on being in love with Orsino, and one had a volatile mixture. The breakthrough, I think, must have occurred

during the rehearsal of the song, when of course neither
actor had any lines to say, and yet the audience's attention is on them and they have to do something.

Viola was slightly behind Orsino in the staging, and
something wonderful happened. Orsino moved about a
little, made characteristic gestures—leaning on his hand,
ruffling his hair, and so on. Viola, quite unconsciously,
mimicked his gestures. The faint element of the comic
about the mimicry only heightened the pathos and the
psychological intensity of this piece of business. Many of
the audience felt tears come to their eyes. Here we have a
Viola whose idealism of loyalty and whose passionate
identification with her master have made her utterly
vulnerable, so much so that she is unable to resist the
unconscious invasion of her personality by the manner-
isms of the beloved. Suddenly the vehemence of her
advocacy of Orsino's love-suit to Olivia makes perfect
sense. She *is* Orsino!

From this point of view we have almost an entirely
different play—one in which Orsino is much less of a
jackass, Viola quite as much a victim of the "whirligig of
time" as Malvolio or Olivia are, and the whole play shot
through with passionate and tender feeling, much further
away than usual from the hard bright cynicism of the
Commedia or of the contemporary English comedy of
Ben Jonson.

Interesting though this reinterpretation might be in
itself, an even more fascinating problem is raised, it
seems to me, by this anecdote. Anyone who has ever
taught Shakespeare in performance can surely match my
tale, so it is not an exception by any means. The problem
begins to unfold when we ask which interpretation is
right—mine, in which Viola is in control, or the students'
one, in which Orsino, though unconscious of the truth, is
in the driver's seat of the scene.

But of course this is no problem, is it? The question of

multiple interpretations has been treated with immense
literary sophistication by the likes of Norman Rabkin,
John Russell Brown, Stephen Booth, Susan Snyder, Harry
Levin, Stanley Fish, Norman Holland, Marvin Rosenberg,
and others. Perhaps it is seventy years late from a philosophical point of view, but the triumphant relativism of
these critics seems to carry all before it. Naturally, they
say, it is ridiculous to ask "which is right?" Many
different interpretations can be right at the same time.
Not that just *any* interpretation is right, they say; but
even contradictory interpretations can coexist within the
same work of literature, constituting a fertile tension, or
an energized field of meaning, or a rich matrix of ambiguity, or, to paraphrase Rabkin, a dramatization of the
limits of thematizing, an overlay of patterns, a paradoxical embrace of contradictory *Gestalts.*[1]

Clearly there is much in our experience of reading
which gives immediate intuitive assent to such propositions. Yes, that is how it is, we say to ourselves. But wait.
Such a tension, field, matrix, overlay, or embrace may be
critically appealing but it is quite unplayable on the
stage. Give an actor a field or matrix and the play will die
on the vine. My lecture on Viola was a success, though it
did take one view of her; and my students' scene was a
smashing success in its context, not in spite of its critical
unambiguity but *because* of it. Relativism avoids choice
between interpretations, but acting, like action itself,
mandates it. The critic can afford to luxuriate in the
immortal Ogygia or Never-Never land of the potentiality
of meaning; but an actress, like Odysseus, must choose
and act and commit herself to the limits and mortality of
a particular choice of actuality. The critics give us a
divine plenum of possible interpretations, but this divine
plenum is quite impossible to perform.

Testimony from many areas of the study of performance bears out this point. In acting theory, Stanislav-

sky; in general performance theory, V. W. Turner and Richard Schechner; in the field of the oral narrative, Lord and Parry all imply that the act of performance not only radically transforms the "text" (whether written or memorized) but also actualizes it into a single unique reality or manifestation; and this single manifestation for the moment blots out all other interpretations, adapting itself precisely to its immediate audience and socio-cultural context. The text or liturgical canon may indeed at another time flame out in performance in an entirely other incarnation, but it is indeed part of the mortal gaiety of performance that to become flesh the text must take to itself the tragic limits of particularity and exclusive being.

The religious language of the last paragraph is no accident. When my students acted out these Shakespearean scenes, Shakespeare's own indifference to the text of his plays—almost inconceivable from a twentieth-century literary perspective—suddenly made all kinds of sense. The sacrament of the Mass does not take place inside the breviary, but at the altar. The roots of Shakespearean drama in medieval religious theater stood clear. Shakespeare is an oral poet, and his plays are speech acts which create and empower a community, as an oral religious ritual does. The truth of a performance is performative, in the philosophical sense. It enacts itself by its statement, and possesses an absoluteness which is as free of the fundamental undecidability and logical incompleteness of analytic truth, as it is of the necessary falsifiability and contingency of empirical truth. Like the words of a sacrament, the words of the play really and truly bring into being for that audience or congregation a new reality, whether it is the fictional (but real) character of Viola or the spiritual (but real) body and blood of Christ.

Shakespearean theater sprang up just when the antinomianism of the English Protestant Reformation, the new relativism of London's international trading community (analyzed in *The Merchant of Venice*), and the skeptical hubris of scientific humanism (celebrated in *Doctor Faustus*) were breaking the ancient sacramental unity, the brotherhood of Christian communion. Yet in a sense Shakespeare's plays are also substitutes for the divine drama of the Mass: Shakespeare's great image of the art of theater, the statue come to life in *The Winter's Tale,* is an isomorphic transform of the Eucharistic transubstantiation. The communal "performative" speech-act by which the priest stipulates the metamorphosis of bread and wine into body and blood—or rather, by which he reassumes the authority of the dead Christ to do so—has its secular analog in the fictional space of the Globe Theatre, when an actor, "his whole function suiting with forms to his conceit," as Hamlet says, embodies a dead king. Shakespearean drama is ontologically more the heir of medieval ritual than of medieval secular art. It is medieval ritual fictionalized, placed in a Renaissance perspective and performative space. A Shakespeare play is not a book but a social and fictive ritual.

Not that we have any less cause to thank Heminges and Condell for making Shakespeare into a text. The point is that though indeed all those interpretations the critics speak of do indeed coexist in some abstract sense, held in eternal tension within the timeless realm of the text, the actuality of the plays is not in the text but in their performance. This is something a medieval playgoer would understand at once, but which we must struggle to rediscover.

This issue has important ramifications in other regions of criticism and in critical theory at large. Some historical analysis may help clarify those implications.

Where does the relativist divine plenum of interpretation come from? Partly, perhaps, from some implications in Lessing's *Laocoon*. The essence of an art form can be found paradoxically only in its existence, in its medium of expression. "Pure" art is a sort of description of its own technical means. From this idea ultimately derives that special attention to the act of reading—the act itself as a sort of fetish, often loaded with sexual and political significance—which is the stock in trade of many contemporary European theorists, like Barth, and American fiction writers, like Gass.

Once reading is separated from the other senses and from the values of personal life and social activity, it becomes, paradoxically, free to interpret how it wills, while at the same time the text, as a mere hermeneutic system of differences, loses all its relevance to actual human concerns. Dramatic performance breaks the magic spell of the reader's hermeneutic isolation, unless, through certain modern rehearsal/performance techniques, the audience is excluded and the performance becomes a sort of multivocal "reading" by the actors. Normal performance, however, by its simplicity of action, returns the artwork to the whole person and rescues it from the indeterminacy of the linguistic left-brain permutation machine.

Related to this historical development is the structuralist emphasis on the text. The hermeneutic miracles of structuralist analysis work only on an object that will lie still and not move as the elegant logical microtome shears apart its delicate tissues. The text is, in a sense, anything that will lie still in this way. Dramatic performance pays by its transience, its sacrifice of itself to the air, to get in return a kind of vigor and life that make such analysis impossible. Instead interpretation becomes a matter of synthesis: playgoers do not come out of a good play discussing binary oppositions, but arguing about divorce or heaven or the state, newly rearranged in the play's light, or laughing or weeping at their own lives.

The New Critical premium on ambiguity has also contributed to the "divine plenum." Ambiguity does indeed have certain uses, providing artistic space within an artform which is heavily traditional and in which there is a routine and mechanical consensus on the meaning of its elements—an artform like the short lyric poem in the early twentieth century, for instance. But what was a limited virtue for a particular set of cases was generalized to cover all literary art, and has been the cause of considerable damage. To use a physical metaphor, ambiguity is like physical disorder—in highly organized and ordered systems, a little disorder can be useful (for instance, evolution by genetic mutation). But if the general tendency of the physical universe is an entropic descent into disorder, order and unambiguity are precious and need to be saved. *Any* group of words has anarchic proclivities toward tedious ambiguity: to make them mean something definite is the miracle, and to cultivate indiscriminate indeterminacy of meaning is as if in an attempt to liven up our genetic evolution we were to infect our healthy tissues with cancer. Ambiguity is not necessarily a virtue even in the lyric poem. The chief virtue of poetry is to perform a definite act within the indeterminate potentiality of the world. Ambiguity is *given*, there is no need to seek it; art realizes a concrete act out of the unreality of the physical universe. It is, of course, one of the glories of literature to use ambiguity against itself, as when a whole group of ambiguities is made to fall into phase and thus indicate a meaning beyond the reach of direct statement. But here it is the unambiguity of the whole that is the virtue, not the ambiguity of the parts.

Perhaps the best test of the validity of a literary ambiguity is performance. Performance cannot afford the luxuriant malignancies of the private reading, and thus drama can perhaps lead us to a notion of literary meaning not so heavily dependent on the "encoding error" type of ambiguity.

Post-structuralist and deconstructionist critical theories have gone a step further and have positively celebrated the collapse of meaning which follows the "divine plenum" of interpretation. There is an interesting decadence in this movement which parallels such cultural excrescences as punk rock and nuclear escalation, in its positive affection for self-destruction.

At bottom we find the existentialist impulse of our century, with its denial of essences and of ontotheology, and its consequent relativism and indeterminacy. But the new comparative studies of culture, combined with new understandings of perception and of the chemical reward-system of the human brain, seem to indicate that our very nature, our existence itself, is predisposed to essential values, ideals, and the creation of entities which elegantly explain the confused and ambiguous complexity of experience. Thus to be true existentialists we must be true essentialists, and this formulation perfectly describes what a stage actor does in preparing a part, when the actor creates an *objective*, a purpose, to which existence and experience become subordinate, and ignores the plenum of other possible objectives and purposes.

This is not to say that the New Critical, Structuralist, and Deconstructionist methods are totally ineffective and invalid, only that their range of validity is limited to works of literary art that share their existentialist ideology and express it stylistically. Such methods fail to touch such elements of literature as communication, the relationship of author and audience, its truth, and most of all the creation and maintenance of communal value by performative speech acts. Perhaps indeed these reflections point to certain contradictions inherent in much modernist literature. When we imagine the first-person anti-heroes of Gide, Camus, or Sartre, for example, contacting their editors at Gallimard, haggling with their agents over royalties, waiting with bated breath at Les Deux Magots for the reviews in the great Paris literary journals, hoping for book-adoptions by the schools, the reality of such memoirs as theirs becomes impossible. In their performance—their publication—they are unplaya- ble! And if these accounts are thus by their own confes- sion only fictions, then their authors are surely in bad faith if they cover themselves with the mantle of their fictional character's values (or lack of values). Norman Mailer, more literalistic and more honest, got himself into precisely this difficulty when he posted literary bail for a killer who promptly did it again.

The question "can this scene be acted?" thus leads us to a kind of literature which must, of its nature, be unambiguously instantiated, that is, actualized, in a communal context, and must create or maintain values by means of "performative" speech acts.

It is this quasi-religious function which is most tell- ingly revealed to us by oral performance: a choice of meaning which alters the world and which attends away from all other interpretations. An understanding of the medieval roots of Shakespeare's drama in liturgical action can open up not only fruitful critical approaches to Shakespeare but also a new conception of the arts of words as value-creation and as a super-temporal conver- sation within the human community.

Such a "kalogenetic"—value-creating—"ontogenetic," "performative" conception of literature may radically affect our pedagogy, suggesting the *performance* of texts to make them come alive, a return to oral and communal modes of learning, an understanding of the discussion and criticism of literary texts as part of their performance and as a direct conversation with their author, a reemphasis on the value of personal talent, authority and charisma, a sense of teaching as a sacramental act, and a critique of Deweyan theories of training, technique, specialization, and academic certification.

Even more important, perhaps, this conception of literature implies a new theory of the reader; one which may rather neatly resolve the problem of the moral role of literature and at the same time remove the chief objection to "reader response" theory, its tendency toward relativism and indeterminacy.[2]

John Gardner in his *On Moral Fiction*[3] complains of literature which demoralizes and corrupts its reader by a persuasive enactment of a false and pessimistic world view. The verdict of most literary folk who read his book was, I think, that the alternative to allowing such literature to continue was censorship, and that censorship is so great an evil in itself that Gardner's very premise had to be vigorously rejected. Literature, they insisted, was of so hypothetical a nature that it could not corrupt anyone— or, more subtly, anyone capable of translating the fictional events of a story into a program of action would either have the sense not to do so, or would not need a fictional justification for his or her misdeeds anyway.

But I do not believe that those who made this response were entirely happy with it. If literature cannot corrupt human life, it is hard to see how it might improve it. George Steiner has pointed with a certain gloomy satisfaction to the spectacle of the extermination camp commandant relaxing over his evening Beethoven.[4] Is art simply a pleasant but valueless froth upon a world of historical events which require much stronger stuff to make any kind of moral difference?

Yet as Keats said, we hate poetry which has a palpable design upon us: and perhaps justly. The didactic relationship between writer and reader may itself be an immoral one by its very nature, as Plato insisted in *The Republic*, for a reader should not submit his or her conscience to an authority whose validity is unknown or unproven.

As it stands at present, the "reader response" theory of criticism does not offer much help with this problem. The reader must indeed try to be the best possible reader for a given work of literature; or rather, the raw material of a work of literature includes not only words but also the reader's linguistic and other expectations. But "best" in this case has no moral content, and it is just as praiseworthy, in the theory, to ingeniously, and rewardingly, disappoint a reader's expectations of a morally positive outcome as it is to disappoint our vicious hopes for an evil conclusion. Further, a different reader means a different work of literature.[5]

But if we envisage the reader as acting, or performing, the role of ideal reader, a number of new perspectives open up. First of all, the notion is intuitively appealing. Michael Polanyi, in his book *The Tacit Dimension*,[6] describes the effect of a really great musician or dancer as having the power to make the audience feel as if *it* were playing the music or dancing, and as if *it* possessed the miraculous insight and skill and second nature by which the bow is guided against the strings or the body is turned to the music. Suppose the great writer has the power to make the reader into a virtuoso performer? Certainly the performer cannot bring to the performance anything which does not come from his or her own nature and experience: but that performer, to act the role well, must feel and follow a dedicated fidelity to the meaning the author embodied in the work; and there is nothing arbitrary or relative about such an intention.

Now there is an undeniably moral element in this activity. In Cyril Tourneur's play *The Revenger's Tragedy* the avenger is corrupted by the evil roles he plays to compass his revenge. Actors frequently report the need to exorcise themselves of a part they have been playing. Similarly, they can be ennobled by a role, and much religious ritual is predicated on the truth that we tend to become what we perform, and thus it is worth performing a part of which we know we are unworthy. May not a reader, then, by acting the role of the ideal reader, be in a position to be thus morally affected?

But this moral effect is a very subtle and indirect one. To play a dark or evil character can, paradoxically, be a profoundly redeeming experience. Hamlet surely grows morally through his work portraying the hissing revenger, the homicidal lunatic; Edgar in *King Lear* attains similar insight through his role as Tom, so that he is finally able to act the part of Michael the Archangel without disgracing himself. More to the immediate point of this essay, Viola grows profoundly in moral stature by acting the role of the opportunistic young courtier, Cesario.

We may now be in a position to assert the moral power and proper moral role of literature without requiring that it preach, either explicitly or implicitly. The morally valuable kind of literature is that which ennobles its reader/performer, and the morally evil kind is the kind which seduces into corruption the "actor" of it; not directly as a person, but indirectly through the performance. Since such distinctions cannot possibly be demonstrated in denotative chapter and verse, they are impervious to any system of censorship. Further, one might even say that they can act as a marvelous "test in advance," of incipient new moral problems and solutions; a way of doing even terrible acts without really doing them, and finding out how one might be changed by them without fully going through the change. If we considered Kafka's *Metamorphosis* as a piece of direct moral statement, for instance, it would not be hard to make a case that it is morally evil and corrupting, as a counsel either to callousness or to despair. But, strangely, when we "perform" it imaginatively as a reader, it can, I submit, have an effect of profound and positive moral change. Indeed for this to happen we must be strong and perhaps experienced "performers," and the weak and suggestible might be damaged. But it seems to me that this is a responsible and realistic way of talking about literature, as well as an optimistic one, and that it contains sufficient internal and systematic safeguards against authoritarian misuse to warrant its introduction of strong moral language.

Even if we did not take the matter as far as this, the classroom experience of which I gave an example at the beginning of this essay presents us with an interesting hermeneutic question. On the face of it, we have two different interpretations: the one arrived at critically and the other arrived at "performatively." Current critical theory can easily—indeed enthusiastically—embrace the possibility of two different legitimate interpretations, when they are both arrived at critically. But there is a radical difference in kind between *these* two that escapes critical theory. The "reading" I proposed to my class was implicitly one of several possible readings: a sample from among the "divine plenum" of valid interpretations. But the performed interpretation, while it is on stage, insists on its own absoluteness, its choice of a particular concreteness, its almost tragic limitation to the confines and contingencies of a particular act. Instead of the *reader's* experience of a pleasing ambiguity which he, as a single and integral consciousness, observes, there is the theatrical experience of a single and integral event before us, which, if the performance is a good one, throws our own lives and selves, and our own relations with each other and our world, into question.

Thus the aesthetic experience in the minds of my class and myself at that moment was composed simultaneously of a field of critical interpretations, exemplified by one of them (mine), and of a single dramatic interpretation, involved with the complexities of our lives as persons. Perhaps it was appropriate that the issue arose with the characterization of Viola, who can, and does, play many different roles, but who is—and indeed welcomes her fate as—a woman forced to act to survive on a foreign shore.

NOTES

1. Norman Rabkin, *Shakespeare and the Problem of Meaning* (University of Chicago Press, 1981).
2. I owe the germ of the following idea to Michael Wood.
3. Basic Books, 1978.
4. *Language and Silence* (Atheneum, 1970).
5. See Stanley Fish, *Is There a Text in this Class? The Authority of Interpretive Communities* (Harvard University Press, 1980).
6. Routledge and Kegan Paul, 1967.

INTERCHAPTER V

The other literary period which I have chosen to illustrate the rediscovery of natural classicism is the American Renaissance: I have concentrated particularly on Thoreau.

One of the fundamental principles of natural classicism is that self-awareness, self-reference, control—in a word, reflexivity—is not in opposition to nature's own spontaneous creativity: rather, it is its driving force and inner principle. The human experience is not at odds with nature but paradigmatic of it. Human nature is what nature defines itself as when it is given its best opportunity to elaborate, its most varied materials, and its most efficient schedule. If we wish to understand the animating drives of nature we can go to no better place than ourselves. Thus the anthropologist is in a sense the most comprehensive kind of scientist; and if literary criticism can aspire to be a science, it is as a branch of anthropology.

Thoreau was one of the first to find his way back to this conception of the relationship between the human and the natural. He was a contemporary of the founder of American anthropology Lewis Henry Morgan, and the date of his *Walden* coincides roughly with that of Darwin's *Origin of Species:* by introspection and close observation of nature Thoreau independently intuited both the anthropological perspective and the essential spirit of evolution.

Reflexivity as Evolution in Thoreau's *Walden*

"I would fain say something, not so much concerning the Chinese or Sandwich Islanders as you who read these pages, who are said to live in New England." (*Walden*, p. 2.)

Thoreau the Anthropologist of Experience

As Victor Turner points out, "experience" is a volatile word, as hard to contain within a single definition as an incandescent plasma, yet perhaps as productive if it can be controlled. Its antonyms indicate its range of meanings: text (as in "did you read that in a book or was it a real experience?"); the socio-cultural norm (as in "my upbringing tells me one thing but all my experience tells me another"); knowledge (as in the French opposition of *savoir*, to know, and *connaître*, to be acquainted by

experience); naiveté; ignorance; untestedness; inno-
cence; innate ideas. In this essay I propose to examine
what Henry David Thoreau meant by "experience"; it
was one of his favorite words, and his thoughts upon it
are, I believe, of interest not only to the literary reader
but also to the anthropologist.

In one sense the phrase "the anthropology of experience" is a contradiction in terms. If "anthropology"
means "the study of human society and culture" and if
"experience" means "first hand knowledge, untainted by
socio-cultural *givens*," then the phrase is equivalent to
"the social life of the solitary" or "naming the unnamea-
ble." These phrases do have a sort of poetic germ of
meaning, though, despite their paradoxical appearance;
and it is no coincidence that Henry David Thoreau was
fond of them both. "I have a great deal of company in my
house," he said, "especially in the morning, when nobody
calls." (*Walden*, p. 148) And:

> It is a ridiculous demand which England and
> America make, that you shall speak so that
> they shall understand you. Neither man nor
> toadstools grow so. . . . I fear chiefly lest my
> expression may not be extra-vagant enough,
> may not wander far beyond the narrow limits of
> my daily experience. . . .
> The volatile truth of our words should continu-
> ally betray the inadequacy of the residual state-
> ment." (Walden, pp. 346–7)[1]

It does not, I believe, stretch the facts to describe
Thoreau as an early "anthropologist of experience," setting out to study the inner man as his contemporary
Lewis Henry Morgan set out to study the outer. Natural
classicism implicitly predicates the existence and validity of an anthropology of experience: and one of the wisest

guides to that field was the man whose greatest achievement, *Walden*, coincided with the birth of American anthropology.

For Thoreau social reality was rooted in, sprung from, and fed upon a presocial ground, and it was his ambition to discover that ground; or to put this more radically, he wished to speak of how the speakable was grounded in the unspeakable. His great metaphor for the process by which the unspeakable and the pre-social give birth to the speakable and social is *cultivation*, whose three senses, the agricultural, the social, and the psychological, he explicitly relates. Typically, he is not content to allow the metaphor to remain in the linguistic sphere; he must, besides, dig up two-and-a-half acres of ground (wherein he found several Indian arrowheads, testifying to the past presence of "some extinct nation") (p. 169) and plant beans there. As he said, he did it to provide himself with "tropes and expressions" (p. 176), describing himself, like Jesus, as a "parable-maker." He made "the earth say beans rather than grass" (p. 170); he "was determined to know beans" (p. 175). Note the extraordinary reflexiveness of his experience—his grounds are his ground; he is an animal nourished by a crop he is cultivating, which cultivation is both an example and a symbol (a use and a mention) of the process of cultivation by which the human race became human; he is a writer whose metaphorical language cultivates his physical activities and renders matter into meaning; and he is also a critic of language who enjoys pointing out how his own tropes both express and exemplify the process of self-cultivation he has embarked upon. He is, so to speak, the anthropologist, the object of anthropological study, and the fieldwork all rolled into one; and his autobiography, *Walden*, is simultaneously a work of self-description and a work of self-construction.

If social reality is rooted in a pre-social ground, and if that ground is experience, then the most literally fundamental anthropology would indeed be the anthropology of experience, although like Kurt Gödel's critique of axiomatization in mathematics, it would approach the boundaries of its own discipline, and be forced to distinguish between truth and legitimate provability within the rules of the system. This is exactly what Thoreau was trying to do:

> I went to the woods because I wished to live deliberately, to front only the essential facts of life, and see if I could not learn what it had to teach, and not, when I came to die, discover that I had not lived. I did not wish to live what was not life, living is so dear; nor did I wish to practice resignation, unless it was quite necessary. I wanted to live deep and suck out all the marrow of life, to live so sturdily and spartan-like as to put to rout all that was not life, to cut a broad swath and shave close, to drive life into a corner, and reduce it to its lowest terms, and, if it proved to be mean, why then to get the whole and genuine meanness of it, and publish its meanness to the world; or if it were sublime, to know it by experience, and be able to give a true account of it in my next excursion. (p. 98)

Significantly and paradoxically, it is only by envisioning a point of view *outside* life ("when I came to die," "in my next excursion") that Thoreau is able to conduct his investigation of it. Gödel was only able to resolve the famous paradox of the statement that claims to be unprovable by distinguishing from the provably true a kind of truthfulness that is not based on the logic of the system within which the statement is made.

If these paradoxes seem familiar to the anthropological reader, it is probably because they are an isotropic transformation of what is known as the hermeneutic circle, encountered whenever a field researcher settles down to study in an alien society (or, for that matter, whenever a newborn baby does the same thing in its own). A society is, among other things, a system of signs, each of which gets its value from its context among the others. If that system were unchanging and incapable of reflexive description and self-criticism, anthropology (and the education of children within the society) would be impossible because before any given sign could be understood, other signs, which constitute its only adequate translation, would have to be understood first. It is only because the signs are variable, because the society itself has not "made up its mind" what its signs mean, and is still, through its reflexive genres of ritual, carnival, play, art, and so on, deciding on their meaning, that a chink in the armor of contextual significance is afforded through which an anthropologist (or baby) may creep. The initiand's mistakes fall within the acceptable range of error for the system, and in the process of successive correction, both the initiand and his society are reciprocally changed. Education cannot avoid being a test of the very ideology it indoctrinates.

Even the most uninventive and non-innovative "neutral" description of a custom by a native informant—even when that description is not available to an outsider at all, but is expressed in the context of a secret ritual and heard only by initiates—assumes a point of view that is necessarily, by a Gödelian logic, outside the system it describes and therefore potentially subversive of it. The mere statement of dogma is itself slightly heretical. This is perhaps the very reason why initiation rites are indeed so often secret.

The fact that there is a kind of truth about a system of signs[2] which is distinguishable from correctness within the system, and that the formulation of that truth within the language of the system changes the system, carries exciting implications for anthropology, which Thoreau explores. As I shall suggest, the comfortable relativism whereby anthropologists often avoid the clash of different value systems by asserting their incommensurability becomes untenable; and the old theory of cultural and social evolution receives unexpected support.

I began by suggesting that Thoreau believed experience to be the ground from which social reality springs. Of course this formulation is not entirely accurate, because for Thoreau experience itself is conditioned by social reality. To press Thoreau's metaphor, the "ground" itself, as Thoreau, who was a surveyor by trade, knew well, is provided with cardinal directions, use, beauty, significance, economic value, and even ruins, fertilizers, and buried arrowheads, by the society that inhabits it. So the initial mistaken or partial formulation must be corrected as we pursue our own hermeneutic spiral toward mutual intelligibility.

But social reality and experience are not simply in a circular "chicken and egg" relationship either. Or rather, the "chicken-egg" relationship is not what it used to seem. The priority of one over the other is no longer a nonsensical concept; wherever we draw the line between the chicken and its ancestral species, at whatever crucial genetic mutation or recombination, we find something that we have legitimately, if nominalistically, defined as not a chicken, laying something that we have legitimately defined as a chicken egg, which will hatch out as an Ur-chicken. So the egg came first. But we have been

forced to resolve an Aristotelian puzzle by means of a
Darwinian solution, to invoke trans-specific change as an
answer to a problem of intraspecific change. The question
has been answered at the expense of the system that
spawned it. Thoreau uses an almost identical method to
resolve the problem of the relationship of experience to
social reality.[3]

For Thoreau, like his contemporary Lewis Morgan,
society was continually undergoing a process of evolutionary development. "The civilized man is a more
experienced and wiser savage." (p. 45) Individual experience was the leading edge of that development. Experience was where social institutions were tested (if
necessary, to destruction) and where new institutions
took their root:

> No way of thinking or doing, however ancient,
> can be trusted without proof. . . . I have yet to
> hear the first syllable of valuable or even ear-
> nest advice from my seniors . . . Here is life, an
> experiment to a great extent untried by me; but
> it does not avail me that they have tried it. If I
> have any experience which I think valuable, I
> am sure to reflect that this my mentors said
> nothing about. (p. 12)

But Thoreau's emphasis on the primacy of experience
should not be taken as a belief in "raw sense data" or
Lockean "impressions" impinging upon the mind's
tabula rasa. Like Emerson and Samuel Taylor Coleridge
before him, he had rejected the positivism of David
Hume; he believed that experience was an *activity,* the
mind's own active questioning of the world, the inner
equivalent of scientific experimentation. His limnologi-
cal survey of Walden Pond is the objective correlative of

his inner quest for understanding. But experience is even more than an active quest. It is a creative act of novel synthesis:

> I know of no more encouraging fact than the unquestionable ability of man to elevate his life by a conscious endeavor. It is something to be able to paint a particular picture, or to carve a statue, and so to make a few objects beautiful; but it is far more glorious to carve and paint the very atmosphere and medium through which we look, which morally we can do. To affect the quality of the day, that is the highest of arts. (p. 98)

Instead, therefore, of invoking sensory perception as a corrective against social custom, he asserts that both are dead and passive, and corroborate each other's deadness and passivity, in the absence of the active and volatile force of creative experience. The vicious circle of expectations governing perceptions which in turn confirm expectations, reproducing each other without novelty, is broken by the idea of evolution; the hermeneutic circle becomes an evolutionary spiral; and experience, in Thoreau's sense, is the locus both of mutation and selective testing.

I propose to explore the anthropological implications of Thoreau's view of experience, first by a discussion of Thoreau as an object of anthropological research, as an early anthropologist, and as an explorer of the fundamental myths of anthropology; second, by setting Thoreau's ideas within their historical context and by an analysis of Thoreau's philosophy of experience in the light of its location near the source of pragmatist epistemology; and third, by a close reading of the "melting sandbank" episode in *Walden*.

Walden as Anthropology

If we were anthropologists doing a field-study of nineteenth-century New England we might well use Thoreau as a gifted native informant. He is a mine of information (usually salted with irony) on Concord customs, crafts, economics, politics, rituals, ideology, fashions, language and dialect, psychology, history, country-city relationships, land-use, and architecture— though he has intriguing and significant omissions, such as kinship and sexuality.

These are significant omissions, because we should, as anthropologists, be astonished at a certain remarkable characteristic of this society, which achieves its most intense form in our native informant. This characteristic is the emphasis placed on the individual person as the fundamental active force in society: not the family, clan, sexual partnership, village, lineage, society, cult, caste, religious organization, guild, union, corporation, lodge, or age cohort. Thoreau avoids family and sex because, one would begin to suspect, family and sex present him with the greatest immediate threat to his personal independence. For Thoreau, the final moral authority, more than in any other society we might have studied, is the individual, and therefore the central social actions, decisions and changes must not only be confirmed at the individual level in order to be properly ratified, but must, preferably, be initiated there as well. "To march to a different drummer" (p. 348) was Thoreau's phrase:

> Wherever a man goes, men will pursue and paw him with their dirty institutions, and if they can, constrain him to belong to their desperate odd-fellow society. It is true, I might have resisted forcibly with more or less effect, might

> have run "amok" against society; but I pre-
> ferred that society should run "amok" against
> me, it being the desperate party. (p. 186)

Of course, further study of the natives would reveal the vestiges and embryos of powerful institutions of collective moral decision. But we would note that many of the most respectable spokesmen of the social norm (not just hermits like Thoreau) were also praising self-reliance and the primacy of individual conscience—Emerson, for instance—and that the prestige of individual conscience outweighed other sources of norms even when its power was at a disadvantage with them. Thoreau takes positive delight in puncturing such sacred cows as progress, social responsibility, and philanthropy ("the only virtue" he says dryly, "which is sufficiently appreciated by mankind."). (p. 82) And significantly, he is sure of his moral ground, and it is his opponents that are on the defensive, not he.

It is, as anthropologists have shown, around the most powerful sources of moral authority in a society that the greatest density of ritual, myth, and ideological-orectic symbolism clusters. If ritual, myth, and symbolism have the double function of transmitting and transforming the values of a society, than it is natural that they should adhere to the institutions which are most active and powerful. Anthropologists are familiar with the rituals and myths of caste, kinship, cult, age or sex cohorts, and so on. But when it is in none of these units, but in the individual, that the driving force of society is found, what are the myths, rituals, and symbols of that peculiar social institution, the individual person? Can an individual even *have* myths, rituals, symbols? Are they not collective by their very nature? We have returned to Thoreau's own paradox, of having company when nobody calls.

It is at this point that we must abandon our own pose as objective scientists, for whom a Thoreau is at best a gifted native informant. For we are as much in the dark as he is, or rather, more, because he has trained himself and is a specialist in the anthropology of the individual. We must become his apprentices as he sets out into the wilderness, as anthropologists do in Borneo or Central Africa, the Sahara or the tundra; as he builds his house, helped by the natives; as he lays the economic and caloric groundwork of his study; and as he settles down to observe his little community in the woods. The difference is that the community is a community of one, and that the researcher and the object of research are identical. Or, we might ask after we have followed him a while, are they?

> With thinking we may be beside ourselves in a sane sense. By a conscious effort of the mind we can stand aloof from actions and consequences; and all things, good and bad, go by us like a torrent. We are not wholly involved in nature. I may be either the driftwood in the stream, or Indra in the sky looking down on it. I *may* be affected by a theatrical exhibition; on the other hand, I may not be affected by an actual event which appears to concern me much more. I only know myself as a human entity; the scene, so to speak, of thoughts and affections; and am sensible of a certain doubleness by which I can stand as remote from myself as from another. However intense my experience, I am conscious of the presence and criticism of a part of me which, as it were, is not a part of me, but spectator, sharing no experience, but taking note of it: and that is no more I than it is you. When the play, it may be the tragedy, of life is

over, the spectator goes his way. It was a kind of
fiction, a work of the imagination only, so far
as he was concerned. This doubleness may
easily make us poor neighbors and friends
sometimes. (p. 146)

I have quoted this extraordinary passage at length not
only for its inherent interest but also because it contains
a powerful corrective to many of our most apparently
useful assumptions about human social behavior. If a
person can have commerce with oneself, then whenever
we describe social interaction we are leaving out a crucial
participant in the scene if we neglect the other in the self.
If we are persuaded of the truth of Thoreau's analysis, we
can no longer assume that a person will follow his own
interests, for he may himself be a battle-ground between
different perceived interests, or even a little society of his
own, *creating* values and interests where they had not
existed before. The economic model of man breaks down,
for every man contains a critic of his own values. One of
Thoreau's first acts in *Walden* is to undermine the value-
and reality-claims of the discipline of economics, an act
as subversive to a Marxist position as it is to the capitalist
one that dominated nineteenth-century Massachusetts.
He reveals the economic bottom line itself to be the most
flimsy of metaphysical constructions.

Of course Thoreau may be deceiving himself when he
claims to be able to stand apart from himself and view
himself objectively. But if we accept the hypothesis of
self-deception we place ourselves in the embarrassing
logical position of having escaped the complications of
one explanation by resorting to another still more complicated. Thoreau here supposes only a dynamic doubleness in the self, but "self-deception" is so problematic a
notion that it requires at least three independent actors in
the psychological drama: a deceiver, a deceived, and an

inner authority that makes the deception necessary; and
a further outside source of absolute truth is needed also
in order that we can assert that the "deception," by
contrast with the truth, is indeed a deception at all. Not
that Thoreau would deny the possibility of self-
deception; rather, self-deception begs even more metaphysical questions than genuine self-knowledge. If we
wish to deny the possibility of two actors within the self,
it will not do to assert that there are three, *pretending* to
be two!

If we accept that the "anthropologist of the self" can
constitute a little society, composed of the self as known
and the self as knower, two fascinating questions arise,
both of which Thoreau explores. The first is this: What
are the relations between knower and known *over time?*
And the second is this: What are the rituals, myths, and
symbols of this little society?

The first question, of time, takes us to the heart of
Thoreau's discoveries. He saw at once that no study of
experience can avoid being simultaneously a study of the
present moment and of universal time in general. The
instant the self as knower has become part of the past and
of the contents of memory, he found, it becomes accessible in turn to being known, and a new self-as-knower,
whose objects of knowledge now include the old self-as-
knower, has sprung into being. The present moment is
constituted by the completion of this cycle. Self-
knowledge is a constant process of transformation of
container into contents, and of generation of a new
container; a continually expanding mandala whose leading edge is the self-as-knower and whose contents are the
self-as-known.

The paradox of the Laplace calculator, which contains
a record of all the information in the world and which can
therefore accurately predict future events, is that it must
also be able to predict what will occur as a result of the

predictions that it has made; or to put the same thing in
different terms it must include, as part of the information
it contains, a complete account of its own construction,
records, and process of calculation. The paradox is resolved only by the reflection that the universe itself is
such a calculator, performing its calculations at a rate
which constitutes the rate of time—that is, as fast as
possible—announcing its predictions in the form of their
enactment as real events, and expanding just fast enough
to accommodate the new "wiring" it requires for the
increased volume of calculation. This mechanistic account gives a fair idea, I believe, of what Thoreau and
Emerson meant by "nature," if we may add that the
human self was for them part of the "new wiring" that
the universe must add to itself in order to keep up with
its own self-comprehension, and that the accumulation
of self-comprehension in general was what we mean by
God. A few quotations will give the flavor.

> . . . at any moment of the day or night, I have
> been anxious to improve the nick of time, and
> notch it on my stick too; to stand on the
> meeting of two eternities, the past and future,
> which is precisely the present moment; to toe
> that line. You will pardon some obscurities, for
> there are more secrets in my trade than in most
> men's, and yet not voluntarily kept, but insep-
> arable from its very nature. (p. 20)

> For many years I was self-appointed inspector of
> snow storms and rain storms, and did my duty
> faithfully . . . (p. 21)

> It is true, I never assisted the sun materially in
> his rising, but doubt not, it was of the last
> importance only to be present at it. (p. 20)

There were times when I could not afford to
sacrifice the bloom of the present moment to
do any work, whether of the head or hands. I
love a broad margin to my life. Sometimes . . . I
was reminded of the lapse of time. I grew in
those seasons like corn in the night . . . They
were not time substracted from my life, but so
much over and above my usual allowance. I
realized what the orientals mean by contemplation and the forsaking of works. For the
most part, I minded not how the hours went.
The day advanced as if to light some work of
mine. . . . My days were not days of the week,
bearing the stamp of any heathen diety, nor
were they minced into hours and fretted by the
ticking of a clock: for I lived like the Puri
Indians, of whom it is said that "for yesterday,
today, and tomorrow they have only one word,
and they express the variety of meaning by
pointing backward for yesterday, forward for
today, and overhead for the passing day."
(p. 121–2)

God himself culminates in the present moment, and will never be more divine in the
lapse of all the ages. (p. 105)

"So soul," continues the Hindoo philosopher,
"from the circumstances in which it is placed,
makes its own character, until the truth is
revealed to it by some holy teacher, and then it
knows itself to be Brahma." (p. 104)

Thus Thoreau discovers in the relations between
knower and known, when the same person is both, a
mystical conception of the human experience of time

that intimately connects it with the evolutionary process of nature as a whole. "Frame," or "reflexivity," and "flow" are here identical. The distance between the knower and the known is the distance the universe expands during the present moment.

The second question, of the rituals, myths, and symbols of *Walden*, is easy to answer. The very activity of contemplation is Thoreau's central ritual. Its participants are the two sides of the self. To embody and objectify that activity Thoreau borrows or adapts rituals from societies whose active unit is larger than the self: the "first-fruits" ritual of the Mucclasse Indians, in which they burn their domestic implements at a certain time each year, fast, and then kindle new fire (p. 74); the fifty-two year purification of the Mexican Indians (p. 75); the ritual bath of "King Tching-thang" (p. 96); and so on. Like his contemporary Herman Melville he rifles the new ethnographic riches of an expanding cultural world for materials to build a vital American syncretism.

Thoreau draws his major symbols from the Concord Woods and from his own way of life: the cycle of the seasons, the sacramental bean-field, the cabin he builds over his head, the melting sandbank (to which we shall return), and above all the pond itself, which he calls "earth's eye" (p. 202) and which becomes a complex symbol of the individual self. His long discussion of the color of the pond's water (pp. 191–3) is at once a piece of careful scientific observation and a lofty and mystical allegory of the nature of the soul. The doubleness of its color, which he attributes to the dialectical relation of earth and sky, is the objective correlative of the doubleness of the soul.

The great mythic text of Thoreau's cult of the individual soul is *Walden* itself. The genre best fitted to such a cult is autobiography, nor was Thoreau the only American to achieve a masterpiece in that genre.[4] The composition of *Walden*, which took place over a period of seven or eight years, was the central activity of the life that the book describes. *Walden* is not a retrospective memoir, but a celebration of a life as it is being lived, a life which includes the composition of the book. Again, in the very circumstances of its creation, the Walden myth is profoundly reflexive while at the same time immersed in the flow of being. Thoreau's description of night-fishing on the pond, where his meditations are suddenly brought back to reality by the jerk of a fish on the line, beautifully catches this reconciliation:

> It was very queer, especially in dark nights, when your thoughts had wandered to vast and cosmogonal themes in other spheres, to feel this faint jerk, which came to interrupt your dreams and link you to nature again. It seemed as if I might next cast my line upward into the air, as well as downward into this element which was scarcely more dense. Thus I caught two fishes as it were with one hook. (p. 190)

Thoreau and the Birth of American Anthropology

As a systematic field of study, the discipline of anthropology arose in Europe and America during the nineteenth century. Of course there had been Ancient Greek, Moslem, European, Indian, Chinese, and Japanese travelers' tales and accounts of "barbarian" customs, but it took a peculiar kind of civilization to produce anthropology proper. This fact is, oddly enough, rather embarrassing to

anthropologists, for it suggests a uniqueness in Western
civilization that appears to contradict the institutional
ideology of the field, that all societies are comparable and
that values are culturally relative. But however noble that
prejudice—and it is noble, for it supports a generous and
open-minded humanism—if it is in conflict with the
truth it ought to be corrected. European/American civilization is uniquely privileged in having produced, paradoxically, the discipline which asserts that no society is
uniquely privileged. The problem can only be escaped by
denying the *raison d'être* of anthropology, which is that
it actually gives a better account of a society to the rest of
the world than that society gives of itself unaided, or by
denying the plain fact that the discipline of anthropology
was an institution of Western society. Until other societies learned from the West the principles and techniques
of the field, Western civilization possessed, in addition to
the enthnocentric point of view it shared with other
cultures, a unique, if however imperfect and partial, point
of view that could see itself as one of a number of cultures
whose values made sense in their own terms but not
necessarily in others'. Of course every society is unique
in its own way; but the realization of that fact by the West
gave it an asymmetrical position of epistemological superiority, a reflexive capacity not shared by other societies. To give an absurd analogy, it was as if all languages
except English were in the beginning mutually untranslatable, and that they only became accessible to each
other via the universal skeleton-key of the English language. The great dangers of such a line of thought are
obvious, but they should not discourage us from facing its
logic.

What I wish to suggest is that the dangers may be
exorcised by a study of the cultural origins of those
modes of thought that made anthropology possible. In

such a study Thoreau would figure as an interesting litmus test in one sense, and as a pioneer in another.

The anthropology of experience may be a new topic in current anthropology, but I wish to suggest that it may also be at the very roots of the discipline itself: that it was only when we learned how to be harmoniously and creatively alienated from ourselves that we became able to understand the ideas of cultural aliens. The individualistic artistic and scientific genres of Western society[5] are to ritual what ritual is to the ordinary social life of a culture, and they sometimes achieve a separation from that ordinary life that is sufficient to permit us to step over imaginatively into the margins of another culture altogether. Once the step has been made, a bridge can be built: and that bridge is anthropology.

Thoreau stands at that point in American intellectual history when the prerequisites for the birth of anthropology had begun to fall into place. Through immigration, economic expansion, the influence of Europe, and forces inherent in its own constitution, the narrow puritanism of New England had given way among the intellectuals to a variety of lofty Theisms, Swedenborgianism, Pantheism, Fourierism, Scientific Rationalism, and the Romantic religion of Nature. These forces cohered into the movement known as transcendentalism, whose leading light was Emerson. At the same time an extraordinary cultural renaissance was underway. In literature alone, Thoreau's contemporaries included Dickinson, Melville, Henry Adams, and Poe. Richard Henry Dana was his classmate at Harvard. He knew Walt Whitman, Nathaniel Hawthorne, and Henry James the elder, the Swedenborgian theologian and father of William and Henry; and one of his closest friends was Ralph Waldo Emerson.

Certain common qualities mark the work of these very different writers: a robust individualism, an ebullient and

optimistic relativism, a sturdy confidence in the possibility of successful syncretism, introspection, a lively interest in and friendship for the sciences, a fascination with
religion, and a mystical bent. It was in this fertile soil that
American anthropology could put down its roots: far
enough away from the narrow ethnocentrism of the
Pilgrim Fathers, yet still new enough to the wide world to
encourage intense curiosity about other cultures; in
touch, through the whalers and traders of New England,
with the exotic lands of the Orient and the "primitives"
that Melville celebrates in *Typee* and *Omoo*, but still
nourished by the great classical tradition of Greek and
Latin learning preserved and transmitted at Harvard and
the liberal arts colleges. The young Lewis Henry Morgan,
who was educated at Union College, transformed his
alumni fraternity from the neoclassical "Gordian Knot,"
which followed the ancient Greeks, into "The Grand
Order of the Iroquois," which interpreted Lakes Indian
customs in terms of the classical virtues. Thus began his
life-long interest in the Indians.[6]

For the first time since the Renaissance, when the
societies of pagan antiquity had come to serve as models
in the initiation of the elite, the West had grasped alien
cultures as possibly exemplary or superior to its own. The
profound orientalizing of our poetry, architecture, religion, and cuisine, and our attempt to imitate imagined
Amerindian virtues in our personal relations, dress, and
recreation is a consequence of this remarkable nineteenth-century movement. Castaneda's Don Juan has a
New England ancestry.

Thoreau cites Gookin, who was the superintendent of
the Indians subject to the Massachusetts Colony in 1674,
on the comfort, convenience, and economy of Indian
architecture, and contrasts their domestic economy favorably with that of his compatriots:

> In the savage state every family owns a shelter
> as good as the best, and sufficient for its coarser
> and simpler wants; but I think that I speak
> within bounds when I say that, though the
> birds of the air have their nests, and the foxes
> their holes, and the savages their wigwams, in
> modern civilized society not more than one
> half the families own a shelter. (p.34)

As we can see from this passage Thoreau, like Morgan,
implicitly assumes that contemporary savages live as did
our own ancestors, and that through an evolutionary
process the savages arose from the brute and civilized
man from the savage. Thus to go "back," as he claims to
do, to the economic condition of the savage, in search of
the place where we took our false turning, is the phyloge-
netic equivalent of his ontogenetic attempt to discover
the roots of his personal experience. Thoreau is being
historically, as well as personally, reflexive; just as he is
seeking the foundations of his own experience, he is
seeking the foundations of the experience of his culture.
What I wish to argue is that, however faulty Thoreau's
theory of cultural evolution may have been, he is right in
assuming the cultural journey cannot properly take place
without the personal one. Except ye become as a little
child, ye shall not enter the kingdom of another culture.
   If it is true that some form of personal voyage of
self-discovery must accompany any genuine understanding of another culture, then we may have the beginnings
of an explanation for the uniqueness of the West in
having generated an anthropological tradition. Perhaps it
is precisely the contraction of the unit of social initiative
to the individual that is essential to the early development of anthropology; and perhaps it was only in the
West that this contraction took place. One might even

speculate about the roles of democracy and Protestantism in encouraging this contraction: democracy because ideally the fundamental act of political decision is the individual vote, and Protestantism—especially Puritanism—because of its emphasis on the personal encounter with God and the central role of individual conversion in the salvation of the soul.

In this light the central *agon* of the anthropological myth becomes much more intelligible. More than in other sciences whose myth often involves teamwork, the anthropologist is alone, almost marooned or shipwrecked in the culture he studies. He undergoes, in the myth, an experience of personal conversion that involves culture-shock, self-confrontation, a profound alienation from his own culture, a sense of being only a child in his newly adopted culture, an initiation into its mysteries, and an acceptance by it; eventually he becomes its spokesman, interpreter, and protector against the culture from which he originally came. (I say "he" for stylistic reasons: the myth works better with a female anthropologist, who is by virtue of her sex already somewhat marginal in her own Western society.) The personal memoirs of such anthropologists as Malinowsky will, I believe, bear out this analysis.

Essential to the myth is the aloneness of the researcher; the individual person is the largest social unit within which the experience of conversion can take place, and it is only that conversion which enables a student of another culture to interpret between it and his own. This myth, I believe, is in process of changing, partly through the work of Victor Turner and Richard Schechner, among others, who have attempted, by reproducing alien rituals through dramatic means, to enlarge the unit of conversion to the size of a small group of persons.[7] If they are successful, the results, I believe, will surpass the achievements of the individual researcher by the power of the number in the group: but individual self-confrontation becomes even more crucial for the success of the project. Schechner's almost psychoanalytic rehearsal process is perhaps designed to bring about the necessary personal crisis. Though the autobiographical, the dramatic, and anthropological genres seem far apart, they possess deep affinities.

The birth of American anthropology required not only an appropriate psychosocial preparation, but also an appropriate philosophical one. And here again we find Thoreau in attendance at the birth, wittingly or not.

American pragmatism took its origins in the encounter between British empiricism, native Yankee technical know-how, transcendentalism, and Kantian epistemology. Less passive in its notion of truth than empiricism, pragmatism had benefited from America's experience of having recently transformed its own physical environment: what is the case is not only what one perceives but also what one does. From transcendentalism came a dynamic notion of Nature and a confidence in the match between the natural order and human understanding; as Thoreau puts it, "The universe constantly and obediently answers to our conceptions; whether we travel fast or slow, the track is laid for us. Let us spend our lives in conceiving then." (p. 105) From Kant came the idea that the categories of our perception cooperate in the generation of the concrete world, and that certain *aprioris* must be synthetic.

Thoreau is already, I believe, a pragmatist in many senses. Like the pragmatists he believed the truth was provisional and volatile in its essence, and depended upon practice for its validation: for Thoreau experience was the inner form of *experiment*, the active "frisking" of Nature for answers, by which alone truth is discovered. Like Peirce, Thoreau saw the world as a system of mutually validating signs:

> But while we are confined to books, though the
> most select and classic, and read only particu-
> lar written languages, which are themselves
> but dialects and provincial, we are in danger of
> forgetting the language which all things and
> events speak without metaphor, and which
> alone is copious and standard. Much is pub-
> lished, but little printed. (p. 121)

From here we might trace the development of semiologi-
cal theory through Peirce and European phenomenology
and into European anthropology, where it crops up, for
instance, in Lévi-Strauss' understanding of the world as
text.

More important still was the contribution of pragmatist ideas to anthropological *method*. The participant
observer, who alters the system he studies and is reciprocally altered by it, whose truths are what works best, and
who penetrates the hermeneutic circle by a process of
successive approximation and correction, is most comfortably and consistently accommodated within a philosophically pragmatist framework. Other philosophical
systems allow for anthropological method, but only with
difficulty, and they do not encourage it as pragmatism
does. Here is Thoreau's impressionistic description of the
method:

> The intellect is a cleaver; it discerns and rifts
> its way into the secrets of things. . . . My head
> is hands and feet. I feel all my best faculties
> concentrated in it. My instinct tells me that my
> head is an organ for burrowing, as some crea-
> tures use their snout and fore-paws, and with it
> I would mine and burrow my way through
> these hills. I think that the richest vein is
> somewhere hereabouts; so by the divining rod

and thin rising vapors I judge; and here I will
begin to mine. (p. 106)

Experience, for Thoreau and the pragmatists, is truth;
and if they are right, the anthropology of experience is the
anthropology of truth.

The Sand Bank

In the penultimate chapter of *Walden*, entitled "Spring,"
Thoreau gives us an extraordinary description of a bank
of sand in a railroad cutting as it thaws out in the spring
sunshine—a description which is also an extended metaphor of the evolution of the universe, of the creative
evolution of human experience, and of linguistic expression as a continuation of that evolution.

He begins with a detailed, scientifically precise description of the thawing sand and clay as they form their
complex patterns of deposition. Even the fact that the
phenomenon occurs in a railroad-cutting is significant:
for human invention (of which the railroad was, for
Thoreau, the obvious example) is an extension of the
creative process of nature. It is not only the content of
the passage that we must pay attention to, but also its
form:

> Innumerable little streams overlap and inter-
> lace one with another, exhibiting a sort of
> hybrid product, which obeys half way the law
> of currents, and half way that of vegetation. As
> it flows it takes the form of sappy leaves or
> vines, making heaps of pulpy sprays a foot or
> more in depth, and resembling, as you look

> down on them, the laciniated lobed and imbri-
> cated thalluses of some lichens; or you are
> reminded of coral, of leopards' paws or birds'
> feet, of brains or lungs or bowels, and excre-
> ments of all kinds. It is a truly *grotesque*
> vegetation, whose forms and color we see imi-
> tated in bronze, a sort of architectural foliage
> more ancient and typical than acanthus,
> chiccory [sic], ivy, vine, or any vegetable
> leaves . . .(p. 326)

The intensity of perception is almost hypnotic, and
Thoreau reminds us of our own perceiving selves as we
see with him: "as you look down on them . . . "you are
reminded." The sequence of images follows the course of
evolution, from the physical laws of currents, through
the vegetable kingdom and into the animal kingdom of
birds' feet and leopards' paws, concluding with the prod-
ucts of human art. And there is a subtle playing with the
evolution of language itself, with the etymological relations of "overlap" and "lobed," and "interlace" with
"laciniated," with the origin of the artistic word "gro-
tesque" in the natural "grotto" or cave, and with the
phonological relations of the labial consonants p, b, f, v.
    As the passage continues, these implicit meanings,
through the process of feedback between experience and
contemplation, become explicit and put out leaves of
exegesis as rich and various as the leaves of multicolored
mud and sand bursting out of the frozen inanimate mass
of the bank. The suggestion of natural evolution implicit
in the sequence of images now becomes explicit:

> What makes this sand foliage remarkable is its
> springing into existence thus suddenly. When I
> see on the one side the inert bank—for the sun
> acts on one side first—and on the other this

luxuriant foliage, the creation of an hour, I am
affected as if in a peculiar sense I stood in the
laboratory of the Artist who made the world
and me—had come to where he was still at
work, sporting on this bank, and with excess of
energy strewing his fresh designs about. . . .
You find thus in the very sands an anticipa-
tion of the vegetable leaf. No wonder that the
earth expresses itself out- wardly in leaves,
it so labors with the idea inwardly. The atoms
have learned this law, and are pregnant by it.
(p. 327)

Next the etymological relations themselves become
explicit. Thoreau takes up the phonological connection
of *leaves, labor,* and *law,* and develops it, his own
language exfoliating as he does so:

Internally, whether in the globe or animal
body, it is a moist thick *lobe,* a word especially
applicable to the liver and lungs and the *leaves*
of fat, (λειβω, *labor, lapsus,* to flow or slip
downward, a lapsing; λοβος, globus, lobe, globe;
also lap, flap, and many other words) *externally*
a dry thin *leaf,* even as the *f* and *v* are a pressed
and dried *b.* The radicals of *lobe* are *lb,* the soft
mass of the *b* (single lobed, or *B,* double lobed)
with a liquid *l* behind it pressing it forward. In
globe, *glb,* the guttural *g* adds to the meaning
the capacity of the throat. The feathers and
wings of birds are still drier and thinner leaves.
Thus, also, you pass from the lumpish grub in
the earth to the airy and fluttering butterfly.
The very globe continually transcends and
translates itself, and becomes winged in its
orbit. (p. 328)

Here, as in the "Bean-Field" passage, analysis reveals a remarkable layering of reflexivity. In a language which, through his own metaphorical usage, is evolving as he employs it and *because* he employs it, Thoreau describes the evolution of language using as a metaphor the evolutionary process of the natural world—of which linguistic evolution is both a part and a reflection—here evoked through the description, in this very language, of an experience of natural productiveness on a spring morning; and the process of thought in the passage, turning back on itself repeatedly, in a helical fashion, adds another depth to the triple pun on "spring."

He goes on to a minute description of the rivulets of liquid clay and sand:

> If you look closely you observe that first there pushes forward from the thawing mass a stream of softened sand with a drop-like point, like the ball of a finger, feeling its way slowly and blindly downwards, until at last with more heat and moisture, as the sun gets higher, the most fluid portion, in its effort to obey the law to which the most inert also yields, separates from the latter and forms for itself a meandering channel or artery within that, in which is seen a little silvery stream glancing like lightning from one stage of pulpy leaves or branches to another, and ever and anon swallowed up in the sand. It is wonderful how rapidly yet perfectly the sand organizes itself as it flows, using the best material its mass affords to form the sharp edges of its channel. (p. 328)

This careful observation—again with its reminder of the process of observation itself, "if you look closely"—is not merely an enumeration of particulars, but a graphic account of a universal creative process. Or rather, these particulars are the "minute particulars" in which William Blake discovered the universal. There is an uncanny resemblance between Thoreau's conception of the creative process and Blake's. In *The Marriage of Heaven and Hell* one of the "Memorable Fancies" describes creation as the work of demons who melt the interior of their cave, extracting precious metals, and then cast the molten fluids out into the abyss, where they take what wonderful shapes they will. Thoreau, like Blake, insists that no mold is needed, for the solidifying liquid contains in its own nature a perfectly adequate set of formal principles: "You may melt your metals and cast them into the most beautiful molds you can; they will never excite me like the forms which this molten earth flows out into." (p. 330) The silvery icicles that Samuel Taylor Coleridge describes at the end of "Frost at Midnight" constitute a similar image of the nature of creativity.

What principles can be derived from Thoreau's account of the thawing sand? The first is that the past of a given flow of events, combined with its texture, are all the constraints that are needed to produce more and elaborate forms of existence. No Aristotelian Final Cause is required to draw out these shapes: they are *expressed*, pressed out, not drawn forth or externally molded. The creative process needs no metaphysical grounding but itself. Like the twigs of a tree, historical sequences propagate themselves outward into the future, drawing their sustenance from their past. One of the most striking images in Darwin's *Origin of Species* is that of the tree of reproductive descent. Here that tree, the tree of life, is identical to the tree of knowledge.

The second principle is that the creative process is dialectical, being composed of an active energy, what Blake calls "the Prolific"—in Thoreau's image, the glittering lightning-like stream of water—and an inert material deposit, Blake's "Devourer," here imaged as the clotted sand, which both retards and records the flow of energy, and by periodically damming it up provides it with variation and rhythm.

The third principle is that creation always involves a sort of paradox of self-transcendence—the sand continually overwhelms itself, the globe "transcends and translates" itself—like the mysterious paradoxes of self-awareness discussed earlier.

The fourth principle is that our human experience is not a passive process but an active and creative one. Our very bodies, our sense organs, Thoreau suggests, are an elaboration of the same playful creative force:

> What is man but a mass of thawing clay? The ball of the human finger is but a drop congealed . . . is not the hand a spreading *palm* leaf with its lobes and veins? The ear may be regarded, fancifully, as a lichen, *umbilicaria*, on the side of the head, with its lobe or drop. The lip– labium, from *labor*–laps or lapses from the sides of the cavernous mouth. The nose is a manifest congealed drop or stalactite. (p. 329)

Thoreau's century was too delicate to allow him to extend his metaphor to its obvious genital conclusion, but he had it in mind: ". . . more heat or other *genial* influences would have caused it to flow yet farther" (p. 329; emphasis mine); "Who knows what the human body would expand and flow out into under a more genial heaven." (p. 329)

"Thus," says Thoreau, "it seemed that this one hillside illustrated the principle of all the operations of Nature. The Maker of this earth but patented a leaf. What Champollion [the decoder of the Rosetta Stone] will decipher this hieroglyphic for us, that we may turn over a new leaf at last?" (p. 329) For Thoreau moral and practical action ("turning over a new leaf") cannot be detached from the active discovery and probing of Nature ("turning over a new leaf") and the reading and interpretation of the book of Nature ("turning over a new leaf"). These ideas are not only associated, they take the same words. Here we find an interpretation for "experience" that perhaps adequately contains the many meanings I listed at the beginning of this paper. When we are truly experiencing we are growing by a reflexive process, in which we are only separated by our consciousness from nature in order to share in nature's own creative process of self-transcendence.

Notes

1. All quotations from *Walden* are taken from the Merrill edition, 1969. It was at some time between 1846 and 1854 that Thoreau wrote these words, which makes them almost exactly contemporaneous with the composition between 1843 and 1851 of Lewis Henry Morgan's *League of the Ho-de-no-sau-nee or Iroquois*.
2. It was Charles Sanders Peirce who described the world as a system of signs, who defined the sense of a symbol as its translation into another symbol and who was thus the father of anthropological hermeneutics. Peirce was a member of the same circle of Harvard intellectuals that had included Thoreau. Clearly Thoreau has an historical, as well as a theoretical, interest for anthropology.
3. Again, an historical note dramatizes the progress of the dialectic: *The Origin of Species* (1859) was published five years after *Walden*. Of course Darwin could not have read *Walden*; but Darwin and Thoreau were both naturalists and were both responding to the same logical questions and the same evidence from early ethnography and biology. Thoreau knew Darwin's work and quotes him on the Indians of Tierra del Fuego (*Walden*, p. 15).
4. Benjamin Franklin, Henry Adams, and Thoreau were the origi-

nators of a great tradition, in which we find modern poets like Berryman, Lowell, and Plath, and novelists like Pirsig, Bellow, and Mailer.

5. It may seem odd to speak of contemporary Western scientific genres as "individualistic"; but a comparison between the institutionalized irreverence and originality of modern research and the authoritarian conformism of ancient science, that Francis Bacon took to task, will make the point clear. Galileo was the victim less of the church than of his old-science colleagues.

6. Carl Resek, *Lewis Henry Morgan* (University of Chicago Press, 1960), p. 23.

7. See V. W. Turner, "Dramatic Ritual/Ritual Drama: Performative and Reflexive Anthropology, *"Kenyon Review,* New Series, I. 3., Summer 1979.

INTERCHAPTER VI

The ideas espoused by this book clearly apply directly to contemporary culture; they imply a reinterpretation of our cultural history, a reevaluation of our
present (which turns out to contain much greater
cause for hope than is often thought), and a kind of
program for our cultural future.

Such Stuff as Dreams: Technology and the Future of the Imagination

Consider the process by which a modern integrated circuit is made. A wafer of silicon is doped with impurities, exposed to light which is shone through a template mask to form a pattern of shadows, treated with new impurities which differentiate between the irradiated and unexposed areas, etched by a bath of corrosives, blanketed with a new surface of silicon, exposed to another pattern of light, and so on, until a marvellously complex three-dimensional system of switches, gates, resistors, and connections has been laid down; which may be destined to form part of a computer which will in turn help design new integrated circuits. The technical term for this process of manufacture is "photographic." Essentially an integrated circuit is a very complex silicon photograph. Photographic techniques are now being used to make all kinds of very tiny machines—pumps, solar energy collectors, measuring equipment, and so on.

We normally think of a photographic process as one which makes pictures of things rather than things themselves. A photograph is significant as a piece of information, but as an object itself it's just a bit of sticky paper. But our silicon photograph doesn't just *represent* something—the pattern of light with which it was irradiated—it really, efficaciously, *does* what it is a photograph of. In a sense it is a miraculous picture, like that of Our Lady of Guadalupe or Czestochowa or the Shroud of Turin. It not only represents, but does; it is not just information, but reality; it is not just a piece of knowledge, but a piece of being; it is not just epistemology but ontology. Another term for such devices is "printed circuit," because the process is also a kind of printing. Again, printing is a technology once used exclusively for the transmission of information rather than the creation of new objects.

Consider, moreover, the digital, or "Soundstream," method of reproducing music. The music is scanned every forty-four-thousandth of a second or so; the sound wave activity in that forty-four-thousandth is given a numerical value corresponding to its Fourier transform; and this value is recorded in terms of a binary sequence of laser-burned holes and unburned spaces on the record. To play the music you just scan the holes with another laser, and synthesize a sound every forty-four-thousandth of a second which corresponds to the number you get.

The point is that the digital recording is really just a very sophisticated "score" of the music. There is no way in which the recording reproduces the actual shape of the music, the way the grooves on the vinyl of a normal record do; any more than the five parallel lines, the clef, and the little black ellipses with their tails reproduce the actual shape of the music—or indeed, than the letters on the page reproduce the sound of speech. In a sense, the

digital recording harks back to an old method of reproducing music: the player piano.

But the interesting thing is that digital recordings are
very much more accurate than any analog recording,
which attempts to match the actual shape of the music,
could be. They are literally as accurate as you want them
to be: if you like, you could scan every hundred-
thousandth of a second—though it would be useless, as
the highest pitch we can hear is lower than a twenty-
thousandth of a second in frequency. Moreover, a digital
recording is theoretically almost invulnerable to wear,
whereas an analog recording must suffer and shriek to
give up its musical information.

The paradox is that an analog recording, which is the
actual reverberation of the original performance of the
music—as if we were to put our ear against the wall of
the Sistine Chapel Choir—is less accurate than the entirely new performance generated by machinery from the
meticulous numerical score of a digital recording. It is as
if, knowing the right language, we could write the names
of foods so accurately that if you ate the paper it would be
more tasty and nourishing than food itself.

So: photographs can now, magically, do what they are
pictures of; and a score of a piece of music can be more
accurate than the sound of the music itself. We live once
again in a world of runes and icons, efficacious and full of
virtue; a world in which the distinction between how we
know and what we know, statement and referent, meaning and object, has begun to break down. Indeed, our
quantum physics tells us that these cloud-capped towers,
these gorgeous palaces, these solemn temples, the great
globe itself, are made out of statistical domains of
information—numerical likelihoods called electrons,
photons, and so on; and the Big Bang theory of the origin
says we are all made out of light.

Remember the scene in *Close Encounters of the Third Kind* where Spielberg has the kids' mechanical toys all wake up to their dim electronic awareness, and run about on the floor, and clap their hands and flash their lights? And recall that the music of the Aliens is actually—as you realize at the very end—a simple variation of the Disney tune "When You Wish Upon a Star?" We have met E. T., and he is our toys, our animated cartoons, our computer programs. The Magic Kingdom—Anaheim or Orlando—is the American Eleusis where spirits are invoked to transubstantiate inanimate matter. George Lucas' space cruisers made of light are cheaper and more effective than if they were made out of matter.

Our children are growing up on computer programs and fantasy role-playing games—"Voyager," "Greyhawk," "Dungeons and Dragons." The space program was too slow to bring them to those other worlds, and therefore they constructed them right here on Earth. Play has become increasingly concrete and even practical and profitable. It is almost as if an evolutionary necessity in culture dictated that from our most infantile and inconsequential and unnecessary behaviors—"a waste of time" —comes the solid future of the species. Just as it began to seem as if political, economic, and technological forces were combining to organize the human race into a rational, centralized, and anonymous unity, and the world was, as they say, becoming a small place, counterforces of great power and unexpected provenance have taken us all in an entirely new set of directions. The new electronic technology is by its nature playful, decentralizing, individualizing, and pluralist. The strong hand of the corporation and the still stronger hand of the state, which were once able to coerce the population into their service by cutting off its sources of energy and information, are becoming more and more impotent to get a grasp on the individual. Quite soon a family equipped with its own solar power generator and its own computer will have a kind of practical sovereignty once possessed only by nations.

Once the city, which was the central machine of production and the access to the power of information and communication, could be used by the authorities to maintain their power; proximity to the city was the reward for compliance, and banishment to the state of nature was the most effective punishment. But now there is no way of denying the city to anyone who has the curiosity and energy to appropriate it. The telephone and the C.B. radio have replaced the city street, the home computer with a modem replaces the office block, the dish antenna and videotape recorder have replaced the movie theater, and the digital stereo music system has replaced the symphony hall and opera house. Information is the means of production, and there is now no way of plugging the leaking joints where the public can feed on the rich flow of free information.

We are reentering at last the ancient animist universe, populated by genies and geniuses of place, in which every object possessed a spirit or daemon that one might control and use. But the nymphs and dryads are now microprocessors, inhabiting our machines and tools and toys; our cars, our cooking stoves, our clocks, our chess sets, and our typewriters. Soon every human artifact will have its own helpful and dedicated little intelligence, its own *nisus* or animating will; and we shall surely not stop there. Already electronic prostheses are a regular part of medicine, and they have begun to be used in livestock management and agriculture. We are teaching Nature how to speak with us, at the same time as we are learning the languages of natural species.

The world is becoming a *bigger* place, more densely packed with information. A few years ago the amount of information contained in the world's libraries, computer memories and so on doubled every ten years: now the doubling-time itself has gone down to eight years and is continuing to shrink. ·This process has a cosmological significance, because the universe itself is made of information: Matter and energy are only more or less simple forms of information, and are by no means as fundamental as they were once thought to be. And whereas matter and energy can indeed decay according to the laws of entropy, paying for their durability of form by their eventual death into more primitive states of organization, information itself is not only immortal but also self-propagating. On the level of matter and energy, the world is running down; on the level of information the world is growing and becoming more and more elaborately organized. And *our* activities, tiny as they appear in space and time, are a significant part of that growth.

Pascal said that the silence of these infinite spaces terrified him. But we now know that those spaces, large as they are, are not infinite; and that space itself is generated by an evolutionary process which is more primary than space itself. Once the universe was no bigger than a baseball, and before that it was smaller than an atom. What counted then was not how big or how old it was, but its capacity to generate new information: to derive in turn, from its single law of relation, first gravitation, then the strong and weak nuclear forces, and at last electromagnetism. Measured in terms of space and time humankind is indeed, as the scientists traditionally remind us, a tiny speck in the vastness of the cosmos. Measured in a more fundamental way, by density and complexity of information, we are already the largest objects in the universe. Indeed we are the cortex or cambium of the universe, its skin, its bud, its growing surface, and our new laws, of morality, esthetics, government, games, take their appointed place next to their predecessors, the laws of biology, chemistry, physics, mathematics. Our laws, though latecomers, are no less real for that; it is a matter now of embodying them in their constituency, as a new statute gradually takes its place in the legal system through judicial interpretation and precedent. As Thoreau put it, punning between the leaves of the trees, the leaves of books, and the "new leaf" we shall all turn over:

> No wonder that the earth expresses itself out-wardly in leaves, it so labors with the idea inwardly. The atoms have already learned this law, and are pregnant by it . . . The very globe continually transcends and trans- lates itself, and becomes winged in its orbit. Even ice begins with delicate crystal leaves, as if it had flowed into moulds which the fronds of water plants have impressed on the watery mirror. The whole tree itself is but one leaf, and rivers are still vaster leaves whose pulp is intervening earth, and towns and cities are the ova of insects in their axils. (*Walden*, p. 327)

The evolutionary biologist David Cairns-Smith has recently suggested a very exciting hypothesis. To put it in an oversimplified way, there were, before the DNA-based life that we know today, more primitive forms of self-replicating and metabolizing chemistry, of which the organic molecules, proteins, and amino acids of contem-porary life were once only part of their phenotype, their somatic machinery. Domains of electromagnetic polari-zation in certain clays, he suggests, could print replicas of themselves in growing columns which would in gross structure and behavior differ according to the pattern of the polarization. These structures and behaviors could differentially affect the survival of the whole organism, and thus the three forces of evolution—mutation, reproduction, and selection, could come into play. Cairns-Smith is able thus to explain the otherwise highly improbable origins of DNA.

Not least among the fascinating intellectual implications of this idea is the notion that what is now the genotype—the program—of a living organism was once only part of its phenotype—the expression of this or blueprint in physical terms. Indeed, we do not need to go to Cairns-Smith's work for an illustration of this idea. There are many cases in the study of viruses and bacteria where a piece of machinery used by the genetic material to promote its survival has actually become incorporated into the genetic material itself, as in the case of the plasmids; or where the messengers of the DNA perform some of the functions of DNA itself, as when viral RNA takes part of the responsibility for carrying the genetic inheritance.

A fascinating analogy suggests itself: Perhaps our cultural and traditional way of storing and passing on information—through speech, the development of socially-maintained individual personalities, writing, and electronic data processing—is now taking over the central genetic tasks of our species; just as the organic molecules that were once its tools superseded the genetic functions of the clay ur-life, if Cairns-Smith's theory is correct.

The distinction between being and consciousness, which to Descartes and Berkeley seemed so absolute as to require divine intervention to enable them to communicate, has now become only a matter of degree. Being has dissolved before our eyes as we examined it more and more closely, until, in quantum physics, matter proves less durable than the light in which we see it; and evaporates into energy, pure event, if we try to take it apart any further. Matter, then, was only an arrangement, a mutually-supporting collection of probabilities, in the

first place; and its only existence was as and in its
relations, internal and external. The universe is made up
of the differential sensitivities of its components to each
other. Our clever toys, our microchips, are only a concrete demonstration that the physical world is inherently
sensitive and potentially aware. And if we are to take the
theory of evolution seriously, which says that a conscious human being is an advanced ape, a sophisticated
vertebrate, a highly-developed bit of matter, a complex
arrangement of energy, then the corollary must also be
true: the apes are primitive men, the phenomenon of life
is undeveloped human awareness, matter and energy are
unorganized or diffused forms of human consciousness.
The universe is only and always its own registering,
measuring, calibrating, and recording of itself; and we are
the most active example of that process.

One consequence of this view is that the old notion of
humankind's alienation from Nature was only a cultural
illusion, which is now utterly exploded. That Nature
from which we were supposed to be alienated never
existed: the great quantum experiments—the parallel-
slits light experiment, the polarizing filter light experiment—show that Nature has not made up its own mind
about what it *really* is, and is quite happy to have us help
it do so. That whole tradition of philosophy which saw us
as cut off from our "true" way of being has in fact
collapsed, and simply has not realized it yet. *We* are
Nature, and we are as at home here in the world as
anything has ever been at home: for the whole world is
made up of such as we. Its physical components are, just
as much as we are, tourists, outsiders, amateurs, getting
by on a smile and a shoeshine, and deriving what being
they have from the recognition of their fellows. All
nature is second nature.

The new quantum theories of cosmology suggest that
the probabilistic and chance-governed behavior of the

elementary particles is a sort of "living fossil" of the state of the whole universe in its first moments of existence during the Big Bang. In other words, the order and determinateness of the physical world as we know it through conventional physics and chemistry did not at first exist, and evolved out of a chaotic prior state. Given a random chaos not only in the physical world but also in the rules (or lack of them) which govern it, lawful regimes tend to persist and propagate themselves into the future, by definition, while chaotic regimes are inherently unstable and evanescent. The laws of physics and chemistry—and of biology and human society—evolved because they promoted survival.

At the very beginning of the universe, there existed an infinite number of possible states, each with a probability of $1/\infty$. Even nothingness was only one possibility, sharing the same infinitesimal likelihood of being true. "Existence" itself, as a sharply defined state completely incompatible with nonexistence, had yet to establish itself clearly. All the possibilities "existed," with an infinitely small efficacy. The quantum-statistical nature of the electron, for instance, is a remnant of that indeterminacy, as is the statistical-mechanical character of the pressure of gases, indeed any physical process when we analyze it to a point at which our unit of measurement is smaller than the acuity of the system's minimum behavior as a system. The sharpness of reality is the result of a harmonious synchronizing of many fuzzy events.

Human technology is in some senses the continuation of the process of evolution by which the indefiniteness of the world gave rise to greater and greater certainty. Technology is the realizing of the possible, and our machines are only the last in a series which goes back through the chemical servomechanisms of our bodies and the bodies of animals, the persisting and self-maintaining organization of crystal structures and stable molecules, and the durable coherence of the elementary particles, to that first moment when possibility resolved itself into a burst of identical photons.

We are at a curious juncture in the history of science and technology. The empiricism of the Renaissance gradually, over the next three hundred years, flattened out the ancient hierarchic coherence of the universe, and broke up the great chain of being. Just at the moment when the world seemed to have been reduced to a valueless collection of objective facts—the world view of Modernism—a new order began to come into being. A gigantic hierarchy is appearing more and more clearly, as the jigsaw puzzle pieces of science are put together: geometry the microstructure of physics, physics the microstructure of chemistry, chemistry the microstructure of biology, biology the microstructure of the human sciences.

That new Great Chain of Being is, unlike the old one, dynamic and fluid: it is the great branching tree of evolution. As long as evolution was conceptually confined to the realm of biology, it did not seriously threaten the Modernist conception of the world as "value-flat"; it simply made Life into a mystical anomaly, or a pullulating disease, a "fever of matter," as Thomas Mann put it, in the "frozen chastity" of the inorganic. But now we can construct viruses out of "dead" chemicals, proving they were not as dead as we thought, and the link has been made. All of the world is alive, as it were, and its life becomes more and more intense as it evolves, more and more self-referential, more and more self-measuring and self-certifying; more and more sensitive to the rest of the universe, and thus determinative of its nature.

The destruction of the old coherence can be traced and epitomized in the etymological collapse and fragmentation of the word "art." In *The Tempest* it is Prospero's "art" that makes temporary sense of the airy nothing the world is made of, rendering it into cloud-capped towers and gorgeous palaces, solemn temples, even the great Globe Theatre itself. For Shakespeare "art" meant science, philosophical knowledge, technical power, craft, theatrical sleight of hand, liberal education, magic, and "art" in our modern meaning, all at once. The moment of *The Tempest* was the last moment of full cultural health and integrity until our own time now. "Art," the word, was gradually torn to shreds, until in our century art and science, science and technology, philosophy and science, art and philosophy, magic and science, craft and art, education and art, have all been set against each other, like demons bred out of the corpse of the great mother.

But now that coherence is swiftly returning. Film and science fiction testify to the convergence of science and art. The indeterminacy principle, which destroys the distinction between observation and action, makes all science into technology and all technology into science. Academic philosophy has died and passed its inheritance on to the theoreticians of science and to art criticism; the anthropologists have revealed other cultures' magic as science and our own science as magic. In all the arts, the death of Modernism has given birth to a new rapprochement between craft and art; education is at last being recognized as a valid experience in itself, and art is, once more, properly required to be moral. All of these assertions are prophetic more than scholarly: but watch the event.

Not that the empiricist detour or diaspora was unnecessary. Shakespeare's magic did not work outside the theater, and we needed three centuries of self-imposed alienation, of tearing things to pieces to see how they worked, to be able to come back to a coherent and valuable world, this time with the powers and knowledge we always felt were our birthright—powers and knowledge we had mimed with our magic. But now we have come back we must cast away the habits of our exile—the self-contempt, the illusion of alienation, the hatred of the past, the sterile existentialism, the fear of the future, the willful imposition of meaninglessness on a universe bursting with meaning.

Another way of saying the same thing is that we are undergoing a religious revolution. In about 1600 a new religion appeared on the scene, which we might call materialism. Its practice is what we usually call "economic activity," and its higher religious emotions include the sense of the beauty of Nature and awe at its workings, and the sense of triumph in technological achievement. Its theology was atomistic: like God, the atom of matter was indivisible, eternal, invulnerable, responsible for all events in the world. Unlike God, though, it was not aware, conscious, or personal. As with other great religions—and it was a great and in many ways noble religion, and much of our own best and most significant behavior consists in its observance—it gave rise to magnificent heresies, systems of morality, and even good science: dialectical materialism, existentialism, the theory of evolution.

If it be protested that materialism is not a religion, a cross-cultural view would rapidly convince the objector. People living in the medieval world did not call their everyday rituals religious, or even rituals. They were just the way one lived one's life. Animists or totemists, before contact with Europeans, would say the same thing about their own practices and value system. What enabled materialism to triumph all over the world was precisely the fact that it did not claim to be a religion at all, but labeled other systems as religious; and, just like monotheism, polytheism, animism, totemism, and ancestor-worship, there are elements of it in all human value-systems.

But materialism is now going through the same crisis

that Christianity did four hundred years ago. Christianity resolved its crisis by coexisting with the new religion, to the usual enrichment of both, while accepting certain modifications and limitations in its relevance, the chief of which was the recognition of itself as *a* religion, rather than "the way things are." Perhaps a similar adjustment will take place to the new religious conceptions that are now beginning to burst on the world.

The chief challenge to materialism, as I have already pointed out, was the disappearance of the atom as atomic or irreducible, and the consequent dissolution of matter into event, relation, and information. One of the advantages of materialism was that the further one reduced the complex and ambiguous behavior of the apparent world in the direction of simple atomic events, the more concrete and unambiguous one seemed to get. Religion seeks certainty, and for a long time materialism delivered it. But one more reduction, one last simplification, spoiled everything. Suddenly the world, as it was revealed by quantum physics, had become utterly ambiguous again; and far from offering an escape from the relativism of human perception, the pursuit of material explanations had now totally implicated the observer in the behavior of reality.

Much that is good can be salvaged from the old religion: the world of matter, though it is now revealed as a provisional one, without the appealing absoluteness it once possessed, is still a beautiful and exquisitely ordered one; and it is surely legitimate to give it a share of worship. But if we do so, we must give a greater share to ourselves, both as the supreme product and expression of matter given its chance to do what comes naturally, and as the supreme observer and determiner of the material world. That aspect of religion which desires to worship something outside of, and superior to, ourselves, will not be satisfied any longer with materialism.

And materialism always carried a dangerous and perhaps evil flaw: its fundamental and ultimate realities, the
atoms of matter, were impersonal, insentient, and
unintelligent—that was precisely what made them intelligible. But the elevation of matter also implied a
valorization of those characteristics—impersonality, in-
sentience, unintelligence. We began to regard the personal, the sensible, the conscious, as a second-class reality,
which must face up to the impersonal "real world" and
submit to the "reality principle," or to the blind forces of
economic change, the dialectics of class struggle, or the
survival of the fittest. And perhaps our great political and
technological monsters—Communism, Nazism, the hy-
drogen bomb—are the final expression of that inbuilt
suspicion of the personal: they promised to eradicate
persons from the face of the earth. Even the impiety that
you may sense in this essay comes from the violation of
the materialist theology.

But we *are* entering a new age, one which will see a
reconvergence of the old meaning of "art" upon a more
efficacious basis, and a reestablishment of the great chain
of being with a new, dynamic, evolutionary aspect. It will
be an age of return of the classical philosophy, ethics,
aesthetics, and economics, but with solid scientific foundations, and enriched immeasurably by the cooperation
of all the human cultural traditions.

In fact this is the most startling aspect of the postmodern synthesis as it comes into shape: its classicism.
In the heyday of high modernism the world of the future
seemed more and more impersonal, cool, centralized,
inorganic, tidy, sharp-edged: a world-state with equal
prosperity for all, tall rectilinear buildings, cool atonal or
serial music, abstract art, imagistic free verse which
caught and froze a moment of sensory experience in an
exact verbal image, the "new novel" purified of the
fetishism and hierarchy of plot and character, a leveling

of all sexual, religious and ethnic differences, and a psychological style without repression, without aliena- tion, without ego, absolutely free from the shibboleths of honor, beauty, sexual morality, patriotism, faith, ideal- ism, religion, and duty.

But oddly enough this future now appears more and more dated, even dreary. The marvelous cross-cultural studies of the human ethologists, linguists, and compara- tive religionists have shown that yes, indeed, humankind *does* have a nature; there are cultural universals. But this nature is neither a limitation nor a totally protean adap- tiveness. Rather, it is a system of neurobiological and developmental rules which make possible an immensely productive and infinitely versatile, but characteristically mammalian and human *generativeness*. The rules must be followed, or the freedom, the limitlessness, the generativeness, will not come about. And those rules include not only the grammar of language, but also the classical laws of harmony, melody, color, proportion, poetic meter, narrative, rhythm, and balance. The human nervous system is designed by its evolutionary adapta- tion to cultural selective pressures to be sensitive to certain culturally-universal qualities found in the arts all over the world. The Modernists believed those classical qualities to be arbitrary and reactionary limitations, and tried to sweep them away, thus deeply damaging the art-forms they were trying to liberate, and also depriving them of their audience. But now we are beginning to discover the nature of our humanity as well as the humanity of nature. To put it aphoristically: we have a nature: that nature is cultural: that culture is classical.

Of course we must redefine "classical" to include the tonality of Chinese, Indonesian, and African music, and the visual representational conventions of the Tlingit, the Maori, and the Navaho, and the verse-forms of the New Guinea Eipo, the Eskimos, and the Yanomami. But there *are* rules to be derived from this pan-human study; and to break them is not a daring innovation but a pointless exercise: akin to shining a light in our eyes at a wavelength invisible to the human retina, or to playing a sound to us beyond the capacity of the ear, or to speaking a sentence whose grammar works on no humanly-comprehensible principle. We must change our romantic attitude to the rules, too, and recognize them not as a tyrannical imposition but as our own biologically and culturally agreed-upon code of communication, our constitution, the foundation of our freedom. The great mistake of the Modernists was to identify randomness with freedom. Freedom lies on the far side of order, it is an order which has got so complex that it has become self-referential, and thus self-governing, autonomous. The random is the most complete of tyrannies.

The future now looks quite different from what it once did. Not only is a world-state, thank heavens, quite out of the question; we may even be in the last days of the nation-state, which can no longer fulfill its original function of protecting the population from the external and internal disruption of its productive activities. A much more decentralized world seems most likely, more personal, warm, custom-made, organic, untidy, decorated. Our music will be full of enchanting melody again, though it would sound strangely foreign to the ears of Brahms or Beethoven; more dark-skinned, more rhythmic, with an Oriental quaver, more incantatory, with more improvisation in performance. Our visual arts will be mainly representational, with abstraction usually reserved for the decorative function, but there will be a rich play of modes of representation; it will once more seek after beauty, nobility, truth, and the sense of wonder. Our architecture will recapitulate the pan-human village clutter, with all functions, domestic, religious, retail, industrial, educational, horticultural, political, jumbled in together; no zoning; and it will be splendidly and comfortably decorated. Our poetry will be, as all human poetry was until seventy years ago, richly metrical and rhetorical, full of stories, ideas, moral energy, public statement, scientific speculation, theology, drama, history. Indeed, many of these changes have already begun, though an entrenched rearguard of Modernist reactionaries still holds much of the political and economic power, and middlebrow taste will need decades of deprogramming from its masochistic preferences.

The new world will also be a more oral and aural one, as the written word takes its proper place as only one of a number of modes of verbal information storage and transmission. The arts of speech, of rhetoric, will rise again. The word as performance, as part of the living colloquial present of a culture's experience of itself, will take on greater importance, and the folk arts and popular arts will be reconnected with high art.

There will also be a refeminization of the arts. The Modernist reduction tended to write off sexual differences as trivial cultural impositions, and thus, paradoxically, reformed all of its ideals and norms upon an exclusively masculine model. What followed was a tragic destruction and dismissal of the arts of the traditional feminine culture, and an attempt—pathetic as it now seems—to provide equality for women by demanding that they imitate the achievements of the traditional male culture. Now, however, the scientific study of sexuality and gender, and of human social and biological evolution, is showing distinct statistical differences between men and women. A full, rich, and human culture is impossible upon an exclusively male model, even if women are trained to fit that model; and we are now seeing a rediscovery and revalorization of the female side of culture.

I suspect that some readers winced a few pages ago

when I cited a list of values: honor, beauty, sexual morality, patriotism, faith, idealism, religion, and duty. That wincing reflex is an indication of a set of bio-cultural factors related to value-creation and reward systems which is both fascinating and almost unexplored.

In order to understand these factors we must first make an essential connection. A value system, despite Kant, is a reward system. Not that there is anything base about reward. The nobler a value, the nobler—and the more intangible to an ignoble mind—is the reward which goes with it. The nature of a value will be determined by the nature of the reward. Now the human body, we now know, has a very complex hierarchy of reward systems, the lowest associated with what is evolutionarily most archaic and automatic, and the highest with what is most recent and voluntary.

Materialist ethics came together with materialist biology in the nineteenth century and agreed that there were only two types of rewards: those obviously associated with physical survival, and those obviously associated with reproduction. Two brilliant systems of value—Marx's, which essentially reduced all value to the economics of physical survival; and Freud's, which reduced all value to sexual libido—were the result. Existentialism struggles ambivalently between accepting these rewards as preferable to the more complex socio-cultural value systems; and rejecting them, and all rewards, as bribes to make us give up our freedom, which it identifies with randomness.

Under the pressure of these theories of reward, which postulated very coarse rewards even for very refined behavior, the value systems of world culture themselves changed and coarsened. When an audience winces at the sound of "duty, honor, and beauty," and so on, it is doing exactly what a Victorian audience would do if it heard, instead, words like "passion," "desire," "sexuality," or even "money," "fees," "honoraria." The Victorians, in a last ditch defense of the older, more complex value system against the efficient and economical new reductions, would naturally be pained by references to the enemy's rewards. We, the inheritors of D.H. Lawrence and Albert Camus, feel the same old blush come to our faces when we are reminded of all the old rewards—the joy of duty, the satisfaction of honorable conduct—that we have given up. Not that we are not often honorable and dutiful, but we are so in a spirit of taking nasty medicine with a good grace, and we deeply suspect anyone who enjoys doing their duty.

But a new biology is forcing on us a new value system. The pleasures of eating and sex, which our evolutionary inheritance has provided to encourage us to perform activities which are metabolically rather expensive and time-consuming, are not the only rewards. The study of the chemistry of brain reward has begun to uncover a remarkable variety of rewards, suppressors of rewards, suppressors of the suppressors, linked rewards which in the absence of each other are punishments, and so on. The pleasures of achievement, of insight into the truth, of heroic exertion or sacrifice, of good conscience, of beauty, are *real* pleasures in themselves, not repressed and sublimated derivatives of sexual libido or the fetishism of a food-controlling class. Certainly the higher pleasures *enlist* the coarser and more obvious ones to reinforce them; and indeed society uses the coarser and more obvious ones—food, for children, and sex, for adolescents—as ways of training, calibrating, and stimulating the higher reward systems, "priming the pump," so to speak. But the "endorphin high" is as real a reward as are orgasm, or the pleasures of eating.

Nor are food and sex any longer the simple survival drives they seemed to the materialists. The study of human evolution shows that very early on the division of food played a central role in the religious rituals that defined the human community. What food *represents* soon became more important to us than the two thousand calories, the proteins and vitamins we required for mere survival. A Hindu would die rather than eat of the sacred cow. Food, as the anthropologists Mary Douglas and Claude Lévi-Strauss point out, has become more than bread alone. So too sex. The comparative study of sexual behavior shows that, far from possessing a feeble and watered-down version of brute sexuality, we are the most sexual of all animals—we are in heat all the time, we copulate face-to-face, females have as powerful a libido as the male. Our sexuality is much more powerful than that of our closest relatives, the chimpanzees and gorillas: far more powerful than is needed for straightforward reproduction. Many anthropologists now suspect that our sexuality evolved in tandem with our brains, and that it took on an important social and cultural function: to encourage the creation of family and social groupings that could nurture the young through the extended human infancy, and promote cooperation through personal affection. Nevertheless, without the discovery of the higher reward systems, theories of sublimation could still keep motivation on a materialist basis. It was the brain-chemicals that broke the old ideology.

But there is a terrible tragedy here. The endorphins were discovered because certain researchers into the physiology of narcotics and drug addiction asked the obvious, and brilliant question: Why should the brain have receptors designed precisely to respond with extreme sensitivity to the sap of an Oriental poppy? What evolutionary necessity could make such sensitivity adaptive? The answer, of course, was that those receptors were designed to respond to something else entirely, and that the poppy-resins simply happened to possess a molecular resemblance to that something else: an opiate produced by the brain itself to reward itself for doing its very hard work. The tragedy is this: the materialist theory of value had the result of cutting off many of the pleasures produced by the brain-chemicals. Just as our sexual and digestive deprivations were finally being satisfied by the new morality and the economics of abundance, we were being starved of the pleasures of the mind and spirit and soul. Twentieth-century culture is full of an angst, an unsatisfied and inexplicable yearning, which we can now identify as a thirst for those essences as glory, sanctity, conscience, heroism, which were forbidden to us by the doctrines of existentialism. Worse, we began to replace those pleasures with their artificial counterfeits; and as the doctrines of materialism triumphed first among intellectuals, then among the population at large, so did the use of opium, cocaine, mescalin, and cannabis. Of course those individuals at the bottom of society, who felt themselves outcasts from its value system, have always used such drugs when they could get them.

We are only now beginning to realize the horrible effects of tampering with the brain's own endogenous reward system by means of drugs. It touches us, with the hard thrill of permanent damage, in the very center of our will, our freedom, our selfhood. It eats the soul, because the soul is a process of transformation between what is and what ought to be, a hunger that is elevated when it is satisfied, and the drug destroys the tension and the hunger and thus the process of transformation. Who can forget those rats, which would ignore females in heat and starve to death, pressing the pedal which would deliver their shot of mental happiness? Or the teenage mugger, sniffing and shaking with his addiction, interested in nothing but the high?

But—turning again to the future—as the theory of

reward changes to encompass those higher brain rewards, so we will once again educate the young to administer their own endogenous opioid rewards to themselves, and the demand for the artificial substitute will decline. For after all the real thing is, the chemists say, fifty times more powerful than the false, though harder to obtain.

What are the brain-rewards for? This is one of the most fascinating questions in the current study of evolution. Some of them—the pleasures of honor and duty—clearly have a function in the promotion of social cohesion and community. Others—the pleasures of insight and puzzle-solving—reward us for our naturally human scientific and technical capacities. Others—love and tenderness—encourage us to nurture what we have reproduced rather than abandon it. Others still—the pleasures of beauty and creative synthesis—are rewards for the world creating activity which is our single greatest specialization as animals. But they all require a cultural medium that feeds and encourages them, if they are to develop into their full expression.

The origins of the peculiarly human use of endorphins as a reward for ethical, intellectual and aesthetic activity can be plausibly located in early hominid ritual behavior. Many of the higher vertebrates engage in complex rituals, usually at some point in their life-cycles where two contradictory behaviors are evoked by the same situation —for instance aggression and sexuality, territoriality and sexuality, territoriality and flight, flight and sexuality, and so on. The ritual always involves inappropriate, out-of-context or non-utilitarian behavior, "as-if" behavior, which creates an alternative non-factual or non-present model of the situation: for instance, in the triumph ceremony of the geese, where the courting male makes a symbolic attack on a nonexistent hostile rival or enemy.

The early human mating/hunting/housewarming ritual evidently involved more strongly than with any other species the creation of alternative worlds. We see those worlds later on the walls of the caves of Altamira, Lascaux, Zimbabwe, the Chumash Indians. And the ritual began to be passed down traditionally as well as genetically, and therefore it could change quite swiftly from generation to generation. Since success in the ritual led to success in mating and reproduction, it thus exerted a powerful selective pressure—an intra-specific selective pressure, like that which produced the brilliant scales of the stickleback, the feathers of the peacock, the antlers of the elk. The ritual very rapidly domesticated the human species, causing its cortex to mushroom out to three times normal size, and producing the loss of body hair, upright posture to carry the fetish objects of the ritual, a long period of infancy to program the brain, greater life-span to instruct the young, the face-to-face sexual posture to encourage the development of personality, extension of the period of being in heat to the status of permanence, so as to increase the social intensity, and most of all the development of the endogenous brain-reward system to encourage the expensive activity of alternate world construction.

It is this development which explains the addictiveness of the activity of computer programming. For the creation of a program is the most direct way yet devised for a human being to create alternative world-models, to try out the future in advance, to play, to enter the subjunctive or extraterritorial space of "as-if." This is why it is so great a boon to public education, which has largely destroyed all its old techniques for stimulating and calibrating the inner reward system.

Any good teacher will recognize the phenomenon of the potentially gifted student, whose self-reward capacities have been stunted from birth by parents and teachers who would not challenge them and who feared to inculcate in the student an undemocratic pride and pleasure in achievement. As you force the unaccustomed juices of pleasure—in learning, in truth, in beauty, in work—to flow, your students are almost incredulous. Surely you do not expect them to *enjoy* it? It's obscene. You're teaching vile and monstrous joys. And in fact you are giving them their inheritance; an inheritance paid for by millions of our remote ancestors in their caves, humanizing themselves by ritual, the development of kinship structures, the agonizing and delicious effort to articulate the wordless.

Paradoxically, then, materialism as the supreme religion began to sicken when we were able to make thinking machines, and died when we began to see ourselves as machines for the production of spirit, soul, value. Materialist politics is dying too, as we came to see our traditional cultures as machines to support and promote that productive process of soul-making. All over the world the revolutionary forces are now what the reductionist revolutionaries of the nineteenth century would call "reactionary:" they champion complex cultural and traditional value-systems—ethnic, religious, and political—against reductionist materialism, whether liberal, fascist, capitalist, socialist, or communist. What makes the Vietnamese, the Shiites, the Poles, the Iranians, the Afghans, the Israelis, the Palestinians, the Irish such dangerous adversaries is not materialistic socialist ideology but religion, traditional education, kinship structure, patriotism, the sense of beauty, honor, heroism, duty, and all the rest: the endorphins blazing in the head like a lantern, more fiercely than any sexual passion, or thirst, or hunger for bread.

To a materialist or an existentialist all those values and beliefs are only games, a distracting play by which we hide death and the reality of our material condition from ourselves. But the strange thing about the human race is that it is more deeply motivated by a game than by a reality, and fears losing more than it fears death. From the point of view with which we began—the collapse of knowledge and being, information and reality, representing and doing—the paradox is no paradox. Reality was always a game, and our games continue the evolution of reality. We evolved as idealists, teleologists, essentialists, because we survived better that way. Essentialism is the only practical form of existentialism. Teleology is the best policy. Less idealistic animals have less control over the future.

This essay began by showing how technological change might alter some of our fundamental philosophical distinctions—between knowledge and being, animate and inanimate, epistemology and ontology. It continued by showing how the sciences themselves confirmed these changes; and then it demonstrated how, when we understand our own bodies and brains as a chemical technology directed toward higher goals, our useful and serviceable materialist ideology must be laid aside for a more personal and humanly responsible view of the world. Let me conclude by showing how in one field of human activity, poetry, the changes I have described might have specific effects.

Some effects I have already described: once our biogenetic predilection for metered verse, narrative, drama, and communal meanings is understood, poetry will gravitate back towards its ancient center, represented by the *Ramayana*, the *Heike*, the *Iliad*; it will take back into itself the capacities of the novel, which only developed because poetry had given up plot.

Other changes are foreseeable. In his most famous poem, "A Blessing," James Wright describes an Indian pony:

> She is black and white,
> Her mane falls wild on her forehead,
> And the light breeze moves me to caress her
> long ear
> That is delicate as the skin over a girl's wrist.
> Suddenly I realize
> That if I stepped out of my body I would break
> Into blossom.

This poem is imagistic, and it expresses, finally, a terrible alienation from the world of nature, a gap which the anthropomorphic imagery (the skin over a girl's wrist) attempts, with self-conscious futility, to bridge. After all, to join the horses Wright must step out of his human body. Keats said the same thing in "Ode to a Nightingale." Now Homer is not imagistic because his characters are at home in the world, and his natural objects—olive trees, mountains, caves—take their place in human purposes. Imagism attempts to anticipate human interpretations of objects and show them in themselves, naked to the naked senses. The attempt is of course always unsuccessful, because, as we know now, nature doesn't know any better than we do what it should look like. But the failure feels to imagists like the consequences of a fall, a casting-out from our proper nature as nature's insiders.

Of course we were always nature's insiders, and our solidarity with nature is based on the fact that nature, like us, is fallen and is still falling, outwards from the chaos of the Big Bang, into order and complex beauty and freedom. Once we realize this the image will be released from its old ideological bondage and can take its place in the human story, the human argument; pure imagist poetry will have lost its ideological basis and will become a minor if delightful form of decorative verbal art.

The nature of metaphor and symbol will also change.

Before the materialist revolution we robustly persisted in the belief that objects possessed the powers that the poetic imagination conferred on them: we believed in magic, magical properties, efficacy by correspondence. The rose was sick with love, the sword hated its enemies, jewels could enchant or heal, the moon was intelligent and a little mad. Our world made more human sense to us than it did to the materialists, but it was almost completely intractable and inhabited by uncontrollable powers.

For the materialists, metaphor and symbol are terribly sad reminders of that human sense of the world that was lost, of our alienation from nature. The rose does not really love, nor the sword hate, nor the jewel heal, nor the moon enchant; they only arbitrarily symbolize these things. Metaphor is technical failure. All significance is a pathetic fallacy, canals on Mars that we put there by the weakness and hopefulness of our eyes. There is no magic any more.

We had to choose, as Freud saw, between technical power and psychic health.

That time is now over. We shall be making intelligent and crazy moons, and passionate roses, and fierce swords with microprocessors in their hilts, and medically efficacious jewels. No doubt we will build canals on Mars, and make it into exactly the place of Edgar Rice Burroughs' poetic visions, if we so choose. Metaphor and symbol will become a program for technical transformation, and invented technology will be the new metaphors and symbols of the world. In one sense, our poetry will become less obviously metaphorical and symbolic—only because the metaphors and symbols will not be plastered on to the outside of reality, but will be a concrete and accepted part of its plot, as the technical hardware is in a science-fiction novel. Facts will be significant, and symbols will be facts. It is not that we shall rise above

nature—one of the goals of Modernism—rather, we shall
be nature, naturans, naturing. We will once more see life,
as Edgar says in *King Lear*, as a miracle; as magic, but at
the same time an "art lawful as eating," like the enchant-
ment that, in *The Winter's Tale*, brings the statue of the
dead queen to life.

INTERCHAPTER VII

The natural classical perspective implies that there should be a science of beauty; that beauty can be a legitimate subject of scientific investigation, and that such a science will offer powerful solutions to problems in other disciplines, and a richer understanding of the world. I propose that this science be called "kalogenetics," from the Greek "καλος," beautiful or good, and "γενεσις," creation, origin, or begetting. Many contemporary researchers are, in fact, already engaged on the work of such a science. The last essay attempts, by providing the rudiments of an annotated bibliography of the new science, to summarize many of the central ideas in this book.

Kalogenetics: Bibliographical Notes on Recent Developments in the Scientific Study of Aesthetics

This essay, to repeat, does not purport to be an exhaustive bibliography. Such a bibliography would not in any case be possible at this stage in the infant science I have dubbed "kalogenetics," for the boundaries of that science are still unclear and subject to redefinition; moreover, as a body of research and knowledge it possesses as yet no institutions, libraries, or organization. On the other hand it has been the chosen arena of many of the most interesting and original contemporary thinkers, and these notes are intended not only as a guide to the general reader but also as a sort of directory for those contributors to the new science who may not yet be aware of each other's presence and lines of research.

A second warning is also perhaps required. The notion of a science of beauty is already so controversial that it would seem safest to confine it to the interface between the traditionally humane study of society and the traditionally "hard science" study of living organisms. Obviously, any attempt to provide a scientific basis for the study of aesthetic phenomena must take the royal road through biology: the perception of beauty is first and foremost a capacity belonging to living organisms, one which must have been selected for and genetically preserved by biological evolution. But the new investigators of the beautiful and the artistic do not stop there. They also make interesting claims about the objective characteristics of beauty in the physical world at large, and about the relationships between the beautiful and the fundamental strategies of physical morphogenesis and survival. These claims, in turn, have begun to revolutionize our humanistic understanding of beauty, and rescue the study of aesthetics from the rather dusty back shelf of academic philosophy where it has languished for so long.

The reader is also warned that much of the current research on the scientific foundations of aesthetics is as yet unpublished and is still tentative and speculative. In some cases I shall refer to work-in-progress, giving the researcher's name only.

One of the first places that an investigator of the scientific basis of aesthetics might look is in the field of animal behavior. Do animals experience beauty or perform intentionally beautiful actions? Much animal behavior has been characterized by scientific observers as essentially playful; Konrad Lorenz's excellent popular book *King Solomon's Ring* (Methuen, 1964), gives many examples—and the realms of play and the aesthetic obviously intersect broadly. Generations of poets and painters in various human cultures have celebrated the grace and beauty of animals: could it all have been simply in the eye of the beholder? These questions have been largely ignored by scientists, I suspect for two reasons: one being the dogmatic assumption by aesthetic philosophers that the aesthetic is a realm confined to the human

mind, and the other being the materialist bias of many
scientists, who are, for metaphysical reasons of their
own, more inclined to explain the behavior of an object
by its material composition than by its structure and
organization.

Thus in the promising field of aesthetic animal behavior, the researcher is reduced to following a few isolated
clues: Konrad Lorenz's interesting discussion of the mating and aggressive displays of various species, especially
tropical reef fish, in his *On Aggression* (Methuen, 1963);
W. H. Thorpe's article "Duet-Singing Birds" in *Scientific
American*, August 1973; J. S. Huxley's classic "The
Courtship Habits of the Great Crested Grebe," in *Proceedings of the Zoological Society of London* 35 (1914);
Thomas Gilliard's "The Evolution of Bowerbirds" in
Scientific American, August 1963; and even David
Attenborough's provocative, if offhand remark in his
recent television series *Life on Earth*, to the effect that
flowers are designed to appeal to the aesthetic tastes of
bees. If, as Jacob von Uexküll argued in his seminal
Umwelt und Innenwelt der Tiere (Springer, 1921) the
world of an animal is circumscribed by the capacities of
its affectors and receptors, then for the foraging bee such
qualities as variety, symmetry, color harmony, precise
detail, redundancy of pattern, complexity in simplicity,
unity, and even accurate mimicry, are clearly part of the
bee's world. And these qualities, especially when brought
together, are equally clearly involved in human visual
aesthetics.

If a philosopher were to object that the aesthetic is
essentially "for its own sake" and cannot be utilitarian in
purpose, that objection might profitably be taken up with
other aestheticians as an unproven argument which begs
many questions. The whole existence of the bee is in an
adaptive sense "for its own sake" anyway. The distinction between the utilitarian and the intrinsically valuable

might begin to disappear if the qualities comprising beauty were to be recognized as necessary to and even constitutive of the continued survival in time and against entropy of organized physical structures. The fact that beauty seems to be most strongly associated with reproductive activity—even when the observer is not aware that a reproductive function is involved—is of special interest here. Animals, and even plants, seem to concentrate their capacities to produce what we call the aesthetic into the structures and behaviors of reproduction: mating songs and dances, the plumage and pigment of sexual display, flowers, perfumes, nectar, and so on.

Sociobiology and human ethology, like the field of animal behavior, contain promising opportunities for research into these questions: but they too have avoided them for the most part. Darwin, near the end of *The Origin of Species*, speculates about the adaptive origins of our liking for bright colors in the sugar-energy content of ripe fruit, and suggests an interest in sexual preferences based on reproductive fitness. Konrad Lorenz draws parallels between animal and human aesthetic preferences which, I believe, have been unjustly dismissed by many biologists; to my ear they often have the ring of the careful naturalist's intuitive sense of the truth—those unscientific hunches that are confirmed by later scientific paradigms. Similar analogies have been made by Lorenz's successor Irenaeus Eibl-Eibesfeldt, in his classic textbook *Ethology: the Biology of Behavior* (Holt, Rinehart, 1970). But on the whole human ethology and sociobiology have ignored aesthetic matters.

The case has not been much better in the fields of paleoanthropology and human evolution, but the most recent work in these areas shows an increasing interest in aesthetics. S. L. Washburn and Phyllis C. Joy's *Perspectives on Human Evolution* (Holt, Rinehart, 1968), a useful collection of essays, is already provocative on these issues, and John C. Eccles' *The Human Mystery* (Springer, 1979), begins to tackle them in an exciting speculative fashion (Eccles, however, is a neuropsychologist, not a paleoanthropologist). Best of all, to my mind, is Peter J. Wilson's excellent book *Man, the Promising Primate* (Yale University Press, 1980), which fully grasps the fascinating philosophical issues raised by the fact that our evolution, as a species that is capable of determining to some extent the nature of reality itself, was partly our own doing; we created ourselves by selectively enacting the promise of ourselves. I shall return to this book later on, but will note here that Wilson's position implies that aesthetic choice can be a determinative force in evolution, and that the aesthetic may well be the most comprehensive and active mode of the cognitive.

The field of cultural anthropology is presently the scene of an interesting and important debate which is central to "kalogenetics." The old socioeconomic theories, which dismissed aesthetics as merely a superstructure designed to justify and rationalize economic power and social inequality, have now largely been exploded. Economic valuations turn out to be only a crude statistical summation without predictive power; a close examination of economic value returns us at once to the mysterious realms of human desire, aspiration, spirituality, ideology, and cosmology. In place of the old reductionism, several new approaches now compete for the allegiance of the cultural anthropologists. Their explanations of human preference cover a broad range. The most extreme cultural-relativist position is represented brilliantly by Clifford Geertz's *The Interpretation of Cultures* (New York: Basic Books, 1973); and *Negara: The Theatre State in Nineteenth-Century Bali* (Princeton, 1980). The most solidly ethological position is represented with equal brilliance by Eibl-Eibesfeldt. For the former, culture is a great game, arbitrary in its rules, fully determinative of human behavior, and almost infinitely variable from one part of the world to the other. For the latter, culture is innate, the expression of a genetic program having behind it the wisdom and experience of millenia of selection, to be violated only at the risk of deforming human nature. Between these two positions lie the functionalists, who retain enough of the old economic-determinist ideas to put limits on the arbitrariness of culture as envisaged by the relativists: culture for the functionalists is not a game to be played but a system of technology reconciling human psychological needs with the demands of ecological survival. The question of what those needs are and how they are created is, of course, begged. The structuralists, most signally represented by Claude Lévi-Strauss: *The Raw and the Cooked* (Cape, 1970); *From Honey to Ashes* (Cape, 1973); *The Origin of Table Manners* (Cape, 1978); *The Naked Man* (Cape, 1981); *The Savage Mind* (Weidenfeld, 1972), limit the playfulness of culture in another way, by postulating a universal inner logic of binary opposition and mediation in all human culture, which is in its own sense as tragically determinative of human behavior as any innate "drive" or ecological "necessity."

Of special interest to the student of "kalogenetics" is the work of a group of anthropologists connected with the late Victor W. Turner. In Turner's *The Ritual Process* (Aldine, 1969), *The Forest of Symbols* (Cornell University Press, 1967), *The Drums of Affliction* (Oxford University Press, 1968), *Dramas, Fields and Metaphors* (Cornell University Press, 1974), and *From Ritual to Theater* (Performing Arts Journal Publications, 1982), he spells out a complex position best summarized by the notion of "social drama." For him culture is not merely an epiphenomenon of economics, nor an arbitrary game, nor the expression of a genetic program, nor a technology of adaptation, nor a variation of an abstract structure, but rather a drama played out by individuals modifying and adapting, at the cost of personal sacrifice, the cultural traditions, innate drives, and existential constraints that surround them. The chief weapon that the individual possesses in this drama is the capacity to join with others in creating a ludic—a playful—anti-world, a "liminal" space where the rules are temporarily set aside and human community can assert itself against social structure. Turner traces the development of the arts and much of our capacity to appreciate beauty to these fundamental strategies of liberation. His position becomes both problematic—and extremely fertile in testable hypothesis—in those cases where an older ludic order confronts a newer one, or where structures created out of the liminal drama actually prove to make good sense in understanding and affecting the physical universe. What happens when art becomes good science, and where should our sympathies lie when a revolutionary iconoclasm confronts an ancient and beautiful ritual game?

In his later years Turner became increasingly interested in the role of the human brain, its anatomy and function, in the generation and maintenance of the liminal mood which for him was the means of cultural creativity and liberation from perceived necessity, social, innate, or economic. Thus for him, as for all those researchers in this field whom I find most interesting, the biological inheritances of humankind, especially the peculiar features of the human nervous system, are not so much constraints as means of liberation; and I would add, that process of liberation is also a process of nomogenesis or order-creation which is at the heart of our experience of beauty.

But before we follow Turner's lead in the direction of neuroanatomy and psychophysics, it is worth mentioning the work of some of his collaborators. Mihaly

Csikszentmihalyi's *Beyond Boredom and Anxiety: The Experience of Play in Work and Games* (Jossey-Bass, 1975) examines the sense of "flow" which artists, sportsmen, and skilled workers experience when their creative and integrative faculties are operating more perfectly than they are able to analyze cognitively. John J. MacAloon's *This Great Symbol: Pierre de Coubertin and the Origins of the Modern Olympic Games* (University of Chicago Press, 1981), deals with the Olympic Games as a sort of pan-human aesthetic ritual of the body. The late Barbara Myerhoff's very moving *Number Our Days* (Dutton, 1979) describes, using models from cultural anthropology, the often *ad hoc* ritual life of a community of elderly old-country Jews in Southern California, probing sensitively at the common roots of social, religious, and aesthetic creativity. Also to be recommended is Sally F. Moore and Barbara Myerhoff, eds., *Secular Ritual* (Humanities Press, 1977). Finally, Barbara Babcock, in a number of articles, has investigated the phenomena of reflexivity and explicit self-awareness in religious, social, and artistic activity.

Before we leave the anthropologists I should mention four more names. The first is George Peter Murdock, who has composed an extraordinary list of the major topics of pan-human, cross-cultural interest: a list which in some ways sums up the central subjects of all classical representational art—see "The Common Denominator of Cultures," in *Perspectives on Human Evolution*, Vol. I, edited by S.L. Washburn and P. C. Joy (Holt, Rinehart, 1968). The second and third are Andrew Strathern and Marilyn Strathern, who have translated hundreds of lyric poems from New Guinea, and have also described in aesthetic terms the ritual costumes of New Guinea tribesmen—*Self-Decoration in Mount Hagen* (Duckworth, 1971)—in religious, social, and artistic activity.

In the last few years the advent of new and sophisti-

cated measuring techniques, instrumentation, and experimental design have revolutionized the study of brain
activity. The functions of the columnar structure of the
cortex have been investigated by a combination of methods, including the recording of evoked potentials in
individual neurons, the dissection of cat and frog brains,
and behavioral and psychophysical studies of perception
in human beings and animals. The cortex turns out to be
a very active, synthesizing organ, which creates highly
coherent gestalts even when the perceptual givens
are fragmentary and ambiguous. The investigation of
patients with brain lesions—especially "split-brain"
patients—together with studies of blood-flow in the
brain, and more recently, the use of sophisticated CAT
scanning, ultrasound, and NMR scanning devices, have
helped to provide detailed maps of brain functions. Positron tomography has begun to reveal specific neuroreceptors.

Very recently some attempt has been made to assess
the relevance of the new brain science for the study of
aesthetics. Little has yet been published on this subject,
but I shall list a few of the most exciting lines of research,
most of which are associated with the Werner Reimers
Stiftung group of researchers.

Ernst Pöppel of the Institute for Medical Psychology in
Munich has been collecting beautiful experimental data
for some years on the temporal discrimination of the
auditory cortex, examining the way it organizes information into a hierarchy of periodicities, and imposes a
coherent subjective time sense on the acoustic world. His
collaborator and colleague Ingo Rentschler has been investigating the equivalent spatial rhythms in the visual
system, showing how the visual cortex attends optimally
to certain densities and combinations of detail frequency
in a picture or visual scene. Both workers are fully
cognizant of the implications of their studies for aesthet-

ic preference in poetry, music, and the visual arts. Terry Caelli, of the University of Edmonton, has developed a remarkable "filter" theory of the perception of spatial separations which may even confirm the intuitive practice of painters who convey certain moods by detail frequency and composition. The subtle interplay of cultural, neurobiological, and electromagnetic elements in the perception of color and in the preference for certain color combinations is being studied by Semir Zeki, Heinrich Zollinger, and John McManus. Jerre Levy of the University of Chicago has brilliantly extended the early work of Roger Sperry on hemispheric specialization; she has been mapping the cognitive, emotional, and aesthetic capacities of the two sides of the brain, showing how left and right collaborate in the coherent construction of a plausible universe and a plausible response to it. O.-J. Grüsser has actually studied artists whose brains have suffered lateral lesions, and has made fascinating observations on them that combine insights from psychology, art criticism, and neuroanatomy. Robert Turner of the University of Nottingham, Colwyn Trevarthen of the University of Edinburgh, and others have begun work on a project using Nuclear Magnetic Resonance scanning to study the myelinization of nerve fibers in the corpus callosum—the body that connect the left and right sides of the brain—under the influence of acculturation in the first five years of life.

The recent discovery that the brain creates its own pain-killers and stimulants—that class of neuropeptides known as the endorphins, whose subjective effects are mimicked by heroin, morphine, and cocaine—has also revolutionized the study of aesthetics. There is an excellent summary of the progress of the chemistry of pleasure in the chapter entitled "Joy" in Melvin Konner's *The Tangled Wing: Biological Constraints on the Human Spirit* (Holt, Rinehart, 1982). It has been known for some time that there exist "pleasure centers" in the brain; James Olds and Aryeh Routtenberg interpret these centers as being part of an endogenous self-reward or self-motivation system. See James Olds' "Behavioral Studies of Hypothalamic Functions: Drives and Reinforcements" in *Biological Foundations of Psychiatry*, Vol. I, edited by R. G. Grenell and S. Babay (Raven, 1976); A. Routtenberg's *Biology of Reinforcement: Facets of Brain Stimulation Reward* (Academic Press, 1980); Solomon H. Snyder's "Opiate Receptors and Internal Opiates" in *Scientific American*, March, 1977; Floyd Bloom's "Neuropeptides" in *Scientific American*, October, 1981; and Roger Guillemin's "Peptides in the Brain: The New Endocrinology of the Neuron" in *Science*, 202, 1978. Lionel Tiger, in his *Optimism: the Biology of Hope* (Simon & Schuster, 1979) sees the existence of these "rewards" as part of a policy among the higher animals adaptively designed to promote species survival. If, as seems increasingly likely, the experience of beauty is the subjective aspect of endorphin reward in certain contexts, then it begins to make sense to ask the question, What behavior or activity are we being rewarded for when we recognize something as beautiful or when we create something beautiful? And why should our experience as a species have selected for that behavior or activity? Certain kinds of stress, indeed, can trigger endorphin "rewards," as J. C. Willer *et al.* point out in their paper "Stress-Induced Analgesia in Humans: Endogenous Opioids and Naxolone Reversible Depression of Pain Reflex" in *Science*, 212, 1981. Why should we be genetically programmed to risk potentially damaging stress in order to perceive or create the beautiful?

Again we encounter the mysterious connection between beauty and survival, and thus between beauty and being itself. Evidently the old ideas of motivation and aesthetic preference, mostly based on some version of

Freud's sublimation theory, will have to be revised. The sense of beauty is not just a repressed version of the urge to survive or to reproduce oneself, unless we take "survival" and "reproduce" in a sense far beyond Freud's. Could it even be the other way around, that sexual reproduction is only a partial version of the tendency of beautiful order to endure in time?

This view receives some support from the work of a remarkable group of researchers, who have christened themselves "biogenetic structuralists." They include experts on brain function, neurochemistry, child development, human evolution, endocrinology, and anthropology. Their most important book, *The Spectrum of Ritual*, edited by E. G. d'Aquili, C. D. Laughlin, Jr., and J. McManus (Columbia University Press, 1979) examines ritual practices systematically from a variety of viewpoints. Perhaps the most interesting essay in the collection is that by Barbara Lex, which traces the relationships between meditative, ritual, aesthetic, and other types of trance states, examines their physiological aspects, and shows how the techniques of ritual and of many forms of art, such as rhythmic driving, are actually a traditional psychic technology of considerable precision and sophistication. Robert Keith Wallace and Herbert Benson make a strong case for this in "The Physiology of Meditation" in *Scientific American*, February, 1972. The traditional forms of artistic and ritual performance are closely keyed to our neural inheritance. This finding is in good agreement with the work of Ernst Pöppel and myself on poetic meter, which shows a pan-human rhythmic pulse of about three seconds in duration, and which is tuned to a three-second information processing pulse in the human hearing system.

Another interdisciplinary group of this type is the Werner Reimers Stiftung study group on the biological aspects of aesthetics, of which I am a member. It includes

KALOGENETICS 251

Jerre Levy, Irenaeus Eibl-Eibesfeldt, the anthropologists Wulf Schiefenhövel and Andrew Strathern, the distinguished neurologist Gunther Baumgärtner, O.-J. Grüsser, the important American musicologist David Epstein, Heinrich Zollinger, Ingo Rentschler, Terry Caelli, and several others, and has received important contributions from Abraham Moles and Simha Arom, whom I shall mention again later. One of the most stimulating issues that the group tackled was the distinction between aesthetic appreciation and simple perception as such. Much of our work had showed that experimental human subjects show a crude preference—which we had no choice but to regard as the raw material of aesthetic judgment—for perceptual experiences which met and fully engaged the sensitivities and capacities of the various senses. That is, they were neither so simple as to bore the nervous system, nor so complex as to overload it. We prefer a detail frequency that gives us plenty to look at or hear but is not so dense as to make us generalize it stochastically into a mere texture; but we also like a range of detail frequencies, including dense textures and simple spaces. We like a hierarchy of acoustic or visual orders, but also like to see that hierarchy disrupted sufficiently as to remind us of its presence, as long as it is not overwhelmed by "noise" altogether. The musicologist David Epstein, whose book *Beyond Orpheus: Studies in Musical Structure* (M.I.T. Press, 1979) applies his ideas to classical art music, has demonstrated these principles in musical tempo variations and especially in rubato. His work is buttressed by Abraham Moles's brilliant application of information theory to sense perception and preference, *Information Theory and Esthetic Perception* (Illinois University Press, 1968), and by Simha Arom's exhaustive study of African drum rhythms.

Moles and Rentschler relate the phenomenon of habituation—the tendency of individual neurons to respond less actively to repeated stimuli than to unique stimuli, and for the nervous system as a whole to "damp out" repeated or continuous sensations—to information theory, which shows that a message can only be transmitted and received if some kind of regular "carrier wave" or medium is distorted so as to convey information. If there is no regular carrier wave the receiver has no basis against which to compare the encoded message; if the carrier wave remains regular and is not distorted, no message is conveyed.

The implication is that we prefer pictures or sounds which carry the maximum amount of information, given our coefficient of habituation, so to speak. Does the beautiful therefore *only* mean the intelligible, the clear, the well-perceived? Was the Reimers group really investigating only perception, and not aesthetic perception? Interestingly enough it was pointed out that Emmanuel Kant had wrestled with precisely this problem in his aesthetic theory.

Our solution was that a proper understanding of perception itself allowed for degrees of internal world-model construction which would place aesthetic appreciation along a continuum which runs from mere collective statistical variation among subatomic particles, through causal reactions in molecular matter, sensation in primitive living organisms, and perception in sophisticated living beings. The greater precision and constructedness of a percept, in comparison to a mere sensation, is analogous to the greater precision and constructedness of aesthetic awareness as opposed to mere perception. Aesthetic appreciation is as far beyond perception as perception is beyond sensation, but is not a different kind of thing altogether.

A further implication is that if we regard the perceptions of the world by higher animals as providing them with a better, more precise, more accurate view of it than

the sensations of lower animals do, then aesthetic appreciation is correspondingly more exactly truthful about
the nature of the universe than is ordinary perception!
The Werner Reimers group was the less inclined to be
incredulous about this inference than most groups of
scholars and scientists would be, for it had already
explored the important role of aesthetic considerations in
the construction of scientific theories and experimental
design.

Harry Jerison, who has investigated encephalization
and the evolution of the brain in present and prehistoric
species in *Evolution of the Brain and Intelligence* (Academic Press, 1973), directly relates brain development to
the increasing need for predator and prey species to
develop coherent models of the world based on various
sensory inputs, models that might enable the individual
to predict accurately the behavior of other animals. The
"outside world" is a plausible but not provable construction of the higher species, justified only by the fact that
its constructors survive better than more solipsistic species. If the sensation of beauty, aesthetic pleasure, satisfaction in complex but symmetrical patterns, were the
neurochemical reward for the metabolically expensive
but highly adaptive process of world-model construction,
then the evolution of the aesthetic capacity would make
perfect sense. And it would not be at all anthropomorphic
to look for it among other species of animals.

The implications of this line of argument for the arts
are very interesting. The arts would stand revealed as a
set of psychic technologies, designed to stimulate, ampli-
fy, and translate into collective socio-cultural reality the
world-model creating capacities of the human brain. We
would expect to see the classical arts linked in a long
tradition with ancient ritual practices, and would be
likely to find, under the rich diversity of cultural variety,
a universal human "grammar" of aesthetics, tuned to

the habituation period, the information processing pulse, the detail acuity, the fatigue rate, and other constraints of the human nervous system. Again, we would be likely to find artistic practices that sensitize and activate the brain's endogenous reward system, and which both enforce and enable extensive cooperation between the two sides of the brain.

As we have seen, the predictions in the previous paragraph are indeed true for the ancient and universal human practice of metered poetry. A close investigation of mythical stories would, I think, show the same qualities of human universality, ancientness, connection with early ritual practices, and attunement to the peculiar capacities of the human nervous system. The materials for such an investigation are already available in Joseph Campbell's magnificent *Historical Atlas of World Mythology* (Times Book,s 1984), Claude Lévi-Strauss's "Mythologiques" tetralogy, James G. Frazer's classic *The Golden Bough* (Macmillan, 1925), and David Bynum's fiercely original and controversial *The Daemon in the Wood* (Harvard University Press, 1978).

Another field in which artistic practice may be seen to meet the predictions of the new science of "kalogenetics" is that of mnemonics—memory technologies. Milman Parry, in *The Making of Homeric Verse*, edited by Adam Parry (Oxford University Press, 1971) and Albert Lord, in *The Singer of Tales* (Harvard University Press, 1960) have demonstrated with beautiful statistical analysis and detailed comparison of Homeric epic with modern Yugoslav oral poetry, that the formulaic structure of oral epic poetry is precisely designed to fit the limitations and capacities of human memory storage.

In another direction, Frances Yates, in *The Theatre of the World* (Chicago University Press, 1969) has closely investigated the Renaissance system for memorizing orations and theatrical performance, showing that it is based upon a mapping of a temporal sequence onto a spatial configuration of "places." Such a system very neatly remedies the limitations of the left brain, which remembers temporal sequences but has a very limited capacity for doing so, by turning to the formidable gestalt mode of preserving information, possessed by the right brain. Furthermore, this enforced bilateral cooperation nicely fits Jerre Levy's prescription for creativity and understanding in neural terms.

To ascertain, train oneself in, and use this ancient "grammar" that lies ready to hand would constitute an artistic practice which I have called "natural classicism." This approach is still, in fact, rather rare in the contemporary arts and criticism. The musical composer George Crumb, in his essay "Music: Does It Have a Future?" in *The Kenyon Review*, Summer, 1980, has argued for what he calls "natural tonality." The operatic composer Philip Glass has rediscovered and used in new ways many of the ancient classical techniques of music. In contemporary architecture, especially in the work of Michael Graves, there appears to be some questioning of the prevailing modernist bias against meeting the classical human needs. The Scottish poet, landscape-architect, and polemicist Ian Hamilton Finlay happily accepts the label "natural classicist," and has founded a society called "The New Arcadians." A group of American poets including Frederick Feirstein, Dana Gioia, Lynda Sexson, Michael Newman, Amy Clampitt, Julia Budenz, Dick Allen, Wade Newman, Judith Moffett, and others have been rediscovering in various ways the wisdom of the poetic tradition. Michael Newman's synthesis of cell biology, neurology, computer games, music, and poetic meter is especially interesting.

One of the fundamental characteristics of that prehistoric ritual practice which gave rise to the arts is *performance*. In fact the study of performance, artistic and

religious—the ancient ritual did not make the distinction
—offers a direct and powerful probe into the inner workings of the arts and is a valuable tool of "kalogenetics."
Konstantin Stanislavski's *An Actor Prepares* (Theater
Arts Books, 1946) is not only a profound piece of insight
into theater, but also a summary of much practical
wisdom passed down orally from one generation of theater people to the next, a tradition that surfaces, for
instance, in Hamlet's advice to the players. Stanislavsky
particularly insists on the fact that an actor must *choose*,
selecting, from a divine plenum of possible interpretations, an actualizable objective, a clear through-line. A
theater performance is an actual human event. It is
"acted" in the sense of pretense, but also "acted" in the
sense that it is a real action. Part of the work of any artist,
perhaps, is to make the tragic choice of a particular
embodiment, creating an enduring, because internally
coherent and redundant, reality in a world which tends
towards ambiguity and disorder. Paradoxically that claim
to a definite outline and coherence also renders an
artwork tragically subject to decay, especially in acting,
where the physical part of the artwork vanishes with the
very reverberation of the lines in the air. Art, so performance studies tell us, rejects that tentativeness that
might preserve it from the forces that erode the definite
and the committed. And it gets in return certain almost
magical powers.

Some of those powers are described by the Polish
theater director Jerzy Grotowski in *Towards a Poor Theater* (Odin Teatrets Forlag, 1968) and Richard Schechner in
Essays on Performance Theory, 1970-1976 (Drama Book
Specialists, 1977) and "Performers and Spectators Transported and Transformed" in *Kenyon Review*, Fall 1981. In
the theater the world can be transformed, remade. To put
it in the terms of physical science, we might describe
theatrical performance—and artistic performance in

general—as being capable of changing the metric or the gauge by which the world is measured. Thus, since the severest and most rigorous scientific method claims that the world is only and always what it is *measured* to be, that physical reality is only a set of mutual measurings and recordings, art can literally change the world. To put it another way still, art is the way in which we alter the sensitivities of our affectors and receptors, and thus change our umwelt itself, and since the universe is only the set of all actual umwelts—for a scientist there is no *Ding an sich*—art has a direct ontological effect.

In *From Ritual to Theater* (Performing Arts Journal Publications, 1982) Victor Turner forges the link between the traditional ritual calibration of the umwelt and the more *ad hoc* transformations of contemporary performance. He goes on to suggest that the methodology of social anthropology—both in teaching and study—should include an experiental, existential performance element. He, Schechner, and others have actually staged Central African rituals, using drama and anthropology students, and report extraordinary successes with the method. There are interesting parallel developments in pedagogical theory and practice in the fields of language learning and Shakespeare studies. In the latter, for instance, Bernard Beckerman, Homer Swander, and many other Shakespeare scholars, including myself, have been using student performance as a vital element in teaching. Performance thus has a powerful cognitive element—there are some things one can know only by performing them. Perhaps indeed the difference between knowing and doing is not as great as we thought. And any "doing" which is not routine or repetition is already within the artistic sphere and is governed by aesthetic criteria.

A philosophical approach to this issue is now possible because of the extraordinary work of the philosopher J. L. Austin, whose suggestively titled *How To Do Things*

With Words (Oxford University Press, 1976) has become very influential in directions at first not recognized. Austin points out that many uses of language are not referential at all, and discusses what he calls speech acts and performative utterances as examples of language which does not merely describe or refer, but brings real new entities into being. Such language might include, for example, the stipulation of the rules of a game, the postulation of a mathematical axiom, the promulgation of a piece of legislation, the verbal sealing of a contract, the value of a currency, the words of a promise, the introduction to a fiction ("once upon a time"), and the words by which a marriage is enacted; and it also perhaps includes (and even justifies) much religious language— the language of sacraments, prayers, vows, and invocations. Performative language shows considerable resiliency against the attacks of traditional analytic or empirical reason. Chess, for instance, is a real entity; yet it was brought into being entirely by performative stipulations. If God is of the order of Chess, then it would be hard for an atheist to deny His existence; though most orthodox religious people would probably prefer the opposition of an atheist to the defense of a "performativist." And yet there is much in religion that hints at the fantastic freedom to create and be created which performative language gives us. "In the Beginning was the Word." Indeed, the critique of analytic reason by Gödel (no system of proof can prove its own validity) and the critique of empirical reason by Popper (anything we know on evidence must be falsifiable) leave the created truths of performative utterances quite untouched. William James may have had an inkling of this argument, as H. S. Thayer hints in his intriguing essay, "The Right to Believe: William James' Reinterpretation of the Function of Religious Belief" in *Kenyon Review*, Winter, 1983.

Peter J. Wilson's book *Man, The Promising Primate,*
which I have already mentioned, uses Austin's theory of
performative utterances to make the exciting argument
that human evolution itself is the cumulative result of
such speech acts. We promised ourselves into our humanity, so to speak, and our religion and aesthetic activities
were the way we performed our being.

The philosophical/religious/scientific periodical *Zygon,* under the remarkable leadership of Ralph Burhoe,
has been exploring the idea of nature as a sort of cumulative self-utterance. Some of the more speculative quantum theorists, like David Finkelstein, in "Coherence and
Possibility: the Logic of the Innermost Universe" in *The
Kenyon Review,* Spring 1982, have pointed out the remarkable amenability of the physical universe to being
"retroactively" determined by the kind of metric we
bring to bear on it, the kind of question we ask it, and
ultimately the kind of theoretical model—the axioms—
we invent as the basis for experimental design. Not that
the universe, which is, after all, made of components
which contain their own primitive assumptions about
the way things are, always gives us the answer we expect.
But it somehow bestirs itself to fit into the framework of
the question. We cannot change an existent fact by a
performative utterance, but we can make new facts, and
by connecting the old facts with the new ones change
much of the bearing and significance of the old facts.

Of course there are weaknesses in this mode of creating truths, the largest being that it creates truths which
are only true *for* a given community of knowers and
known objects; its truths may not be abolished by
counter-example but they can be diluted and attenuated
into triviality by a reduction in the size and scope of their
performative community. If I invent a private language in
which "red" means "green," "red" really does mean

"green" *in* that language and *for* me as its speaker; but the statement has little power outside my community of one.

Certain cosmologists, such as George Gale in "The Anthropic Principle" in *Scientific American,* December, 1981, have suggested that there are scientifically valid senses of the word "determine" in which it makes sense to say that the initial conditions of the universe—which seem to have been critical to its present constitution— were determined by the necessity to bring about observers of the universe, that is, ourselves. We need not go so far as this to say that any organism, living or non-living, which would, by virtue of possessing an internal model of external conditions, be capable of adapting flexibly to or partly determining its environment, would tend to preserve its structure intact as against less sophisticated organisms; and that this principle of selection could have been at work from the first moments of the Big Bang. Something like this is argued in John D. Barrow and Joseph Silk in "The Structure of the Early Universe" in *Scientific American,* April, 1980; and in Joseph Silk and others in "The Large-Scale Structure of the Universe" in *Scientific American,* October, 1983.

Much of this discussion is placed in a convincingly thorough context by the work of J. T. Fraser, the foremost contemporary theorist of the nature of time. Fraser argues that time as we know it is not a simple phenomenon but a hierarchy of superimposed temporalities, ranging from the atemporality of the photon, through the prototemporality of elementary particles, eotemporality and biotemporality, to the nootemporality of human beings; and that the more sophisticated senses of time were evolved as the universe itself evolved. Each new temporality possesses its own metric, order, determinism, repertoire of forms, and characteristic conflicts; there also exist discordancies between different levels.

An accessible account of his argument can be found in his "Out of Plato's Cave: the Natural History of Time" in *The Kenyon Review*, Winter, 1980; it is spelled out in detail in *Of Time, Passion and Knowledge* (Braziller, 1975).

The major point I wish to make here is that if the study of the biological foundations of aesthetics suggests that aesthetic behavior is adaptive, then certain implications follow about the physical universe. Either it passively submits itself to the imposition of aesthetic pattern by the higher organisms, thus encouraging their survival, or else it contains inherently those very laws themselves, so that "aesthetic predictions" of its behavior are adaptively justified by their objective correctness. These two alternatives may in fact be different ways of saying the same thing; but I would like to conclude this essay by discussing various lines of research which suggest that the production of exquisite patterns may be an inherent property, not only of matter, but of mathematical probability itself. According to this view the universe does not merely produce, at random and amid much dross, occasional ordered patterns, and passively provide the conditions within which their survival is selected, but rather it cannot help actively and preferentially generating beautiful kinds of shapes in space and time.

It was the French mathematician René Thom who, over two decades ago, developed a way of graphing and mapping mathematically discontinuous phenomena both in the abstract realm of topology and in physical systems. There is a clear account of Thom's work in E. C. Zeeman's "Catastrophe Theory" in *Scientific American*, April, 1976. The way was now open for a consideration of the laws governing all kinds of mathematically intractable shapes and forms and transformations.

Meanwhile the physicists had begun examining the notion of nothingness armed with the new conceptions of physical reality provided by quantum theory. Even in a region of total vacuum the surface of space-time is inherently unstable, and if it is examined with a sufficiently small yardstick will demonstrate a kind of seething or boiling behavior: waves, folds, and even wormholes and foams appear, as nature is not sufficiently exact to prevent small variation from forming spontaneously on the positive and negative sides of the norm: variations whose sum adds up to zero, but which can, under the right circumstances, prolong their existence almost indefinitely, putting off the moment when the "wave" is flattened out, and the physical debt paid off and canceled. Such is in fact one explanation of the origin of the universe. Various versions of this notion exist, including Alan H. Guth and Paul J. Steinhardt's "The Inflationary Universe" in *Scientific American*, May, 1984.

Manfred Eigen, in his *Laws of the Game: How the Principles of Nature Govern Chance* (Knopf, 1981), takes issue with Jacques Monod's *Chance and Necessity* (Collins, 1972), arguing that Monod ignores both the lawlike and the gamelike features of probability, and that Monod's belief that the world arises by chance fails to take into account potential stabilities that are inherent in the "game" itself. But both are united in the assumption that very delicate and refined kinds of order can arise spontaneously. Their argument is perhaps a version of the distinction I drew earlier, between the universe as an active generator of order, and the universe as a passive selector of it. The disagreement resembles the linguistic debate that was sparked off some years ago by Noam Chomsky's generative linguistics. On one hand were those who still felt that language was a sort of accretion of randomly-arising but useful (and thus preserved) tools, limited in expressive range; on the other were Chomsky's followers, who saw language as a relatively small group of connected laws which, however, possessed the miraculous quality of being able to generate an unlimited and unpredictable repertoire of expressive utterances. Derek Bickerton's "Creole Languages" in *Scientific American,* July, 1983, seems to indicate that certain linguistic rules are indeed innate.

The work of Arthur M. Young deserves mention in this context. In his book *The Geometry of Meaning* (Robert Briggs Associates, 1976) he demonstrates that the classical measure formulae of the physical science of dynamics are related to each other by a powerful symmetry which is, however, incomplete. The series: position, motion, acceleration, must be completed by a fourth entity, which he calls "control." He shows that this entity, predicted by the symmetry, corresponds exactly to what aeronautical engineers (his original profession) call "jerk," and actually use regularly in their work. If we examine the kinds of objects which are capable of producing this series of characteristics we find that we have constructed a primitive map of the evolution of the universe, and that "control" requires the equivalent of a living organism. This idea implies not only that there is a universal necessity to generate higher order forms of complexity, but also that those higher order complexities, at a certain point in evolution, pass an inflection point at which they become more and more autonomous and determinative of their own environment.

M. J. Feigenbaum in his "Universal Behavior in Nonlinear Systems" in *Los Alamos Science,* Vol. 1, no. 1, 1980, introduces a new body of scientific study, which can be loosely characterized as the investigation of chaos. His theory of period-doubling, which provides a mathematical description of processes which begin with an ordered structure but break up into unpredictable eddies or discontinuities, has been shown to be useful in studying such diverse phenomena as jets of liquid and gas, economic and epidemiological cycles, and cardiac fibrillation. The interesting thing is that in such systems the gradations between orderly and predictable behavior and total chaos are a) critically dependent on the values of the initial conditions; b) can be mapped; mappings which c) display very beautiful, elaborate, and symmetrical patterns. Between the areas where the initial values of a system generate a simple stable state or oscillation and those areas ("strange attractors") where chaos is generated, exists a world of delicate morphogenesis. Douglas Hofstadter, in his "Strange Attractors: Mathematical Patterns Delicately Poised Between Order and Chaos" in *Scientific American,* November, 1981 reports these developments with cogency and verve. A more strictly mathematical account may be found in R. May's "Simple Mathematical Models with Very Complicated Dynamics" in *Nature,* 261, 1976.

Perhaps the most stimulating book in this area is Benoit Mandelbrot's *The Fractal Geometry of Nature* (Freeman, 1983). He synthesizes many of the lines of research I have mentioned in the last few pages, naming and analyzing whole classes of shapes whose configuration is the same at whatever magnification we examine them: the fractals, as he calls them. Fractals are the product of a new kind of symmetry, in which the repetitions are not around an axis but at various scales of analysis, so that some aspect of the fine structure is identical to that of the gross structure, and the fine structure is in turn the gross structure of a new fine structure to which it bears the same relation, and so on. Fractals are the spatial expression of any reflexive and thus any hierarchical process. Indeed, this connection between the reflexive and the hierarchical becomes intuitively compelling when one considers fractals: feedback systems create hierarchical forms. Mandelbrot claims that fractal geometry is the very geometry of nature itself, and suggests (p. 239) that quantum mechanical motions follow fractal curves. Further, he claims frequently that fractal forms are "art," and uses boldly aesthetic language to describe his findings. A new synthesis is emerging between game theory, probability mathematics, catastrophe theory, quantum physics, and the study of chaos. The universe, for these theorists, has been since the Big Bang the elaboration of a more and more complex, hierarchical, reflexive fractal curve generated by some universal period-doubling principle embedded in the logic of stochastic processes.

Douglas Hofstadter, in his *Gödel, Escher, Bach* (Harvester Press, 1979), explores another aspect of this emerging synthesis: the creative paradoxes that arise in self-observing and self-generating systems. His term for the way in which lower levels of organization are subsumed under higher levels is "chunked description," which corresponds to Mandelbrot's "fractal," and Feigenbaum's "period doubling." This concept represents, I believe, a contemporary solution of the logical impasse known as the infinite regress, transforming the "observer problem" from a stumbling-block into a potent tool of understanding.

It is my contention that the human aesthetic capacity is essentially an ability to recognize, comprehend intuitively, take part in, and even guide the kind of processes which these thinkers have identified. The pleasure afforded by the golden section in art, architecture and music is related, I believe, to its key role in all sorts of recursive, reflexive, infinitely-regressive, hierarchical, fractal, spiral, and feedback processes. Vladimir A. Lefebvere makes fascinating connections between the human preference for the golden section and the ethical process of reflexive self-correction in "The Golden Section and an Algebraic Model of Ethical Cognition," in *Journal of Mathematical Psychology*, 1985. It is interesting that the foundation principle of classical art should be

that surd whose ratio to unity is identical to the ratio of
unity to the sum of itself and unity. If our biological
adaptation to recognize and take pleasure in beauty is
indeed a means of predicting the behavior of the physical
world on the basis of its actual principles of organization,
then such coincidences should not be surprising.

Bibliography

J.L. Austin, *How to Do Things with Words*. Oxford: Oxford University Press, 1976.

John D. Barrow and Joseph Silk, "The Structure of the Early Universe," *Scientific American*, April, 1980, p. 98.

Gregory Bateson, *Steps to an Ecology of Mind*. New York: Ballantine Books, 1972.

Derek Bickerson, "Creole Languages," *Scientific American*, July, 1983, p. 116.

Floyd Bloom, "Neuropeptides," *Scientific American*, October, 1981, p. 114.

Ralph Burhoe, et al., editors, *Zygon*.

David Bynum, *The Daemon in the Wood*. Harvard: Cambridge University Press, 1978.

Joseph Campbell, *Historical Atlas of World Mythology*. London: Times Books, 1984.

George Crumb, "Music: Does It Have a Future?" *The Kenyon Review*, Summer, 1980, p. 115.

Mihaly Csikszentmihalyi, *Beyond Boredom and Anxiety: The Experience of Play in Work and Games*. San Francisco: Jossey-Bass, 1975.

E.G. d'Aquili, C.D. Laughlin, Jr. and J. McManus, editors, *The Spectrum of Ritual*. New York: Columbia University Press, 1979.

Charles Darwin, *The Origin of Species*. New York: Collier, 1962.

John C. Eccles, *The Human Mystery*. New York: Springer-Verlag, 1979.

Irenaeus Eibl-Eibesfeldt, *Ethology: The Biology of Behavior*. New York: Holt, Rinehart & Winston, 1970.

Manfred Eigen and Ruthild Winkler, *Laws of the Game: How the Principles of Nature Govern Chance*. New York: Knopf, 1981.

David Epstein, *Beyond Orpheus: Studies in Musical Structure*. Cambridge: M.I.T. Press, 1979.

M. J. Feigenbaum, "Universal Behavior in Nonlinear Systems." *Los Alamos Science*, Vol. 1, no. 1, 1980, p.4.

David Finkelstein, "Coherence and Possibility: The Logic of the Innermost Universe." *Kenyon Review*, Spring, 1982, p. 95.

J.T. Fraser, "Out of Plato's Cave: The Natural History of Time." *Kenyon Review*, Winter, 1980, p. 143.

James G. Fraser, *The Golden Bough*. London: Macmillan, 1925.

George Gale, "The Anthropic Principle," *Scientific American*, December, 1981, p. 114.

Clifford Geertz, *The Intrepretation of Culture*. New York: Basic Books, 1973.

——————————, *Negara: The Theatre State in Nineteenth-Century Bali*. Princeton: Princeton University Press, 1980.

Thomas Gilliard, "The Evolution of Bowerbirds." *Scientific American*, August, 1963. p. 38.

Jerzy Grotowski, *Towards a Poor Theater*. Holstebro: Odin Teatrets Forlag, 1968.

Roger Guillemin, "Peptides in the Brain: The New Endocrinology of The Neuron." *Science*, 202, 1978, p. 340.

Alan H. Guth and Paul J. Steinhardt, "The Inflationary Universe." *Scientific American*, May, 1984, p. 116.

Douglas Hofstadter, "Strange Attractors: Mathematical Patterns Delicately Poised Between Order and Chaos." *Scientific American*, November, 1981, p. 16.

——————————, *Godel, Escher, Bach*. New York: Basic Books, 1979.

T.S. Huxley, "The Courtship Habits of The Great Crested Grebe." *Proceedings of the Zoological Society of London*, 35, 1914.

Harry Jerison, *Evolution of the Brain and Intelligence*. New York: Academic Press, 1973.

Melvin Konner, *The Tangled Wing: Biological Constraints on the Human Spirit.* New York: Holt, Rinehart & Winston, 1982.
Vladimir A. Lefebvre, "The Golden Section and An Algebraic Model of Ethical Cognition." *Journal of Mathematical Psychology,* to be published, 1985.
Claude Levi-Strauss, *The Raw and The Cooked.* London: Cape, 1970.
―――――――――, *From Honey to Ashes.* London: Cape, 1973.
―――――――――, *The Origin of Table Manners.* London: Cape, 1978.
―――――――――, *The Naked Man.* London: Cape, 1981.
―――――――――, *The. Savage Mind.* London: Weidenfeld, 1972.
Jerre Levy, "Psychobiological Implications of Bilateral Asymmetry." *Hemisphere Function in the Human Brain.* Edited by Stuart J. Dimond and J. Graham Beaumont. New York: John Wiley & Sons, 1974.
―――――――――, "Interhemispheric Collaboration: Single-Mindedness in the Asymmetric Brain." *Development Neuropsychology and Education: Hemispheric Specialization and Integration.* Edited by C.T. Best. New York: Academic Press, 1984.
―――――――――, "Cerebral Asymmetry and Aesthetic Experience." *Biological Aspects of Aesthetics.* Edited by I. Eibesfeldt, D. Epstein, I. Rentschler, F. Turner, et al. (Not yet published.)
Barbara Lex, "The Neurophysiology of Ritual Trance." In d'Aquili, et al, 1979.
Albert Lord, *The Singer of Tales.* Cambridge: Harvard University Press, 1960.
Konrad Lorenz, *King Solomon's Ring.* New York: Methuen, 1964.
―――――――――, *On Aggression.* New York: Methuen, 1963.
John J. MacAloon, *This Great Symbol: Pierre de Coubertin and The Origin of The Modern Olympic Games.* Chicago: University of Chicago Press, 1981.
Benoit Mandelbrot, *The Fractal Geometry of Nature.* New York: Freeman, 1983.
R. May, "Simple Mathematical Models with Very Complicated Dynamics." *Nature,* June, 1976, Vol. 261, No. 5560, p. 459.
Abraham Moles, *Information Theory and Aesthetic Perception.* Urbana: University of Illinois Press, 1968.
Jacques Monod, *Chance and Necessity.* London: Collins, 1972.
George Peter Murdock, "The Common Denominator of Cultures."

In Washburn and Joy, 1968.
Barbara Myerhoff, *Number Our Days*. New York: Dutton, 1979.
—————————, with Sally F. Moore, editors. *Secular Rituals*. Atlantic Highlands: Humanities Press, 1977.
James Olds, "Behavioral Studies of Hypothalmic Functions: Drives and Reinforcements." *Biological Foundations of Psychiatry*, Vol. 1. Edited by R. G. Grenell and S. Babay. New York: Raven Press, 1976.
Milman Parry, *The Making of Homeric Verse*. Edited by Adam Parry. Oxford: Oxford University Press, 1971.
K.H. Pribram, *Brain and Behavior*, 3 vols. Harmondsworth: Penguin, 1969.
A. Routtenberg, *Biology of Reinforcement: Facets of Brain Stimulation Reward*. New York: Academic Press, 1980.
Richard Schechner, *Essays on Performance Theory, 1970-1976*. New York: Drama Book Specialists, 1977.
—————————, "Performers and Spectators Transported and Transformed." *Kenyon Review*, Fall, 1981, p. 83.
Joseph Silk, et al. "The Large-Scale Structure of The Universe." *Scientific American*, October, 1983, p. 72.
Solomon H. Snyder, "Opiate Receptors and Internal Opiates." *Scientific American*, March, 1977, p. 44.
Konstantin Stanislavski, *An Actor Prepares*. New York: Theatre Arts Books, 1946.
Andrew Strathern and Marilyn Strathern, *Self-Decoration in Mount Hagen*. London: Duckworth, 1971.
H.S. Thayer, "The Right to Believe: William James' Reinterpretation of The Function of Religious Beliefs." *Kenyon Review*, Winter, 1983, p. 89.
W.H. Thorpe, "Duet-Singing Birds." *Scientific American*, August, 1973, p. 70.
Lionel Tiger, *Optimism: The Biology of Hope*. New York: Simon and Schuster, 1979.
Frederick Turner, "Escape from Modernism: Technology and The Future of The Imagination." *Harper's*, November, 1984, p. 47.
————————— and Ernst Pöppel, "The Neural Lyre: Poetic Meter, The Brain and Time." *Poetry*, August, 1983, p. 277.
Victor W. Turner, *The Forest of Symbols*. Ithaca: Cornell University Press, 1967.
—————————, *The Drums of Affliction*. New York: Oxford University Press, 1968.
—————————, *The Ritual Process*. Chicago: Aldine, 1969.

———————————, *Dramas, Fields, and Metaphors*. Ithaca: Cornell University Press, 1974.

———————————, *From Ritual to Theater*. New York: Performing Arts Journal Publications, 1982.

Jacob von Uexkull, *Umwelt und Innenwelt der Tiere*. Berlin: Springer International, 1921.

Henry N. Wagner, et al., "Imaging Dopamine Receptors in the Human Brain by Positron Tomography." *Science*, September, 1983, vol. 221, p. 1264.

Robert Keith Wallace and Herbert Benson, "The Physiology of Meditation." *Scientific American*, February, 1972, p. 84.

S.L. Washburn and Phyllis C. Joy, *Perspectives on Human Evolution*. New York: Holt, Rinehart & Winston, 1968.

J.C. Willer et al., "Stress-Induced Analgesia in Humans: Endogenous Opioids and Naxolone Reversible Depression of Pain Reflex." *Science*, 212, 1981, p. 689.

Peter J. Wilson, *Man, The Promising Primate*. New Haven: Yale University Press, 1980.

Frances Yates, *The Theatre of the World*. Chicago: Chicago University Press, 1969.

Arthur M. Young, *The Geometry of Meaning*. San Francisco: Robert Briggs Associates, 1976.

E.C. Zeeman, "Catastrophe Theory." *Scientific American*, April, 1976, p. 65.

Index

The numbers in parenthesis behind the page numbers refer to footnote(s) on that page.